NEW HORIZONS IN INTERNATIONAL LAW

by

T. O. Elias

Judge of the International Court of Justice, Member of the Curatorium of the Hague Academy of International Law.

1980

SIJTHOFF & NOORDHOFF — ALPHEN AAN DEN RIJN
OCEANA PUBLICATIONS INC. DOBBS FERRY, N.Y.

NEW HORIZONS IN INTERNATIONAL LAW

NEW HORIZONS IN INTERNATIONAL LAW

by

T. O. Elias

Judge of the International Court of Justice, Member of the Curatorium of the Hague Academy of International Law.

1980

SIJTHOFF & NOORDHOFF — ALPHEN AAN DEN RIJN
OCEANA PUBLICATIONS INC. DOBBS FERRY, N.Y.

First printing 1979
Second printing 1980

ISBN 90 286 0039 6 (Sijthoff)
ISBN 0-379-20499-1 (Oceana)

Copyright © 1979. Sijthoff & Noordhoff International Publishers B.V.
Alphen aan den Rijn — The Netherlands

Printed in The Netherlands

FOREWORD

This book consists of a series of studies designed to highlight a number of the more significant aspects of public international law that have emerged during the past thirty years or so. Since the United Nations Organisation came into being in 1945 there have taken place many developments which call for special attention from students of contemporary international law, and it is the aim of the present study to attempt a survey of the field in this series of outline essays, many of which were subjects of lectures while others were research studies designed to deal with matters of concern to those who have considered the subject seriously. The various topics dealt with cannot naturally be regarded as projecting a systematic presentation of the field, but they are rather an attempt at an analysis of concepts and questions that seem to require attention.

Thus there are three main divisions of the book. In the first part are examined certain aspects of the new trends in contemporary international law in which the contributions made by the Third World, especially Asia and Africa, to international law have been outlined with regard to the new initiatives taken by the United Nations Organisation in establishing the International Law Commission and certain economic bodies like the UNCTAD and the UNCITRAL which have been called into being largely by the needs of the developing countries. Also, in this part, an attempt is made to look at the growth of modern diplomatic law within the framework of the International Law Commission and the General Assembly of the United Nations. But probably the most significant development of the period has been the adoption by a Diplomatic Conference of the Vienna Convention on the Law of Treaties, which is important because of its reformulation and progressive development of aspects of the Law of Treaties such as *pacta sunt servanda*, fundamental change of circumstances, new grounds of invalidity of Treaties, particularly the doctrine of *jus cogens* which makes certain types of Treaties invalid *ab initio* in specified circumstances. An interesting aspect of the same subject is the draft Convention on State Succession which attempts to bring up-to-date the law on the subject of the rights and duties of new States in relation to the Treaties they have inherited at independence. Another important new development is the Third Conference on the Law of the Sea which is an attempt to recodify existing customary international law on the subject as well as the various Law of the Sea Conventions of 1958.

In the second part of the book, which is devoted to the judicial process, attempts have been made to examine present trends and future prospects of the International Court of Justice, especially the problem of the varied composition of the Court, the jurisdiction of the Court in regard to whether or not it should be expanded to entertain entities other than sovereign States and to even human individuals. A new development which is also analysed is that of the judicial review function of the International Court of Justice; this has been made particularly important in view of the development of new areas such as international constitutional law and the work of the International Court of Justice in dealing with appeals from other international tribunals like the United Nations Administrative Tribunal.

In another chapter is examined at some length the role of the International Court of Justice as the highest judicial organ of the United Nations charged with the responsibility for the search for peace in all its ramifications. An attempt is made to examine how the Court's jurisprudence is developing towards the achievement of the goal of peace. The part on the judicial process is rounded up with a case study of hijacking in international law, a subject that has become very significant within the last decade or so and the law on which is still at the stage of development.

In the third part of these studies are considered the development and analysis of human rights and humanitarian law. The question of human rights is discussed both from the point of view of the Universal Declaration of Human Rights and the two international covenants on human rights generally, and from the point of view of human rights with special reference to developing countries. The problems posed by decolonization have included the emergence of liberation movements, guerrilla warfare and mercenaries in Viet Nam and other parts of South East Asia as well as in Africa. The Geneva Conventions of 1949 have proved inadequate to deal with these new problems and the International Committee of the Red Cross recently provided the forum for a series of conferences in Geneva which, in December 1977, adopted two Protocols in an effort to up-date the law on the subject. A brief outline of the development of international humanitarian law concludes the present study.

The book is, therefore, no more than an attempt to survey a very wide field in a series of studies designed to draw attention to these new horizons in the field of contemporary international law. It is not a comprehensive or even an exhaustive study of the various topics selected for treatment. It is designed rather to indicate the new trends which require further studies in order to demonstrate the expanding frontiers of public international law. Each of the aspects dealt with is capable of more extended treatment and will no doubt be taken up by students of the subject when some of the topics like modern diplomatic law and the Law of Treaties have been developed by State practice; and, in the case of the Law of the Sea, the final shape and scope of the codified law must certainly await the concluding conference on the subject. One important aspect of the whole matter is the realisation that, because of these new trends in the horizons of public international law, no single treatise or textbook can be regarded as adequately encompassing the entire field of public international law today.

The Hague,
December 4, 1978   *T. O. Elias*

TABLE OF CONTENTS

Part III
Human Rights and Humanitarian Law

TABLE OF CASES
(Alphabetical per court)

TABLE OF CASES
(Chronological)

INTRODUCTION

To the discerning student of public international law today there can be no doubt that certain new trends are visible on the horizon. The aim of this book is to highlight in a series of studies those significant developments in the past three decades or so that deserve special notice in relation to these trends.

International law has been expanding its frontiers not only in terms of its subject matter but also in terms of its content and orientation. In addition to such new areas as international constitutional law, law of international institutions, international economic law, international communications and air law, law of outer space, human rights law and international humanitarian law, there have also emerged new sources of the law and of the ways by which new laws are made by means of declarations, resolutions and the use of consensus at the UN Security Council and the General Assembly.[1] Either because or in spite of this expansion of its frontiers, traditional notions and attitudes are beginning to show a certain resilience and adaptability: the rigid assertion that only sovereign states are the subjects of international law is giving place to the idea that other entities, notably certain international organizations like the United Nations itself, as well as individuals are now also subjects of international law for most practical purposes. One such entity has successfully litigated a case before the International Court of Justice in *Certain Expenses*,[2] while in the *Falsa Case*,[3] certain rights of the individual were recognized, albeit by way of appeal from the UN Administrative Tribunal. Indeed, the European Commission and the European Court of Human Rights have both been entertaining cases brought before them by individual citizens of the States of the Council of Europe. There also exists established machinery, although limited, for the implementation of the fundamental rights of the individual through state action. All these are recent developments in contemporary international law which could not have taken place before 1945.

One significant development in the whole field of international law within the framework of the United Nations Organization has been the express injunction upon the General Assembly in Article 13 of the UN Charter "to encourage the progressive development of international law and its codification". According to the Statute of the International Law Commission which was established for both purposes, "progressive development" means "the preparation of draft conventions on subjects which have not yet been regulated by international law or in regard to which the law has not been sufficiently developed in the practice of States" while codification implies "the more precise formulation and systemization of rules of international law in fields where there already has been extensive State practice, precedent and doctrine" (Article 15). In trying to achieve these ends, the Commission is enjoined in Article 8 to take into account "the main forms of civilization and of the principal legal systems in the world". Chief among its major formulations are the Conventions on Diplomatic and Consular Relations, Special Missions, the Four Conventions on the Law of the Sea, and Relations between States and International Organizations, all of which have resulted in a new body of diplomatic law; the Vienna Convention on the Law of Treaties, and State Succession in respect of Treaties, while ancillary matters are in varying stages of codification and progressive development before the Commission.[4] Thus this institution is a quasi-legislative body specifically charged with the function not only of updating existing rules and practices of customary international law but also of filling in gaps in such law as well as creating new rules to meet the changed and the changing needs of the developing international society.

But the General Assembly, conscious of the possibility of the inadequacy of the International Law Commission to fulfil the task of keeping full pace with the challenges of contemporary international law and the requirements of social justice, later in the same year adopted Resolution 171 (III) of November 14, 1947 (see Appendix I) calling upon States to utilize the Court "to the greatest practicable extent in the progressive development of international law, both in regard to legal issues between States and in regard to constitutional interpretation". The Resolution ends by recommending "as a general rule that States should submit their legal disputes to the International Court of Justice". In this way, the General Assembly has expressly conferred upon the International Court of Justice a new function, that of achieving the progressive development of international law wherever and whenever made necessary by the changing conditions of international life. This express power given to the Court was never before so expressly conferred upon the Permanent Court of International Justice, or even upon the International Court of Justice itself until 1947. As Alvarez observed in the *Corfu Channel Case Merits:* "in consequences of profound changes that had taken place in international relations, a new international law had arisen; it is founded on *social interdependence.* . . . it is the realization of social justice. It is entirely different from the old law, which was strictly juridical; it approaches nearer to the notion of equity, without however being merged in it. This new international law is not a *lex ferenda,* as is often believed; it has a real-existence and it has essential and actual foundation".[5] At that moment, Judge Alvarez thereupon set the Court three functions:

(a) the former function, which consisted in elucidating the existing law, and in defining and confirming it;
(b) that of modifying — in conformity with the existing conditions of international relations provisions which though in force, have become out of date;
(c) that of creating and formulating new precepts, both for old problems where no rules exist and also for new problems.

He warned, however, that in the exercise of these functions, the Court "must not proceed arbitrarily but must gain its inspiration from the greatest principles of the new international law". He concluded: "But the power of the court to remodel international law is merely the application in every branch of that law of the doctrine of the clause *rebus sic stantibus;* the principle at the root of it is the same; it is a principle of social justice".[6] Without necessarily accepting Judge Alvarez's concept and analysis of the new international law in all its detail, one must admit the hard core of his thesis that contemporary international law requires new approaches and new techniques in the resolution of disputes and conflicts between States, and the Court must adapt to the new requirements of contemporary international life which enjoin it to be bold and just in its articulation of the rules and principles of today's international law. The old power structure has crumbled for the most part and what remains of it is in constant need of readjustment and reconstruction. International law is rapidly ceasing to be a game of power politics; it is being subjected more and more to universal influences and modified by a new climate of opinion and a growing awareness of the need for social justice in international relations.

The world community recently demonstrated a significant response to this new challenge when the General Assembly adopted Resolution 3232 (**XXIX**) of November 12, 1974 (see Appendix II) on the Review of the Role of the International Court of Justice as the principal judicial organ of the United Nations. In calling upon all member states to make greater use of the Court, the General Assembly draws attention, *inter alia*, to the recent as well as current amendments of the Rules of Court "simplifying the procedure, reducing the likelihood of undue delays and costs and allowing for greater influence of parties on the composition of *ad hoc* chambers; and to the increasing development and codification of international law in conventions open for universal participation and the consequent need for their uniform interpretation and application. There are also two important points raised by the Resolution: the first is the emphasis on recognition that "the development of international law may be reflected, *inter alia*, by declarations and resolutions of the General Assembly which may to that extent be taken into consideration by the International Court of Justice"; the second is that the power of the Court under Article 38, paragraph 2, of its Statute to decide a case *ex aequo et bono* if the parties agree thereto offers opportunities to State parties to a case before the Court to achieve settlement of their disputes which might not be susceptible of solution in any other way. These two questions supply dynamic dimensions to the judicial process of the International Court of Justice, the one drawing a much-needed attention to a provision of the Statute of the Court which, despite its great potentialities, has never been invoked in any disputes before the Court or its predecessor, while the other gives tacit recognition to General Assembly declarations and resolutions as possible sources of contemporary international law. Although the point awaits authoritative determination by the Court, the invitation thus extended to it by the Resolution is some indication that, in all future cases, references by parties before the Court to relevant General Assembly declarations and resolutions can no longer be ignored as of no legal consequence at all.

We may now turn from what may be regarded as the public affairs of international law and of the International Court of Justice to a brief consideration of two matters relating to the internal affairs of the Court in its new horizon. The first issue of considerable importance relates to the Resolution (see Appendix III) concerning the Internal Judicial Practice of the Court adopted on April 12, 1976.[7] This replaces the 1968 rules of internal judicial practice, governing the methods and stages of the deliberations held by the Court after termination of the written proceedings and before the judgment is given. The main features of the internal judicial proceedings are deliberations between the termination of the written proceedings and the beginning of the oral proceedings at which the judges exchange views concerning the case; the Court also meets in private from time to time during the oral proceedings to enable judges to have further exchanges of views concerning the case; after the termination of the oral proceedings, judges are allowed a period for the study of the arguments, after which deliberations will be held at which the President outlines the issues which in his opinion require discussion and decision by the Court. Judges are then called upon by the President in the order in which they signify their desire to speak. After a reasonable interval, judges exchange written notes indicating their views on the case, including their tentative conclusions as to the correct disposal of the case. A further deliberation is held, additional questions may be asked and a request may be made as to whether a vote should be taken on any question. A drafting committee is then selected by secret ballot and by an absolute majority of votes of the judges present. There are detailed rules for the conduct of the drafting of the judgment. A preliminary draft of the decision is circulated to the judges who may submit written amendments, as a result of which a revised draft is then considered by the Court. Judges who wish to deliver separate or dissenting opinions make the text available to the Court within an agreed time-limit. Upon the termination of the second reading of the draft, judges are called upon by the President, in inverse order of seniority, to give their final vote on the decision or conclusion concerned. Such final votes are normally recorded in person. A separate vote may be demanded on an issue. The procedure just outlined is followed whether the proceedings before the Court are contentious or advisory.

The most important innovation introduced in this latest Resolution of the Court in respect of its internal judicial practices is the *collegiate* system of arriving at decisions or conclusions on the case before the Court, thus replacing the erstwhile individualistic style of deliberation.

The final point is the adoption of a new body of Rules of Court in April 1978 after nearly ten years of labor spent on revision. It would be tedious even to summarise here the fairly substantial changes made in the existing rules. The text of the Rules of Court must be consulted in order to appreciate the new horizon which the Court now offers to contemporary international law.

NOTES

1. See Chapter 3 in my *Africa and the Development of International Law*, 1972, for an extended treatment of this fascinating subject.

2. *I.C.J. Reports 1962*, p. 151.

3. Application for Review of Judgment No. 158 of the UN Administrative Tribunal, Advisory Opinion, *I.C.J. Reports 1973*, p. 166.

4. See *The Work of the International Law Commission*, revised edition, pp. 58–68.

5. *I.C.J. Reports 1949*, p. 4 at p. 40. Judge Alvarez first enunciated his concept of the new international law in his Dissenting Opinion appended to *Conditions of Admission of a State to Membership in the United Nations*, Advisory Opinion, *I.C.J. Reports 1948*, p. 57, at pp. 68–69. He reiterated at some length the same view in his Dissenting Opinion appended to the *Judgment in International Status of South-West Africa*, Advisory Opinion, *I.C.J. Reports 1950*, p. 128, at p. 176.

6. The *Corfu Channel Case Merits*, ibid. at p. 41.

7. Prior to 1968, the internal judicial practice of the Court was governed by the Resolution of the Permanent Court of International Justice of February 20, 1931 (as amended on March 17, 1936) by virtue of a decision of the International Court of Justice of 1946 to adopt provisionally the practice of the Permanent Court.

PART I

Certain aspects of the new trends

Chapter 1

NEW HORIZONS IN INTERNATIONAL LAW

I

The United Nations Charter marks a significant step forward in the development of international law. In a sense, it is both a continuum and new chapter in world history. It does not pretend to usher in a golden age, but it opens up fresh vistas; new horizons in international law are clearly visible.

It is now over thirty years since the establishment of the UN Organization, and it is not inopportune to attempt a survey of the more significant trends in the evolution of international law within this period. If we regard the Charter of the United Nations as marking the beginning of a new era in interstate relations and of the efforts to restructure interstate relations with a view to achieving a new world order, it will be seen that in broad outline certain noticeable trends are discernible on the international scene. Without a doubt, the most spectacular of the new developments have taken place and continue to take place within the framework and under the auspices of the United Nations, and this is rightly so. It is, however, also inevitable that, either because of the impact of the United Nations and of its agencies on the organized life of the international community within the last three decades, or because of the inevitable evolutionary forces operating within a number of independent international institutions and the march of world events, a number of significant developments have also taken place outside the direct purview of the United Nations Organization in the field of international law. It is intended to deal first with the developments under the aegis of the United Nations with which this survey is primarily concerned.

The period may be conveniently if roughly classified into three fairly recognizable, though not mutually exclusive, periods: (a) from 1945 to about 1960, which may be regarded as the formative years during which the UN Organization was trying to find its feet, so to speak, and to map out a program of future action and experiment with a number of approaches to postwar problems; (b) from 1960 to about 1969, in which the greatest developments concerned the phenomenal growth of new states and the preoccupation of the world body was the problem of self-determination of peoples and the battle against racial discrimination — a period that could be described as one of the growing pains of adolescence both for the new states and for the United Nations itself; and (c) the period since 1970, often referred to as the decade of development, especially regarding economic and social growth for the world community in general and the Third World in particular.

In the first few years of the UN Organization, the most important problems were those connected with the unfinished work of the League of Nations Codification Conference of 1924 and the question associated with United Nations membership as a result of the inevitable enlargement of the world body, itself the consequence of the emergence of newly-independent states by the fission of one state into two, as in the case of India and Pakistan, the formation of a new state by temporary union, as with Egypt and Syria, or the emergence of one or two new states as a result of reassertion of sovereignty, as with Outer Mongolia and Byelorussia.

The problems associated with the conditions of admission of a state to UN membership[1] as well as the determination of the General Assembly for the admission of a state[2] will be found to be dealt with in two advisory opinions of 1948 and 1950. In the field of codification, the General Assembly turned its early attention to the provision of Article 13 of the UN Charter which requires that the General Assembly shall initiate studies and make recommendations for the purpose of encouraging the progressive development of international law and its codification. The result was General Assembly Resolution 174(D) by which the International Law Commission was established under an enabling statute. The Commission is enjoined under its statute to "concern itself primarily with public international law, but is not precluded from entering the field of private international law". The Commission has so far worked only in the field of public international law. Working through the Assembly, it submits its work through the Secretary-General of the United Nations in its Codification Division, which supplies the Secretariat of the Commission which also services the Sixth Committee, the body charged with the responsibility of dealing with the Commission's draft prior to the taking of action thereon by the General Assembly. The International Law Commission is required to survey the whole field of international law with a view to selecting topics for codification, its members having been elected by the General Assembly from a list of candidates nominated by the governments of member states of the United Nations; the electors must "bear in mind that the persons to be elected to the Commission should individually possess the qualifications required and that in the Commission as a whole representation of the main forms of civilisation and of the principal legal systems of the world should be assured". The stipulation that the Commission should attempt the "progressive development of international law" is intended to imply the preparation of draft conventions which have not yet been regulated by international law or in regard to which the law has not yet been sufficiently developed in the practice of states. By "codification of international law" is meant the more precise formulation and systematization of rules of international law in fields where there has already been extensive state practice, precedent and doctrine. The International Law Commission is called upon by its statute to establish cooperation with various other bodies, both official and unofficial, and its Article 17(1) authorizes the "principal organs of the United Nations other than the General Assembly, Specialized Agencies, or official bodies established by inter-governmental agreement to encourage the progressive development of international law and its codification". Since the Commission held its first annual session on April 12, 1949, the topics it has dealt with include a Draft Declaration on the Rights and Duties of States, Recommendation on Ways and Means for Making the Evidence of Customary International Law More Readily Available, Formulation of the Nuremberg Principles, Question of International Criminal Jurisdiction, Reservations to Multilateral Conventions, Question of Defining Aggression, Draft Code of Offences Against the Peace and Security of Mankind, Nationality including Statelessness; even as far back as 1949, the International Law Commission included the topic of the Law of the Sea which resulted in the Law of the Sea Conventions of 1958 and 1960; Model Rules on Arbitral Procedure, The Conventions on Diplomatic Intercourse and Immunities, Consular Relations, Extended Participation in General Multilateral Treaties Concluded under the auspices of the League of Nations, The Law of Treaties, Special Missions, and Relations Between States and International Organizations.

All the foregoing are topics in respect of which the International Law Commission has submitted reports, codes and conventions which the General Assembly has adopted at various times and almost all of which have enriched the arcanum of customary international law. It will be noticed that a number of the topics dealt with issues of international law which have continued to be of contemporary relevance; for example, the Question of Defining Aggression in respect of which it was only in 1974 that the General Assembly was able to adopt a formal declaration on the subject, The Law of the Sea

in respect of which the Third Conference has just concluded its fourth
session in New York (in April 1976); while a number of the topics
have been finally disposed of by the Commission and accepted as part
of general international law, especially the Law of Treaties,
Diplomatic Intercourse and Consular Relations, and Special
Missions.

It may be useful to mention that, in accordance with Article 24 of
its statute, the International Law Commission considered ways and
means for making the evidence of customary international law more
readily available; it made detailed and specific recommendations[3] to
the General Assembly in 1950 that the widest possible distribution be
made of publications by the United Nations relating to international
law: the *Juridical Yearbook*, the Legislative Series, *The League of Nations
Treaties Series Index*, *The United Nations Treaties Series Index*, *Reports of
International Arbitral Awards* and, particularly the reports and other
publications of the International Court of Justice. These publications,
it will be agreed, are landmarks in the efforts to disseminate and
publicize public international law in its development under the
spreading wing of the United Nations. This very welcome development as a result of the establishment of the International Law
Commission has greatly increased the range of activities in
international law as well as increased the volume of the literature on
the subject in a manner never experienced in the pre-1945 era.

II

One of the most notable initiatives taken by the UN Organization in
this early period was the preparation and adoption of the Universal
Declaration of Human Rights, 1948, proclaiming a number of
fundamental rights and freedoms of a mainly political nature. One of
the historical antecedents for the enunciation of the principles
embodied in the Declaration was President Roosevelt's famous "four
freedoms", declared by him towards the end of the Second World
War; but the *motif* was no doubt similar to the human yearnings and
aspirations for the greater recognition of the "rights of man"
adumbrated by Thomas Paine and enshrined in the proclamations of
the leaders of the French Revolution of 1789, especially as put
forward in the writings of Rousseau and his followers. As the Second
World War ended, the leaders of the Western Alliance seemed
determined to eradicate war and to ensure peace and security for
mankind in immediate postwar years; in the political language of the
time, they seemed anxious to make "the world safe for democracy",

which in the language of the UN Charter means the assurance of "international peace and security". The Universal Declaration represented a new thinking in international relations and a fresh hope for a better world. Principles and concepts of equality between state and state and between state and citizen were articulated and, in many cases, defined and elaborated not only as matters of political expediency for the Member States of the UN Organization, but also as principles of guidance for action in the relations between the state and the individual. It was little wonder, therefore, that, almost immediately after the proclamation of the Declaration, most of the newly-independent states — beginning with India and Pakistan in 1949 through Malaya and Nigeria to the present day — have all included chapters on fundamental human rights and freedoms in their various constitutions. The language and the basic ideas of freedom and equality, which in some cases have been merely set forth briefly in the UN Declaration, have been more fully elaborated upon in these constitutions. So pervasive has been the effect of the Declaration that the inclusion of legislative provisions in the constitutions of the newly-independent states has not been confined to the Third World. More advanced countries like Canada have adopted Bills of Rights similar to the pioneer enactment of the United States, while the Council of Europe has also elaborated its own Convention of Human Rights administered by both a Commission and a Court of Human Rights. The good beginning made in this area of what has come to be known as Humanitarian Law has since been supplemented by the International Covenant of Economic, Social and Cultural International Rights, the Covenant of Civil and Political Rights (1966) and the Convention on the Elimination of all Forms of Racial Discrimination — all designed to enlarge the boundaries of the rights and freedoms of the individual within an all-embracing rule of law.[4]

The emergence of the new states has, as we have mentioned above, led to a number of problems not only within the United Nations itself, but also in its Specialized Agencies and there has been a noticeable increase in the accession to UN conventions as a result of this enlargement of UN membership. Two major developments of the same fifteen-year period have been the unprecedented emphasis laid upon the Principle of Universality involving the extension of participation of all UN members in the work of the Organization and of its agencies, and the even more important Principle of Non-Discrimination which enjoins equality of rights among all Member States of the Organization. The principle of universality enables all members to accede to international conventions as well as membership of international institutions on the basis of equality and without regard to ideological differences, the only reservations being confined to those organizations of a regional character established for a special purpose.

With regard to the problems of non-discrimination, the overwhelming UN preoccupation of the period between 1946 and the 1960's has been about decolonization, and it is significant that the Charter provisions enshrining the principle of self-determination and the equal rights of peoples have resulted in more than doubling the original UN membership of fifty-one states to well over 100. By resolution, the General Assembly on December 14, 1960, adopted the Declaration on the Granting of Independence to Colonial Countries and Peoples, emphasising the conviction that the continued existence of colonialism prevented the development of international economic cooperation, impeded the social, cultural and economic development of dependent peoples and militated against the UN ideal of universal peace. The Declaration proclaims that "all peoples have the inalienable right to complete freedom, the exercise of their sovereignty and the integrity of their national territory"; it further affirms that the subjection of peoples to alien subjugation, domination and exploitation constitutes a denial of fundamental human rights, is contrary to the Charter of the United Nations and to the Universal Declaration and is also an impediment to the promotion of world peace and cooperation. This was a new language being taught by the whole community of nations to one another, big and small, old and new, and its message was strident and unmistakable. Soon the majority of UN Member States began to accept and assert the principle that all peoples have the right to self-determination and by virtue of that right they freely determine their political status and freely pursue their economic, social and cultural development. In order to ensure implementation, a special Committee of Seventeen was set up and so were a number of committees to examine conditions in non-self-governing territories: the Committee on Information from Non-self-governing Territories was established in 1949 for the purpose of examining the information transmitted to the United Nations by members administering non-self-governing territories in accordance with Article 73(e) of Chapter XI of the United Nations Charter;[5] the Special Committee on South-West Africa, was established in 1961 to render similar services and in particular to deal with petitions from that territory, even though the South African Government has consistently refused to place South-West Africa under Trusteeship or to submit reports and petitions to the United Nations; and the Special Committee on Portuguese Territories which was also established in 1962 to deal with the problems of those territories. All three Committees were merged in 1962 with the Special Committee of Twenty-four. Looking in retrospect at these worthwhile efforts of the United Nations to grapple with the problems of decolonization, efforts scoffed at by a few sceptical members with responsibilities for these dependent territories, it can be seen that encouraging results have marked the expectations of those who believed independence for all dependent peoples was the only hope for a peaceful and just world.

We may mention in parenthesis here the role played by the International Court of Justice, beginning with its advisory opinion of 1950 in which it declared that the territory of South-West Africa[6] has an international status independent of the Union Government of South Africa, that South Africa continued to have international obligations regarding the Territory, and that the functions of supervision over South Africa's administration should be exercised by the United Nations. The International Court of Justice, after a period of vacillation and of much-criticized opinions, reached the epoch-making decision in its advisory opinion in *the Namibia case*[7] in which it proclaimed in very clear terms the principle of self-determination as a recognized legal concept within the framework of the United Nations. We shall refer to this in greater detail later on.

III

The structure of the UN Organization under the Charter was designed to vest the Security Council with executive powers to make decisions for the maintenance of international peace and security while the General Assembly was to be a forum for the ventilation of international problems and issues in more or less parliamentary debates leading to determinations after the fullest discussions. For this purpose the Security Council was entrusted to the five major Powers as Permanent Members, assisted by ten other members elected from time to time. The delicate balance between the power of the General Assembly to make recommendations on practically all questions after full debate, except in cases requiring sanctions, and the power entrusted to the Security Council to take binding decisions soon became disturbed — especially with regard to the establishment of peace-keeping forces under UN auspices in the Congo, Cyprus and the Middle East. A strong debate ensued as to the relative powers of the two bodies in respect of which of them should have the monopoly of decisions to organize and supervise measures for the maintenance of peace. When the majority of the members, after a decade of controversy between the East and the West regarding admissions to membership of the Organization, realised that the *veto* power was likely to prove a handicap to the making of quick and sometimes expensive decisions to establish a peace-force where needed, the General Assembly took a number of bold initiatives in resolutions by means of which it assumed the power to establish peace-keeping forces and to make definitive recommendations as to its own authority in certain matters not unconnected with questions of security. This position taken by the General Assembly received a measure of legal backing in a number of decisions and opinions handed down by the International Court of Justice and criticized by some as based on teleological interpretations of the Charter provisions. Attention may be called to the advisory opinion defining the competence of the General Assembly for the admission of states to the Organization,[8] the problems associated with the payments for the peacekeeping forces which was the subject-matter of another advisory opinion,[9] and the general principles upon which the advisory opinion in the *Namibia Case*[10] was based.

Thus, the original intention to construct a world order in which the Security Council would act to regulate world peace having been checkmated by these developments in the General Assembly and as a result of certain decisions of the International Court of Justice, a period of cold war confrontation ensued between the East and the West on the one hand and, on the other, between the great Powers and the small ones, particularly those of the Third World majority. It soon became clear to far-sighted UN members in all camps that positive action was needed to overcome this *impasse* with a fresh initiative for collaboration and cooperation, even on however limited a scale.

One suggestion was that the difficulties being encountered in the working of the two UN bodies were mainly attributable to many provisions of the UN Charter. Inspired by high ideals and aspirations for the brotherhood of man, they were now seen to be inadequate for the realistic administration of a postwar world which had thrown up unforeseen problems such as the new impetus for self-determination of peoples, equality of states and incessant demands for economic and social justice for all. These developments, it must be confessed, had not been fully anticipated. This was why many members of the UN Organization urged that the remedy lay in a number of radical amendments to the Charter provisions which would ensure the necessary adjustments to the new situation that confronted the world.

One important target for immediate anendment was and still

remains the abolition of the *veto power* in the Security Council. Not surprisingly, however, none of the five permanent Members were ready for that change, or indeed for a number of other amendments to the Charter. After protracted discussions and deliberations, the General Assembly, on December 17, 1963, adopted amendments to Articles 23, 27 and 61 of the Charter. These amendments came into force on August 31, 1965. Under the amendment to Article 23, the membership of the Security Council was enlarged from eleven to fifteen; under Article 27, provision was made that decisions of the Security Council on procedural matters should henceforth be carried by an affirmative vote of nine (formerly seven) members and by the same number on all other matters, including the concurring votes of the five permanent members of the Security Council. One further important concession to the new members was the amendment to Article 61 by which the membership of the Economic and Social Council was increased from eighteen to twenty-seven.

Important as these amendments were at the time, the General Assembly was already debating parallel action for making some desirable changes in both the fundamentals of policy and also of the *modus operandi* of the UN Organization. The new thinking was characterized by "coexistence", a word first used by the socialist countries and soon adopted by the vast majority of UN members to postulate a new era of interdependence and cooperation between divergent legal systems and political ideologies. Most members suddenly awoke to the realization that the alternative to peaceful coexistence would be chaos and world war. So it was that in 1973 the General Assembly established the Special Committee on Principles of International Law Concerning Friendly Relations and Cooperation among States, which consisted of Members from twenty-nine States and which, after a preliminary meeting in New York first met in Mexico later in the same year. The membership was soon raised to thirty-one.[11]

The seven principles this committee was to study and elaborate were (a) the principle that States shall remain free in their international relations from the threat and use of force against the territorial integrity or political independence of any state, or in any other manner inconsistent with the purpose of the United Nations; (b) the principle that States shall settle their international disputes by peaceful means in such a manner that international peace and security and justice are not endangered; (c) the duty not to interfere in matters within the domestic jurisdiction of any State, in accordance with the UN Charter; (d) the duty of States to cooperate with one another in accordance with the Charter; (e) the principle of the equal rights and self-determination of peoples; (f) the principle of sovereign equality of states; (g) the principle that States shall fulfil in good faith the obligations assumed by them in accordance with the UN Charter.[12]

The Charter is "the fundamental statement of those principles", and the Committee was to undertake, pursuant to Article 13 of the Charter, a study of the principles of international law concerning friendly relations and cooperation "with a view to their progressive development and codification, so as to secure more effective application". After almost seven years of conference discussions and debates on the various questions set for the Committee, the General Assembly, by Resolution 2625 (XXV) of October 24, 1970, adopted a Declaration embodying fairly detailed elaborations of these seven principles. The most controversial is the one requiring that States shall refrain in their international relations from the threat or use of force, as to which divergent views were held by Member States who took the view that the use of force forbidden by Article 2 paragraph 4 of the Charter is military force alone and by those States who argued that force also includes economic, political and forms of force other than the military. The latter were concerned to point out that there should be safeguards in the use of force against peoples of dependent territories in the exercize of their right of self-determination, in the use of force in territorial disputes and boundary problems, and in the acquisition of sovereignty by force. A compromise was arrived at that "every State has the duty to refrain from any forcible action which deprives peoples referred to in the elaboration of the principle of equal rights and self-determination of their right to self-determination and freedom and independence". One other problem was the question of acquisition of territory resulting from the threat or use of force and the recognition of such acquisition; the compromise adopted is that in such cases the threat or use of force is illegal provided that the UN Charter provisions or any international provision prior to the Charter regime and valid under international law are not affected. As regards the use of force by dependent peoples, the compromise was that dependent peoples "are entitled to seek and to receive support in accordance with the purposes and principles of the Charter", a statement differently interpreted by Western Powers on the one hand and the African States on the other. The Western Powers interpret it to mean that dependent peoples are entitled to receive non-military support only, whereas the African States see in this statement the recognition of the right of dependent peoples to receive military support.

One question which is still being agitated among students of the

Declaration regards its legal or non-legal character. Are the principles merely political or moral principles or are they legally binding? There can be little doubt as to the legal basis from which the principles were originally extracted, since the original resolution itself notes that the UN Charter is the source. The same resolution insists that the committee should endeavor to achieve progressive development and codification in the formulation of the seven principles and this task could only be discharged by the legitimate reformulation and extension of Charter principles.[13] As Rosenstoc has observed:

> The text of the Declaration on Friendly Relations is incomplete if viewed as a blueprint for world order. Too many issues are not covered; too many of those that are covered are dealt with in a vague manner. Moreover, there is room for debate as to the nature of the binding force of the Declaration among States. Finally, the text is largely oriented towards the preservation and protection of state sovereignty rather that the development of new norms and new mechanisms more suited to the increasingly inter-dependent world of today and of the future . . . . In spite of these *caveats*, the text represents a very substantial contribution to clarification of the key concepts of international law involved — so much so that a significant number of states pointed to the provisions in the course of recent debates in the United Nations as an example of the type of evolution which at this stage better served the needs of the international community than a formal Charter review.[14]

The question of the binding character of this Declaration is bound up with the wider issue of the legal force of all United Nations Declarations, for example the Universal Declaration of Human Rights of 1948, and certain formal resolutions of the General Assembly. The International Court of Justice has made pronouncements on a number of occasions declaring the binding force of these General Assembly determinations on specific issues in certain well-defined circumstances, into which we need not enter here.[15]

IV

We may now turn to some other landmarks in the 1960–1970 period of evolution of international law, the most noticeable being the Law of the Sea, Diplomatic Law and the Law of Treaties. These three were in the original, provisional list of fourteen topics drawn up by the International Law Commission in 1949,[16] and each was studied and finally submitted by the Commission to the General Assembly in that order. The topics on the Regime of the High Seas and the Convention on the Regime of Territorial Waters were adopted in 1958 as the Convention on the Territorial Sea and the Contiguous

Zone, the Convention on the High Seas, the Convention on Fishing and Conservation of the Living Resources of the High Seas and the Convention on the Continental Shelf; the Vienna Convention on Diplomatic Relations and The Vienna Convention on Consular Relations, in 1961 and 1963 respectively, and the Vienna Convention on the Law of Treaties in 1969; one other 1949 topic, namely, Succession of States and Governments, has since been subdivided and limited into two subjects now under separate study under the titles of Succession of States in Respect of Treaties and Succession of States in Respect of Matters Other Than Treaties.[17] Diplomatic Law has also since been supplemented by the Convention on Special Missions in 1969 and by the Convention on the Representation of States in their Relations with International Organizations, which was adopted at Vienna in 1975.

These three large pieces of progressive development and codification efforts do without a doubt fill important gaps in contemporary international law. The resultant four conventions on the Law of the Sea extended the boundaries of the customary law and practices of the uses of the high seas and territorial waters, the continental shelves and the exploitation of the living resources of the high seas. Two important aspects not dealt with are (a) the definitive delimitation of the Fisheries Jurisdiction and (b) what is now concurrently styled as the concept of the Economic Zone, both of which are the present preoccupation of the Third Law of the Peace Conference, the fifth session of which was held in Geneva in the summer of 1976. The third aspect of the law also engaging serious attention is a generally acceptable machinery for the administration of the seabed, especially the exploitation of its marine and mineral resources as "the common heritage of all mankind". It seems that most nations have now accepted 200 nautical miles as the limit of the jurisdiction of coastal States and at least twelve miles as that of the territorial seas. The International Court of Justice made some interesting contributions to this area of the law in the *North Sea Continental Shelf Cases*,[18] the *Fisheries Jurisdiction Case*[19] and even the *Fisheries Judgment*,[20] by drawing attention to aspects requiring clarification and further study.

In view of the greatly expanded professionalism of diplomatic intercourse, there has been better conventional regulation of the diplomat, the consular agent, *ad hoc* representation or mission on technical assistance programs and similar engagements, State representation at international organizations and specialized agencies as well as at international conferences — the last three categories being off-shoots of the traditional first two. Such is the resilience of customary international law that it has so quickly and so diligently risen to the occasion that we now have the present plethora of laws.

But one may be permitted to claim that the one most outstanding achievement of the United Nations in the field of progressive development and codification has been the Vienna Convention on the Law of Treaties, which is generally regarded as "the treaty on treaties". While still leaving room for the application of customary international law in certain limited areas not specifically covered by it, the Vienna Convention represents the *lex generalis* on the subject of treaty law and, although not yet formally in force, it has been so frequently cited with approval — even by the International Court of Justice — that it is already regarded as part of modern international law.[21] Topics such as the principle of *Pacta Sunt Servanda*, Reservations to Treaties, Fundamental Change of Circumstances, Supervening Impossibility of Performance and the interpretation, amendment and modification of treaties are all defined, refined and put on more acceptable foundations. Part V of the Vienna Convention contains probably the most progressive development and codification elements, in that, in addition to laying down clear grounds of invalidity, termination and suspension of the operation of Treaties, it makes satisfactory provision for the procedure to be followed with respect to these various grounds. By declaring void treaties affected by error, fraud, corruption, coercion[22] and those conflicting with the rule of *jus cogens*, the Vienna Convention proclaims a new universal principle, a new *ordre public* for the moral guidance of States in their *future* treaty relations. Unequal or leonine treaties are no longer permissible in the practice of States. To prevent any abuse by unilateral action, the Convention provides that a claim that a treaty is invalid on the ground that it conflicts with a peremptory norm of general international law (*jus cogens*) must be submitted to the Court of International Court of Justice for adjudication. It is probably needless to retell here the story of the great struggle to secure the adoption of the Vienna Convention in 1969 after nearly twenty years of preparation and two plenipotentiary conferences of almost six months each, in 1968 and 1969, at Vienna. We have told the story elsewhere.[23]

V

The decade since 1970 has been no less a momentous one than its predecessor. It is certainly the era of international economic and social action for the progress of mankind. The UN Commission on International Trade Law with twenty-nine member states was established by the General Assembly in 1966[24] for the purpose of undertaking the progressive harmonization and unification of the law of international trade.[25] The increase in world trade has rendered it even more urgent than before that its unimpeded flow be promoted by every means that will reduce or remove legal obstacles. The Trade Commission, therefore, began with a serious study of four major areas: international sale of goods, international commercial arbitration, international shipping legislation and international payments. The UNCITRAL also embarked upon the question of training and assistance in the field of international trade law. A yearbook and a register of the texts of conventions likely to facilitate the unification of trade law have since been established.[26] Training has been carried on in conjunction with UNITAR in Latin America, Asia and in Geneva, and also at the International Trade Law Branch of the Office of Legal Affairs.

Another important development in the promotion of world economic cooperation has been the establishment of the UN Conference on Trade and Development (UNCTAD). Within its short span, it has made a great impact on world economic relations as providing a better platform than the GATT (General Agreement on Tariff and Trade) scheme, largely through the activities of its Group of 77. Consisting originally of representatives of Third World countries of Africa, Asia and Latin America; although still referred to as the Group of 77, there are now 108 countries in the group. A Ministerial Conference of this group met in Manila in February 1976 to prepare for the Fourth UNCTAD Conference at Nairobi in May 1976 by formulating a common stand for the developing countries vis-à-vis the richer nations. President Ferdinand Marcos of the Philippines said in his address to the Manila conference that he hoped the Group of 77 could be "transformed into a Third World economic system based on the principle of collective economic self-reliance"; he also suggested that UNCTAD be turned into a specialized agency of the United Nations to be called the World Trade and Development Organization.[27]

One of the most urgent tasks of the Third World is to secure the replacement of obsolete economic relations of inequality by those based on equality and fairness. In the last week of January 1976, Dr Henry Kissinger, in an address to the Finance Committee of the US Senate, strongly criticized the Third World nations for using "confrontational tactics" in negotiations with the industrialized nations over their commodities and other products. At Nairobi, in his address to the Fourth UNCTAD Conference, Dr. Kissinger was more positive and understanding when he warned that the industrialized nations should recognize the legitimate claims of the developing nations whose voices had not always been heard in the past. On this last occasion, the US Secretary of State was in a similar mood to that in his address to the Institute of World Affairs at the University of Wisconsin on July 14, 1975: "If the industrial world wants to overcome the attitude of confrontation between nations, it must offer equitable solutions for the problems of the less fortunate parts of the world. Just as we are rightly concerned about the economic impact of exorbitant oil prices, so we should show understanding for the concerns of producers of other raw materials whose incomes fluctuate radically".[28] As Dr. Kissinger rightly said earlier in the same address, there has been a shift from a preoccupation with questions of peace and security to increasing attention to economic and social problems — so much so that nine-tenths of expenditures within the UN system relate to economic and social cooperation. He emphasized:

> Indeed it is in these fields that the work of the United Nations has been most successful and yet the most unheralded. Its specialized agencies have been effectively involved with countless areas of human and international concern: speeding decolonization, spreading education, science, and technology; organizing global cooperation to combat hunger and disease, to protect the environment, and to limit population growth, regulating international transport and communication and peaceful nuclear power; advancing human rights and expanding international law among nations and in outer space and on the seas; preserving the priceless cultural heritage of mankind. It is striking, and of great importance for the future, that the United Nations has been able to respond creatively to so many of the challenges of the modern age.[29]

This phenomenal expansion of international law among nations and on the seas and in outer space is the general theme of this study which, however, specifies significant and particular features of the new horizon. The present Development Decade has been specially marked as such by the UN Organization itself by commemorative action and by important steps to concretize the progress towards and the resolve for the economic and social well-being of mankind.

Two recent outcomes in the legal field are the UN Declaration on the New International Economic Order[30] and its Charter of Economic Rights and Duties of States.[31] These supply the legal framework for the International Law of Development which has been in the offing during the preceding five or six years, since when the United Nations has become seriously involved in the problems of development in the Third World.[32] The new world order necessarily envisages clearer and bolder definitions of the rights and duties of States as between developed and developing ones than have hitherto been attempted or accepted in customary international law. The

Declaration and the Charter reflect the new spirit that has been
abroad underlying the Universal Declaration of Human Rights and
the related convenants, the Declaration on Peaceful Coexistence and
Friendly Relations, and that section of Part V of the Vienna
Convention on the Law of Treaties which declares certain treaties
invalid on certain vitiating grounds — especially those treaties that
conflict with a peremptory norm of general international law (*jus
cogens*). A new world order seems truly to be in the making.[33]

VI

Never before in the history of international relations have so many
peoples of different races and climes joined together to make and to
administer such a plethora of laws for their common welfare, to
organize and execute plans for social and economic development.
Fresh vistas of a brave new world of law and international public
order have been opened up under the aegis of the United Nations,
particularly within the last decade. In addition to the declarations,
charters, conventions, convenants and resolutions which we have
delineated in the foregoing analysis, we must remember a growing
number of non-UN bodies which have, in the period under review,
been churning out new studies and new laws supplementing and
strengthening UN efforts in the field of international law. The Institut
de Droit International, the International Law Association and the
Hague Academy of International Law all antedate the United
Nations and continue to make their own contributions to contemporary international law. The World Peace Through Law group
based in Washington has, within the last twelve years, given wide and
impressive coverage to the work of the United Nations as well as
making international law better understood and more meaningful for
the securing of world peace through the rule of law.

National associations and journals of international law now
abound: the *American Journal of International Law*, the *British Yearbook of
International Law*, the Canadian, Australian and Indian counterparts,
the Japanese, Egyptian and Nigerian *Annuals of International Law* are
making worthy contributions to the expanding frontiers of international law and to the broadening of its application and
acceptability. Regional organizations like the Asian–African Legal
Consultative Committee, the International African Institute, the
Arab League, the Organization for African Unity and the
Organization of American States also contribute to the growing
influence and spread of contemporary international law.

We may mention in concluding our survey of new horizons the emergence of the International Law Commission and the International Court of Justice in their enlarged compositions. We have outlined the work of the Commission in the progressive development of international law and its codification; we have not done more than to indicate something of the evolution of the Court which, in the past five years, has shown a certain measure of judicial activity that seems to have redeemed its decline as a result of the 1966 Namibia decision. It seems such a pity that in an era of more laws, more books, more lawyers and more United Nations and other activities in the international legal field, there should be so much less judicial work for the Court at the present time.

NOTES

1. Conditions of Admission of a State to Membership in the United Nations (Article 4 of Charter) Advisory Opinion 1948, *I.C.J. Reports 1947–1948*, p. 57.

2. Competence of the General Assembly for the Admission of a State to the United Nations, Advisory Opinion, *I.C.J. Reports 1950*, p. 4.

3. *Yearbook of the International Law Commission*, 1950, Vol. II. pp. 367–374.

4. See generally M. Moskowitz's *International Concern With Human Rights*, 1974, p. 8, 40, 111.

5. Two Advisory Opinions of the ICJ on this problem were rendered in the following cases: Voting Procedure on Questions Relating to Reports and Petitions Concerning the Territory of South-West Africa, Advisory Opinion, *I.C.J. Reports 1955*, p. 67; Admissibility of Hearing of Petitioners by the Committee on South-West Afroca, Advisory Opinion, *I.C.J. Reports, 1956*, p. 23.

6. International Status of South-West Africa, Advisory Opinion, *I.C.J. Reports 1950*, p. 128.

7. Legal Consequences for States of the Continued Presence of South Africa in Namibia (South-West Africa) Notwithstanding Security Council Resolution 276 (1970), Advisory Opinion, *I.C.J. Reports 1971*, p. 16.

8. Competence of the General Assembly for the Admission of a State to the United Nations, Advisory Opinion, *I.C.J. Reports 1950*, p. 4.

9. Certain Expenses of the United Nations, Article 17, paragraph 2, of The Charter, (Advisory Opinion, *I.C.J. Reports 1962*, p. 151).

10. Legal Consequences for States of the Continued Presence of South Africa in Namibia, (South-West Africa) Notwithstanding Security Council Resolution 276 (1970), Advisory Opinion, *I.C.J. Reports 1971*, p. 16.

11. General Assembly Resolution 2533 (XXIV) of December 8, 1969.

12. See U.N. Doc. A/AC. 125/L86, May 1, 1970.

13. See M. Sahovic (Editor) *Principles of International Law Concerning Friendly Relations and Cooperation*, 1972 pp. 30–42ff.

14. See R. Rosenstoc, "Declarations of Principles of International Law

Concerning Friendly Relations: A Survey" *A.J.I.L.* Vol. 65, No. 5 1971, at p. 735.

15. See *The Namibia Case, I.C.J. Reports 1971*, p. 16 para. 52; *The Fisheries Jurisdiction Case, I.C.J. Reports 1974*, at pp. 25–26; *The Western Sahara Case, I.C.J. Reports 1975*, paras. 54–59. See, generally, O.Y. Asamoa's *The Legal Significance of the Declarations of the General Assembly 1966* and J. Castaneda's *The Legal Effects of United Nations Resolutions* (1969)

16. *The Work of the International Law Commission* (revised edition), p. 9. The Law of Treaties is to be concluded in its wider aspect by the study currently being undertaken by the ILC on Questions of Treaties Concluded Between States and International Organizations or Between Two or More International Organizations (see *ibid.*, p. 66).

17. *Ibid.*, pp. 60–61.

18. *I.C.J. Reports 1969*, p. 3.

19. *I.C.J. Reports 1973*, pp. 3 and 49.

20. *I.C.J. Reports 1951*, p. 116.

21. See my *Modern Law of Treaties*, 1974.

22. For an account of the controversy over the question of including coercion (or use or threat of force) as a ground of invalidity of treaty, see pp. 174–175. It will be recalled that the Declaration on Friendly Relations drew similar controversy between the Western Powers and the Third World States, see pp. 17–19 earlier.

23. *Ibid.*, pp. 7, 182–185. The writer was the Chairman of the Conference at Vienna in both 1968 and 1969.

24. Resolution 2205 (XXI) of December 17, 1966. In connection with the Report on the work of its Second Session, the General Assembly by Resolution 2502 (XXIV) of November 12, 1969, required the UNCITRAL to keep its program of work under constant review.

25. *Yearbook of the United Nations Commission on International Trade Law*, Vol. 1. See also *United Nations Juridical Yearbook*, 1970, p. 111.

26. Note *United Nations Juridical Yearbook*, 1971, p. 68.

27. See *The New Nigerian*, February 3, 1976, p. 10.

28. "Global Challenge and International Cooperation", at p. 13.

29. *Ibid.*, p. 5.

30. General Assembly Resolution 3201 (S-VI) May 1, 1974.

31. General Assembly Resolution 3281 (XXIX) December 12, 1974.

32. The seeds of the idea were sown under the UN Development Program (UNDP).

33. As an illustration of the concern for a better world in economic and social relations, we may note that in February 1976, the United States, in cooperation with certain Western industrialized nations, began work on a code of conduct for multinational corporations which would condemn bribes to public officials in foreign countries as a means of promoting American business there. This was sparked off by allegations of payoffs by the Lockheed Aircraft Corporation to senior officials in the Netherlands, Italy and Japan for the purpose of promoting the sale of its aircraft in those countries. (See *Dutch News*, of 27/2/76.)

Chapter 2

THE CONTRIBUTION OF ASIA AND AFRICA TO CONTEMPORARY INTERNATIONAL LAW

One of the problems that faced the newly independent states of Asia and Africa in the past two decades was the non-availability on a sufficient scale of trained manpower on the international plane, both at home and abroad, particularly at the United Nations and its specialized agencies. Not all of these new states, however, lacked the manpower: for example India and Japan have had a much longer period of apprenticeship than the others, having taken part in such international congresses as those on the Treaty of Versailles, 1919, and the Congo and Niger Rivers Conventions; their roles at the end of the First World War were still relatively minor ones, however.

From the 17th to the 19th century, international order consisted in the organization of various concerts of Europe designed to ensure that certain power blocs would gain ascendancy in the interest of their nation-states. It would be true to say that international law since Grotius, especially after the Treaty of Westphalia (1648), was largely European both in character and in application. A few years after independence the new states soon began to consider programs of concerted action against their shortcomings on an inter-state basis. The shortage of expertise in personnel in foreign ministries at home and for representational purposes abroad no doubt called for concerted action. There was also the need for a high level of Afro-Asian solidarity on a number of important issues — political, economic and social — all of which clearly required the restructuring of the international legal order.

The first notable attempt at such a concerted effort was the Asian–African Legal Consultative Committee first founded in 1956 with the title of Asian Legal Consultation Committee by seven Asian states under the leadership of India; two years later, its title was enlarged to accommodate African states as well. Today, thanks to the combined efforts of our indefatigable Secretary-General, Mr. B. Sen, and myself, there are some thirty member states of our organization. Among the principal aims of the Committee are the following three:

(1) to consider specific legal problems which may be referred to the Committee by any member government under Article 3(b) of the Committee's Statutes and to make recommendations thereon;

(2) examination of matters before the International Law Commission and other UN agencies in the field of international law and trade law with a view to making recommendations thereon to assist member governments which sometimes have to answer questionnaires and make comments on draft condification and conventions;

(3) preparation of background material and the arranging of exchanges of views on matters of common interest and on important questions which are to come up at diplomatic conferences under the auspices of the United Nations and other agencies.

Other subsidiary functions of the Committee are:

(a) the undertaking of publications on matters of common interest, examples being the Committee's two massive volumes, one each on the constitutions of Asian and of African States;

(b) collection of materials on any legal question for any member state at its request, and

(c) training of officers of member states in research methods in the field of international law, this again being at the request of member states.

In New Dehli, the Legal Consultative Committee's Secretariat is steadily becoming international in both composition and outlook, there being at the moment a mixed staff which, while being of necessity largely Indian, has attracted personnel from at least four other countries as a matter of deliberate policy. Annual conferences of the Committee have been held by rotation in the capitals of the following member states — India, Egypt, Sri Lanka, Burma, Pakistan, Ghana, Nigeria, Iraq and Japan.

As well as having published annual reports of the fifteen sessions already held at the various state capitals, the Committee has also undertaken and issued special reports on such crucial questions as Legality of Nuclear Tests (a study which, in view of the recent cases before the International Court of Justice between France and Australia and New Zealand, has turned out to be prophetic), Reciprocal Recognition and Enforcement of Foreign Judgments (a subject of current importance in view of the increasing social and commercial intercourse between the countries of Africa and Asia), the Rights of Refugees (a development of contemporary relevance to both Africa and Asia where, in recent years, there have been national upheavals in adjacent countries and across frontiers), Relief against Double Taxation and Fiscal Evasion (again a subject of current importance between Africa on the one hand and India, Japan and China on the other, due to increasing economic and financial inter-actions), and the protracted *South-West Africa Cases* (which are a source of common concern to India and Africa as a result of their common experience at the hands of apartheid South Africa. It is significant that even at a time when India had no nuclear weapons, the late Prime Minister Nehru was the first world statesman and lawyer to call the attention of the Committee in 1961 to the need to undertake a comprehensive study of the question of the legality of nuclear tests then being carried out in parts of Africa and Asia. One of the most interesting studies under preparation by the Committee is the *Digest of Judgments of the Courts of Asian and Africa Countries on International Legal Questions*. This important subject has not been given the consideration that it deserves in the writings of international lawyers, and it is most appropriate that the Committee should have undertaken it as one of the sure means of assessing the contribution of the courts of Asia and Africa to the development of international law.

In order to appreciate the significance of the contribution already made by the Asian–African Legal Consultative Committee in the relatively short span of its eighteen years of existence, let us recall its relationship with the United Nations, the International Law Commission, the UN Commission on Trade and Development (UNCTAD), the UN Commission on International Trade Law (UNCITRAL), the UN High Commission for Refugees (UNHCR), the League of Arab States, the Commonwealth Secretariat, the Institute for the Unification of Private Law (UNIDROIT) and the Hague Conference on Private International Law. An interesting recent development has been the practice of these various bodies and of non-Asian and African countries to be represented at sessions of the Legal Consultative Committee by their legal experts in the capacity of observers. There were, for instance, at the January 1974 Tokyo sessions, a total of thirty-nine such delegations from Latin American countries, Scandinavia, Britain, West and East European countries and the United States as well as many Asian and African non-member states. These experts obviously came to ascertain the views of Asia and Africa on the current issues concerning The Law of the Sea, to the Third conference on which the Committee was invited in 1976 by the United Nations as a participant in its own right.

It may be pointed out that this was not the first time that the Committee had been invited to participate in a codification under the auspices of the United Nations. For instance, the Committee took part in the Vienna Conference on Diplomatic Relations in 1961 where the Committee's recommendations on the subject were tabled and discussed as a conference document. Also at both sessions held in 1968 and in 1969, the Committee participated actively in the work of the Conference of Plenipotentiaries on the Law of Treaties in Vienna. The present speaker had the honor of being elected Chairman of the Committee of the Whole at both sessions and was also elected Chairman of the Afro-Asian Group working with the West European, the East European and the Latin-American Groups *pari passu* with the Conference proceedings. It is to the credit of Africa and Asia that, when the prospects of success at this crucial conference looked bleak, it was given to me as Chairman to propose the solution which ended the deadlock and thereby saved the Vienna Conference on The Law of Treaties from imminent collapse. The trouble was that the draft convention combined large elements of progressive development of international law with its codification. The most controversial section of the Convention was Part V which deals with the causes of the invalidity of treaties on the grounds of mistake, fraud, coercion and *jus cogens* (that is, those peremptory norms of customary international law from which states cannot derogate). The Western Powers expressed serious doubts as to the practicability of enforcing claims of invalidity on grounds such as these, and they questioned whether the other provisions of the Draft Convention and those in Part V could be acceptable without at the same time providing an adequate machinery for the settlement of disputes arising out of them. A package deal was then introduced by me which provided that the International Court of Justice should be given jurisdiction to determine disputes between the parties to a treaty as to its invalidity on any of these grounds. At the same time, a detailed procedural machinery for achieving proper adjudication was set out in another provision of the package deal. Both the Western Powers and the Third World (which seemed to want the party invoking the invalidity of a treaty to determine the question without any recourse to a compulsory system of adjudication) were called upon to accept the deal *as a whole*; the alternative would have been chaos. At that poignant moment, both sides showed statemanship and, after a fairly long adjournment of the proceedings, returned to the Conference chamber to accept my proposals.

While we are still on the subject of contributions made to UN Conferences of Plenipotentiaries for the drawing up and conclusion of international conventions, we may note briefly the part the Asian-African Legal Consultative Committee has played and continues to play in the current effort to achieve an acceptable body of modern legal principles to govern the regime of the seas. The Committee has been actively engaged in study of a new Law of The Sea for some five years now, and took up quite early the 1970 UN declaration and the even earlier requests of two member-governments of the committee that a third conference on the subject was both necessary and desirable. Subcommittees of the Committee were set up to study various aspects of the topic in depth. The first comprehensive public discussion of these studies took place at the Committee's session held in Colombo, (Sri Lanka) in January 1971 when a strong contingent from Latin-American countries attended as observers and intervened to press their demand for the 200-mile limit for territorial waters. Other delegations also came from the United States. It was at that conference that the Committee outlined its own distinctive concepts of the Exclusive Economic Zone which embraced not only the outmoded three-mile limit for territorial waters but also included an area of the sea adjacent to the coast which covered fishing grounds as well as the exploitation of the mineral and other resources of the subjacent soil as coming within the boundaries of national jurisdiction. The purpose of the Exclusive Economic Zone is to safeguard the interest of coastal States in the waters adjacent to their coasts without unduly interfering with the other legitimate uses of the sea by other states. The proposal meant that each coastal state should have a territorial sea of twelve miles beyond which there would be this additional economic zone. This zone was not to be regarded as territorial water, since freedom of the high seas as well as freedom of laying some types of marine cables were already established under customary international law. On the other hand, the zone could not be regarded as forming part of the high seas either, because the coastal state should have the exclusive right to exploit, regulate and control fisheries, and take and enforce pollution measures as well as exploit the resources of the sea-bed within the zone. Other states could exercize similar rights of exploitation of the resources within the zone only when so licensed by the coastal states.

We may also recall in this connection that the African Regional Seminar on the Law of the Sea, held in Yaounde in June 1972, adopted the concept of the Exclusive Economic Zone which, be it noted, originated in a Kenyan proposal. Again, in May 1973, the Organization of African Unity, following the draft Declaration on the issues of the Law of the Sea adopted by the Council of Ministers, ratified this Declaration which recognizes the right of each coastal state to establish an exclusive economic zone beyond its territorial waters up to a limit of 200 nautical miles. The matter was taken a stage further when fourteen African States introduced Draft Articles on the exclusive economic zone before the UN Sea-Bed Committee.[1]

Allied to this concept of an exclusive economic zone is that of the *patrimonial sea* which was first adumbrated in the Declaration of the Ministers of Caribbean States in June 1972. The Mexican delegate who attended as an observer at the New Delhi session of the Committee in January 1973 explained the *patrimonial sea* idea at some length. The Committee thereupon decided to make a comparative study of the two concepts. But before this was done, India had made certain proposals for an exclusive fisheries zone which should be complementary to and an elaboration of one of the aspects of the exclusive economic zone. After much discussion aimed at clarification of the limits of the concept, there was introduced before the UN Sea-Bed Committee a Six-Power proposal on the concept of the Fisheries Zone.[2] On the whole, the idea of an exclusive economic zone soon gained wide acceptance among the member states of the Legal Consultative Committee and it would seem that all future discussions on the subject of the law of the sea must take account of it. The general acceptability of the concept of an exclusive economic zone is further underlined by the conclusions of the Fourth Summit Conference of Non-Aligned Nations.

One other aspect of the proposals regarding the law of the sea is the question of the establishment of an international machinery to govern the regime of the sea-bed beyond national jurisdiction, that is to say, beyond the exclusive economic zone. The Committee did not consider that the area of the seabed which should be placed under an international agency should be as large as proposed by the major Powers, or that the powers to be given to the agency should be as all-pervasive as had been envisaged for it. There is no doubt that the United States, the Soviet Union and Japan already possess the most advanced technological know-how in the exploitation of the resources of the seabed beyond national jurisdiction. The Committee was accordingly reluctant to accept the Trust concept put forward by the major Powers which would enable them to use their technology for the exploitation of the resources of the ocean floor as "the common heritage of all mankind". The Committee, both collectively as a body and through its members as individuals, put forward its own detailed proposals at Caracas, and later at Geneva where members of the Committee took part as Chairman and as Secretary of the conferences, and no doubt espoused the cause of Asian, African and Latin-American countries in ensuring a just and acceptable solution to the problems posed by the law of the sea since the last convention was concluded in 1958 and amended in 1960. So intractable have

been these problems of the law of the sea that no formula satisfactory
to all has yet been found. It is not known what a definitive conference
in the future will decide, but the Committee's position should be the
achievement of a balanced system which would ensure fairness and
justice to all.

Before we turn to a consideration of some of the activities of Asia
and Africa in the United Nations and its agencies, let us examine
briefly the work of other regional organizations in parts of both
continents in the last two decades or so. The league of Arab States is
no doubt a political organ primarily, but the importance of certain of
its declarations and resolutions on international issues is that they
connote legal consequences. This is especially so with regard to
Middle East affairs. Take for instance the League's stand that Israel
must withdraw from all occupied Arab territories which it has
occupied since the 1967 war, and remember that this has become the
official position of the United Nations in its resolution on the subject.
This would seem to be in accordance with the customary international law principle that no state may keep any territory
acquired by conquest. Similarly, the influence of the Arab League
must not be underrated in connection with the question of ratification
or acceptance of UN draft conventions; member states of the League
normally follow its lead in such cases, as witness the delay in ratifying
the Vienna Convention on the Law of Treaties because, it is
understood, the League wants to establish an Arabic version of the
text of the Convention before the member states will ratify the
Convention.

The Organization of African Unity is another regional body
which, in addition to being essentially a political organ, provides
specifically for the ultimate use of the UN machinery for dispute
settlements with regard to interpretation of the UN Charter; the
Charter contains a built-in mechanism, in the form of a Commission
of Mediation, Conciliation and Arbitration, for the resolution of
conflicts between its member states. The Commission also makes
important declarations having legal consequences, as for example, its
declaration on the law of the sea in respect of the exclusive economic
zone concept to which we have referred.

One of the results of the conference of the International
Commission of Jurists (of Geneva) held in Lagos in January 1961 was
a proposal by all the African states there present that a Commission of
African Jurists be established. After a preliminary meeting in Lagos
in 1963 on the subject, the inaugural conference was held in January
1964 at which were present representatives of twenty-one independent African States who under my chairmanship unanimously

adopted a convention and a statute. The delegates also resolved to place the Commission of African Jurists under the Organization of African Unity as one of its six specialized commissions. The Organization of African Unity eventually accepted the recommendation. The new organization was intended to serve as a permanent forum for the discussion and study of the many legal and constitutional problems of Africa. The objectives of the Commission of African Jurists may be summarized as follows:

(a) to promote and develop understanding and cooperation among African jurists;
(b) to encourage the study of law, especially African Law, and to advance the concept of justice;
(c) to consider legal problems of common interest and those that may be referred to it by any of its members and by the Organization of African Unity and to make recommendations thereon;
(d) to encourage the study of African customary law in the universities and institutes of legal studies in Africa and elsewhere, and its codification by the African Governments, and
(e) to establish relationships with other international organizations on the basis of non-alignment.

The Commission of African Jurists has not been active so far in the pursuit of its aims and purposes, probably because its proposals for the advancement of the Rule of Law in Africa might be critical of acts or omissions of some of the member governments.

If the preoccupation of the Commission of African Jurists is with the private law sector, public international law is the prime concern of the conference held in March 1967 in Lagos on "International Law and African Problems" under the joint auspices of the Nigerian Institute of International Affairs and the Carnegie Endowment for International Peace. The working papers included Treatment of Aliens, The Methods of Encouraging the Wider Study and Appreciation of International Law in Africa, Government Legal Advising in the Field of Foreign Affairs, Treaties and Succession of States and Governments in Africa, The Relevance of International Law to African Problems and Cooperation in the Utilization of International Rivers in Africa.[3] Of the various papers studied, the one on succession of states and governments is of especial importance because the delegates from Tanzania, in explaining state practice in the East African countries, submitted that neither the automatic succession theory nor the "clean state" theory adequately or accurately described the current practice. They further submitted that, generally speaking, preexisting treaties did not survive the transition from trusteeship to independent Tanganyika **statehood,** whereas there was a continuity of treaty relationships in **Zanzibar** which both antedated and postdated the period of the protectorate. Bilateral treaty relationships in both Tanganyika and Zanzibar survived the union wherever they were not inconsistent with constitutional provisions and wherever they were in accordance with geographical limitations expressed or implied in the treaty; boundary agreements were inherited, provided they were clear and un-ambiguous. Visa abolition agreements survived the grace period, and those that did not were terminated within the ensuing three years; no commercial agreements survived the grace period, but a few were renegotiated after independence. Finally, it was the contention of the Tanzanian delegates that the so-called Nyerere Doctrine of Succession helped to ease the adjustment of fundamentally changed circumstances by permitting a grace period during which all interested parties could review the desirability of continuing treaty relationships, since customary international law recognizes that consent of states is the basic norm of their treaty relationship.[1] When one looks at the Draft Convention on Succession of States in respect of Treaties recently completed by the International Law Commission and submitted to the UN General Assembly, one will find clear evidence of the influence of the thinking of African jurists on the provisions dealing with the "clean state" theory. The other topics received equally extensive discussions at the conference, but it would be impolitic to attempt a detailed review here.

An important outcome of the Lagos conference was the follow-up meeting held, again at the Nigerian Institute of International Affairs, in June 1968 under the joint auspices of the Institute and the Carnegie Endowment for International Peace. It was a more restricted conference in that it was a standing committee meeting of the previous one and it was attended by representatives of Ghana, the U.A.R., Dahomey, Algeria, Uganda, Kenya, Tanzania, Senegal and Nigeria as well as the representatives of the Carnegie Endowment and the Nigerian Institute of International Affairs. After the fullest consideration of the sub-committee's report, it was unanimously decided that there should be established an African Institute of International Law. According to Article 2 of the Constitution of the new Institute, the object is to foster the study of international law and international relations in Africa and to promote African contribution to the development of international law. To this end, the Institute is required to:

(a) cooperate with similar institutes and societies in Africa and in other parts of the world;
(b) be a documentation center for all Africa;
(c) seek to encourage research in the field of international law and international relations in Africa; and
(d) publish studies in international law and on African problems and, in particular, an *African Yearbook of International Law*.

As both the 1967 and the 1968 conferences were held under my chairmanship, I was elected Chairman of the African Institute of International Law with an Executive Council and a Secretariat entrusted to the Nigerian Institute of International Affairs[4]

The proposed documentation center and *African Yearbook of International Law* have had to be held in abeyance pending a decision of the Organization of African Unity as to whether it should foot the bill itself or permit one or more member states to do so. One other reason for the apparent inactivity of the African Institute of International Law may be due to the fact that many of its leading members had, by 1969, became more and more involved with the already established and functioning Asian-African Legal Consultative Committee which began to attract more African government participation at about this time

If we may now attempt a summary of the main activities of the Afro-Asian states in the work of the United Nations, it is no exaggeration to say that their contribution to contemporary international law has been notable. The UN General Assembly began its life in 1946 with fifty-one states of which only Ethiopia and Liberia were foundation members from Africa, although there were a few like India and others from Asia as well. By 1960, the number had grown to ninety-seven and, today, there are some 145 members of the UN Organization, of which forty-seven are Africans and twenty-nine are Asians, totalling seventy-six or more than half of the entire UN membership. While it is true that mere preponderance of numbers does not *ipso facto* signify a greater Afro-Asian contribution to the work of the United Nations than that of the other members, it is my thesis that the Asian–African group of states has made a noteworthy contribution to modern international law. We may classify the spheres of this contribution into the following five categories:

(1) constitutional,
(2) legal and judicial,
(3) economic,
(4) social and cultural.
(5) human rights.

1.   *International Constitutional Law* is a recent phenomenon in the wider field of international law and it has steadily grown out of the multiplicity of international organizations and the various conventions and statutes which create and regulate their activities. Apart from their built-in machinery for determining the respective competences of their constituent organs, there is also the external regulative control in the form of the UN Administrative Tribunal and the collateral powers granted to many of these international organizations to request advisory opinions from the International Court of Justice. All these arrangements are designed to ensure that the United Nations itself, its specialized agencies and the other international organizations act within their proper limits in accordance with their charters and the general principles of international law.[5] Asia and Africa have made notable contributions to the United Nations, the ILO, the WHO, and so on in the development of their institutions along generally acceptable lines.

2.   Under *legal and judicial* we must include the International Law Commission, the International Court of Justice, the UN Administrative Tribunal and other quasi-legal bodies like the UNCITRAL.

The ILC is a creation of the UN General Assembly under Article 13 of the Charter and its main function is to engage in the task of codification and progressive development of international law. Beginning life with fifteen members in 1947, the ILC has since had to increase its membership to twenty-five, so as to ensure that the principal legal systems and the main forms of civilization are represented thereon. There are now five Africans and four Asians on the Commission, that is, more that one-third of the total membership. The ILC, as the principal UN law-drafting body, has done a great deal to widen the horizons of international law and to expand its frontiers by attuning the law to the contemporary needs and aspirations of the whole of mankind. It has modernized almost the whole field of *diplomatic law*, as witness the Consular and the Diplomatic Conventions of 1961 and 1963, the Convention on Special Missions and that on The Representatives of States at the United Nations and at international conferences; *treaty law*, as represented by the Vienna Convention on the Law of Treaties and by the Convention on Succession of States in respect of treaties; *maritime law*, as for example, the Conventions of The Law of the Sea, 1958 and 1960; the draft Conventions on The Rights and Duties of States, Definition of Aggression and many other drafts on various subjects referred to it by the UN General Assembly for study and codification based on progressive development. It would be tedious to stop to analyze the specific contributions of Asian and African participants to the several draft codes and conventions, but anyone who cares to look for these should find them in abundance.

Similarly, even in the judicial sphere, one finds clear evidence of the impact made by Asia and Africa on the International Court of Justice within the last two decades. Of the fifteen members of the ICJ, three are African and three are Asians, making two-fifths of the total membership. Although a number of decisions and opinions of the Court delivered in the last few years have earned worldwide criticism as reflecting more of the old thinking in international law than contemporary norms and aspirations, nevertheless the feeling is now abroad that the notable changes in the law being brought about by the work of the ILC are being reflected more and more in the pronouncements of the Court, particularly within the past four or five years. It is greatly to be hoped that this progressive attitude of the World Court will be maintained in increasing measure in the years that lie ahead.

We need not deal here with the additional law-drafting work of other subsidiary organs like the UNCITRAL which, for example, is confined to trade law. It is sufficient to note that there are such bodies and that the legal work they do is of great importance to contemporary international law.

3. *International Economic Law* is another new branch of international law which has emerged largely out of the creation and operation of economic and financial institutions like the IBRD, IDA and UNCTAD. More specifically oriented towards Asian and African needs are the Economic Commission for Asia and that for Africa. One of the origins of this aspect of the law is GATT (General Agreement on Tariff and Trade). Certain basic norms of economic law and patterns of behavior have grown up which not only define economic and financial relationships between two or more states *inter se* and between one or more states and international financial institutions, but also ensure that equity and fairness inform every aspect of the arrangement in accordance with the UN Charter.

The Economic and Social Council, as one of the principal organs of the United Nations, is empowered to set up commissions in the economic and social field and it has carried out this duty in respect of Asia and Africa. The decisions of ECOSOC are made by a majority of the members present and voting, and the Asian and African states' voices have always been duly heard as and when necessary on matters touching their interests. the enlarged ECOSOC has a membership increased from eighteen to twenty-seven.

4.   The prominence given by the United Nations to the educational, scientific and cultural development of new states is symbolized by the rapid growth of UNESCO, especially in Asia and Africa. Under Article 55 of the UN Charter, one of the main functions of the Organization is to promote solutions of international economic, social, health and related problems as well as international cultural and educational cooperation. The ECOSOC may make and initiate studies and reports with respect to these matters and may coordinate the activities of the specialized agencies and make recommendations to the UN General Assembly.

5.   A new area in which modern international law has expanded its frontiers is in the field of *Humanitarian Law*. Under Article 62 of the UN Charter, the ECOSOC has power to make recommendations to the UN General Assembly for the purpose of promoting respect for, and observance of human rights and fundamental freedoms for all, without distinction as to race, sex, language or religion. Under Article 68, it has set up the Commission on Human Rights. Beginning with the well-known Universal Declaration of Human Rights, 1948, the UN General Assembly has adopted some seven Conventions on economic and social rights, women's rights and other rights covering almost all the known areas of human relationships and endeavors. The present Humanitarian Law conventions are quite ample in their provisions. What remains to be done is to establish a satisfactory machinery for their effective implementation. The efforts of the Third World, especially Asia and Africa, in developing the various charters and conventions are too well-known to require any elaboration here. But we will do well to emphasize in passing the great work of the right to self-determination as a distinctive feature of the achievement of the United Nations since about 1950. There are three chapters of the UN Charter specifically devoted to the interests of dependent peoples: Chapter XI requires that member states which have assumed responsibilities for the administration of non-self-governing territories recognize the principle that the interests of the inhabitants of these territories are paramount and accept as a sacred trust the obligation to promote the well-being of the inhabitants. To this end, member states must undertake to develop self-government, take due account of the political aspirations of the dependent peoples and assist them in the development of their free political institutions. Chapters XII and XIII establish a Trusteeship System for the international supervision of the administration of territories placed under the system through

individual agreements. Such territories were formerly placed under the mandate of certain powers. The basic objective of the Trusteeship system is to promote the political, economic and social advancement of the UN Trust Territories and their progressive development towards self-government or independence as appropriate. Because of the slow pace at which self-government was being granted, the UN General Assembly, at its 1960 session on December 14, adopted a resolution entitled Declaration on the Granting of Independence to Colonial Countries and Peoples which proclaimed that all peoples have the right to self-determination and by virtue of that right they freely determine their political status and freely pursue their economic, social and cultural development. Various committees were established as a consequence and the Special Committee of Twenty-Four was officially known as the "Special Committee on the Situation with regard to the implementation of the Declaration on the Granting of Independence to Colonial Countries and Peoples". By 1964, UN membership had risen from ninety-seven in 1960 to 115; today, it stands at 145. Asia and Africa naturally contributed most to this development. The culmination of their joint struggle was the definitive recognition given to the distinctive legal concept of self-determination of the opinion given by the International Court of Justice in *the Namibia Case* in June 1971.

One the whole, it can truly be said that Asia and Africa, often with the assistance of Latin-American and sometimes of the East European States, have made notable contributions to the development of contemporary international law in the various ways indicated above. One can only hope that one has not exaggerated that contribution.

NOTES

1. A/AC. 138/SC. II/L40.

2. A/EC. 138/SC. II/L38.

3. See D.P. O'Connell's "Independence and Succession to Treaties" in the *British Yearbook of International Law*, 1963, at p. 95.

4. See *The Establishment of the African Institute of International Law and The Documentation Centre: Verbatim Report of the Proceedings of the Standing Committee Meeting of the Nigerian Conference on "International Law and International Problems"*, 1970, Government Printer, Lagos.

5. See e.g. Certain Expenses of the United Nations, Advisory Opinion, *I.C.J. Reports 1962*, p. 151; Constitution of the Maritime Safety Committee of the Inter-Governmental Maritime Consultative Organization, Advisory Opinion, *I.C.J. Reports 1960*, p. 150.

Chapter 3

THE LAW OF TREATIES IN RETROSPECT

Introduction

Following the establishment of the International Law Commission in 1947, the UN Secretariat submitted to the Commission at its first session in 1949 a memorandum entitled "Survey of international law in relation to the work of codification of the International Law Commission" containing twenty-five topics for consideration.[1] Of these the Commission selected fourteen topics, including The Law of Treaties, as forming a provisional list to be studied on a long term basis.

Under Article 13(1) of the UN Charter, the General Assembly is called upon to "initiate studies and make recommendations for the purpose of: (a) . . . encouraging the progressive development of international law and its codification". In embarking upon its task regarding the study of the law of treaties, the Commission considered two alternative approaches: to prepare a code on the subject or to formulate it as an international convention. The first two special rapporteurs submitted preliminary reports which were not, however, discussed because of the successive resignation of each before the Commission had had time to deal with them. It was the third special rapporteur, Sir Gerald Fitzmaurice of the United Kingdom who, in his five reports between 1955–60, suggested that the Commission adopt the form of a code of general character rather than that of a convention. In its 1959 Report to the General Assembly the Commission put the position thus:

> . . . the law of treaties is not itself dependent on treaty, but is part of general customary international law. Queries might arise if the law of treaties were embodied in a multilateral convention, but some States did not become parties to the convention, or became parties to it and then subsequently denounced it; for they would in fact be or remain bound by the provisions of the treaty in so far as these embodied customary international law *de lege lata*. No doubt this difficulty arises whenever a convention embodies rules of customary international law. In practice, this often does not matter. In the case of the law of treaties it might matter — for the law of treaties is itself the basis of the force and effect of all treaties. It follows from all this that if it were ever decided to cast the Code, or any

35

part of it, in the form of an international convention, considerable drafting changes, and possibly the omission of some material, would almost certainly be required[2]

The first fourteen draft articles were adopted on the basis of the first report of Sir Gerald Fitzmaurice and in the light of the code formula set out above. The International Law Commission, however, reserved its position by adding that the adoption of a code was without prejudice to any ultimate decision it might take on the subject. Like his two predecessors, Sir Gerald resigned from the Commission and Sir Humphrey Waldock was appointed to take his place as special rapporteur. The scheme of work was given a new orientation after the Commission had considered the detailed comments submitted on the earlier reports by the UN Member Governments and by the General Assembly. In its 1962 report to the General Assembly, the Commission reversed the process and decided that an international convention would be preferable to an expository code, explaining the change in these words:

> First, an expository code, however well formulated, cannot in the nature of things be so effective as a convention for consolidating the law; and the consolidation of the law of treaties is of particular importance at the present time when so many new States have recently become members of the international community. Secondly, the codification of the law of treaties through a multilateral convention would give all the new States the opportunity to participate directly in the formulation of the law if they so wished; and their participation in the work of codification appears to the Commission to be extremely desirable in order that the law of treaties may be placed upon the widest and most secure foundations.[3]

By Resolution 1765 (XVII) of November 20, 1962, the UN General Assembly endorsed this approach as well as the transmission of the first twenty-nine draft articles to governments for comment. Two further reports and sets of draft articles were submitted to the General Assembly by the Commission in 1963 and 1964. After taking into account the comments of governments and those of the Assembly, the Commission devoted the 1965 and 1966 sessions to the complete re-examination of the entire draft articles[4] and submitted a total of seventy-five articles to the Assembly, at the same time recommending that the latter convene an international conference of plenipotentiaries to study the Commission's draft articles and to conclude a convention on the law of treaties based thereon.[5] By Resolution 2287 (XXII) of December 6, 1967, the General Assembly decided to convene two yearly sessions of the international conference of plenipotentiaries to study and conclude a convention at Vienna in

1968 and 1969 respectively. This was eventually done,[6] and the conference adopted the Vienna Convention on the Law of Treaties on May 23, 1969.

At this stage, it may be pointed out that the importance of the conference lies in the fact that it was the first international plenipotentiary conference under UN auspices in which large numbers of the new member states participated in the work of codification of a general multilateral treaty. Indeed, as we have seen, the particular form in which the Convention was cast by the International Law Commission and finally adopted by the General Assembly and by the Conference itself had been dictated by consideration of the need to facilitate the participation of the new States and of the fact that it

> ... appears to the Commission to be extremely desirable in order that the law of treaties may be placed upon the widest and most secure foundations.

The conference is also significant for the new states in as much as some of them rightly or wrongly complained that they had inherited, and been made parties to, unequal treaties — especially before independence — and there can be no denying the fact that "the law of treaties is itself the basis of the force and effect of all treaties" in the formulation of which they should participate. Also, both in the International Law Commission and the Sixth Committee of the General Assembly, not to mention the Assembly itself, there had been an enlarged membership of the representatives of the new States who had actively participated in the preparation of the various texts of the draft articles at every stage up to and including the conference itself. Indeed, it is significant that the election of the present writer as Chairman of the Committee of the Whole Conference at both sessions in 1968 and 1969 was unanimous. The important role which the Afro-Asians played at the conference itself, both as individuals and as a group, will be referred to later.

Scope of the Vienna Convention

Before we enter into a discussion of the Vienna Convention it would be well to take note of its scope. We begin with a statement of what it does not contain. Thus, the Convention limits the scope of application of the articles to treaties concluded between states only, thereby excluding treaties between states and other subjects of international law, for example, international organizations,[7] as well as those between such other subjects of international law. Also, the Convention does not deal with agreements not in written form,[8] nor does it deal with the application of treaties providing for obligations or rights to be performed or enjoyed by individuals. Also excluded from its provisions are the effect of the outbreak of hostilities upon treaties, succession of States in respect of treaties, the question of the international responsibility of a State with respect to a failure to perform a treaty obligation, and the "most-favoured-nation clauses".[9] All these excluded topics, with the exception of the question of the effect of the outbreak of war upon treaties, have been or are the subjects of independent studies by the International Law Commission.[10]

An omnibus provision specifying the legal effect of international agreements regarded as outside the scope of the Vienna Convention is contained in Article 3 as follows:

> The fact that the present Convention does not apply to international agreements concluded between States and other subjects of international law or between such other subjects of international law, or to international agreement not in written form, shall not affect:
> (a) the legal force of such agreements;
> (b) the application to them of any of the rules set forth in the present Convention to which they would be subject under international law independently of the Convention;
> (c) the application of the Convention to the relations of States as between themselves under international agreements to which other subjects of international law are parties.

Now, with regard to what the Vienna Convention covers, we may briefly enumerate the principal matters as (a) the conclusion and entry into force of treaties, including (b) reservations and provisional application of treaties, observance, application and interpretation of treaties, including (c) treaties and third States, and amendment and modification of treaties; (d) invalidity, termination and suspension of the operation of treaties, including (e) the procedure for the application of the provisions relating to (d) and the settlement of disputes concerning the application or interpretation of the relevant provisions, and the consequences of the invalidity, termination or suspension of the operation of a treaty; and (f) depositaries, notifications, corrections and registration. The Vienna Convention consists of a preamble, eighty-five articles and an annex which sets out the provisions concerning the procedures of the Conciliation Commission established under Article 66 of the Convention for the judicial settlement, arbitration and conciliation of disputes arising out of the operation of the Convention. There were also two declarations adopted by the international plenipotentiaries conference and five resolutions annexed to the Final Act. The declarations are entitled The Declaration on the Prohibition of Military, Political or Economic Coercion in the Conclusion of Treaties and The Declaration on Universal Participation in the Vienna Convention on the Law of Treaties.[11] We shall explain briefly later the background to the adoption of the first declaration about enforced treaties; it is sufficient here to state that the second declaration was adopted in order to ensure that multilateral treaties dealing with the progressive development of international law and its codification or which are of interest to the international community as a whole would be open to universal participation. It is otherwise in the case of treaties dealing with or intended to relate only to a limited group of States parties to such treaties, either on the ground of geographical contiguity (e.g. the Organization of African Unity upon the Council of Europe) or on economic or other limited grounds compatible with regional groupings permitted by the UN Charter. Articles 81 and 83 of the Vienna Convention empower the UN General Assembly to issue special invitations to States that are not members of the United Nations or of any of its specialized agencies or the International Atomic Energy Agency or parties to the Statute of the International Court of Justice to become parties to the Convention. The General Assembly was accordingly to assure the issuing of invitations to ensure the widest possible participation in the Convention.

The Asian-African Legal Consultative Committee and the Vienna Convention

It is fair to record briefly here something of the measure of the contribution which the Asian–African Legal Consultative Committee made to the elaboration of the Vienna Convention on the Law of Treaties.

In accordance with Article 3(a) of its Statute, the Committee has the function, *inter alia*, "to examine questions that are under consideration by the International Law Commission and to arrange for the views of the committee to be placed before the Commission, to consider the reports of the Commission and to make recommendations thereon to the governments of the participating countries". This is to make available to all concerned the Asian–African points of view on the Commission's drafts involving the progressive development of international law and its codification.

When, therefore, the draft convention was under consideration in its final stages the Asian–African Legal Consultative Committee was represented by its Observer at some of the International Law Commission's sessions in Geneva, and the reports of the Commission were considered by the Committee at its 1964, 1965 and 1966 sessions, at the last of which a special rapporteur was appointed to prepare a report for its consideration. This report was, together with a brief from the Secretariat, considered by the Committee at its New Delhi session in 1967. The session also had the benefit of the Secretariat report on the views expressed by the Asian–African members of the Commission throughout its deliberations on the draft articles of the Vienna Convention and also the opinions of the Sixth Committee of the UN General Assembly. After considering the Commission's final draft articles in detail, three subcommittees were appointed to prepare reports on various groups of articles on the basis of which the Committee eventually prepared an interim report in the form of commentaries on those articles which were considered as requiring further study from the Asian–African points of view. The interim report was in due course tabled before the Vienna Conference in 1968. The Karachi session of the Committee held in January 1969 was devoted mainly to the consideration of certain difficult questions arising out of the draft articles of the Convention during the first session. Member as well as non-member governments of the two plenary meetings devoted to a review of the work of the first session. Member as well as non-member governments of the Committee were represented at the session and fully participated in its work on the Law of Treaties. In the end, two fairly large briefs were prepared by the Committee Secretariat and sent to the delegations of Committee members for their information and assistance in connection with the second Vienna Conference session in April and May 1969, at which the Committee was also represented.[12]

There was a clear advantage in the fact that the present writer, who was Chairman of the Committee of the Whole Conference for both sessions, was also unanimously elected Chairman of the Afro–Asian Group of States at the Conference and acted in that capacity for both sessions.[13]

Main Features of the Vienna Convention

With respect to so vast a subject as the Law of Treaties under the Vienna Convention, it is not possible or indeed desirable to attempt in such a brief study as this more than a reasonably descriptive and analytical summary of the principal features for the benefit of students of international law. One's selection of topics for inclusion in such a summary is, therefore, bound to be eclectic, especially when considered from the perspective of those so close to the subject under review. The main topics which we intend to cover are reservations to treaties, interpretation, the principle of *pacta sunt servanda*, supervening impossibility of performance, fundamental change of circumstances, grounds of invalidity of a treaty (including *jus cogens*), functions of the depositary of a treaty and registration of treaties. These do not in any way exhaust the list of possible topics which are of real interest and which are dealt with in the Vienna Convention, but they indicate the areas which are of special interest — either because they represent large aspects of the subject in respect of which publicists hold doctrinal views or because they involve many elements of progressive development of international law and its codification.

We may consider each topic *seriatim*.

Reservations

As is to be expected, the Vienna Convention proper opens with detailed provisions regarding the conclusion of treaties and their entry into force. Most of these provisions are careful and up-to-date reformulations of widely accepted rules governing such topics as the capacity of states to conclude treaties, the use of full powers in the authorization of representatives of states to conclude treaties, the mode of adopting and authenticating the text of a treaty, the expression of consent to be bound by a treaty by signature, by exchange of instruments, by ratification, acceptance or approval or accession and the recognition of an obligation on the part of both sides not to defeat the object and purpose of a treaty prior to its entry into force.

The large and important subject of reservations is then dealt with at some length in five carefully formulated articles which must be regarded as the latest and most authoritative rules on the subject. When signing, ratifying, accepting, approving or acceding to a treaty, a state is entitled to formulate any reservation unless the making of reservation is prohibited by the treaty itself or unless the treaty does not include the particular reservation contemplated by a state party to the treaty or unless the reservation proposed is incompatible with the object and purpose of the treaty. There are well-defined circumstances in which one party may accept a proposed reservation by the other party, since not every intended reservation can be expected to be accepted by the other party. A reservation must be accepted if so authorized by the treaty, unless the treaty requires that all other contracting States are required to signify their acceptance. All the parties to a treaty must be asked to signify their acceptance to a reservation if it appears from the limited number of the negotiating States and from the object and purpose of the treaty that, as between all the parties, the application of the treaty in its entirety is an essential condition of the consent of each one to be bound by the treaty. In the case of an international organization a reservation to a treaty which is a constituent instrument of that organization requires the acceptance of its competent organ. When a party objects to a reservation proposed by another contracting State, such an objection does not preclude the entry into force of the treaty as between the State objecting and the State making the reservation unless the contrary intention is clearly expressed by the objecting State. Sometimes, a State may, by the same act, consent to be bound by a treaty and also specify a reservation to the treaty; in such a case the act of that State is effective as soon as at least one other contracting State has accepted the reservation. In most cases, a reservation made by a party to a treaty is considered to have been accepted by another State if that other State has raised no objection within twelve months after it was notified of the reservation or before the date on which it expressed its consent to be bound by the treaty, whichever is later.[14]

The legal effect of a reservation is to modify the provisions of the treaty with respect to both parties to the extent of the reservation, but it does not modify the provisions of the treaty for the other parties to the treaty *inter se*. If a State objecting to a reservation has not opposed the entry into force of the treaty between itself and the reserving State, both States are not affected by the provisions to which the reservation relates.

A State, party to a treaty, may at any time withdraw its reservation or its objection to a reservation and the consent of any State which has accepted the reservation is not required for its withdrawal, unless the treaty provides otherwise. A withdrawal becomes effective only after notice of it has been received by the other party concerned or, in the case of withdrawal of an objection, only after notice of it has been received by the State which formulated the reservation.

Any reservation, its express acceptance, an objection to it and its withdrawal shall be in writing and communicated to the contracting States and any other States entitled to become parties to the treaty.[15]

Interpretation of Treaties

The provisions relating to the entry into force of the treaty and its provisional application pending its entry into force, though important, need not detain us here except to note that the principle of non-retroactivity of treaties and that a treaty is binding upon each party in respect of its entire territory are entrenched in the Convention.[16] In the case of successive treaties relating to the same subject matter, the general rule is that when a treaty specifies that it is subject to, or that it is not compatible with, an earlier or later treaty, the provisions of that other treaty prevail. There are refinements regarding cases where all the parties to the earlier treaty are parties also to the later treaty but the earlier treaty is not terminated or suspended; in that case the earlier treaty applies only to the extent that its provisions are compatible with those of the later treaty. Where the parties to the later treaty do not include all the parties to the earlier one, the same rule applies but as between a State party to both treaties and a State party to only one of the treaties, only the treaty to which both States are parties governs their mutual rights and obligations.[17] The general rule of treaty interpretation is that a treaty is to be interpreted in good faith in accordance with the ordinary meaning to be given to the terms of the treaty in their context and in the light of the treaty's object and purpose. The context includes the text, its preamble and annexes, any agreement made at the conclusion of the treaty and any related instruments.[18]

Pacta Sunt Servanda

The fundamental principle of treaty law is *pacta sunt servanda*, which stipulates that every treaty in force is binding upon the parties to it and must be performed by them in good faith.[19] The obligation of good faith is invariable, underlying the observance of treaties by all the parties to them. A party does not enter into any agreement or undertaking with another party unless there is an intention to carry it out to the letter and in the spirit. Without the existence of an underlying assumption that promises will be kept, inter-state relations will be impossible to maintain.

No State may invoke the provisions of its internal law to justify any failure on its part to perform a treaty.[20] There is an exception if by the internal law of a State a representative concludes a treaty without the necessary competence. This, however, concerns the conclusion rather than the observance of a treaty. The maxim *pacta sunt servanda* presupposes that the *pact* should be in force, that is, valid according to the ordinary rules governing the conclusion of a treaty.

The placing of this cardinal principle of treaty law at the beginning of the basic provisions and just after the preliminary provisions dealing with the conclusion of a treaty is designed to emphasize its strategic nature in the entire law of treaties. The formulation of this principle did not provoke as much controversy with regard to its purport as it did to its precise wording. The principle underwrites the integrity of treaties as a whole.

Supervening Impossibility of Performance

Another major principle of treaty law under customary international law is that a treaty must be performed according to its tenor unless its performance can be excused in law by supervening impossibility of performance. This is a much controverted ground of invalidity of a treaty which may be invoked by a party.

The rule is that a party to a treaty may claim to be entitled to terminate or withdraw from the performance of it on the ground of impossibility of performance resulting from the permanent disappearance or destruction of an object which is indispensable to the execution of the treaty. A merely temporary impossibility may be invoked only as a ground for suspending the operation of the treaty. Thus, the two conditions for the operation of the rule are that there must be an object that is indispensable for the execution of the treaty and that that object must have permanently disappeared or been destroyed. It is only then that the performance is deemed to be excused by supervening impossibility. If the performance has been delayed or prevented for a while, it is still possible to execute the treaty within a reasonable time.

If the supervening impossibility results from a breach by the party invoking it as a ground for the termination, withdrawal or suspension of a treaty, it cannot be so invoked. It does not matter how the breach has come about; it may result from the breach of an obligation under the treaty in question or of any other international obligation owed to any other party to the treaty. The party invoking supervening impossibility of performance as a ground for terminating, withdrawing from or suspending a treaty must prove that supervening impossibility of performance has not resulted from any breach of that party's international obligation thereunder.[21]

Fundamental Change of Circumstances

This is a plea, much canvassed in the literature on treaty law, which was in need of clarification and restatement. The commonest claim has been for a party to a treaty to say that it was no longer under any obligation to perform any duty under the treaty because circumstances prevailing at the time of the claim had changed radically from what they were at the time the treaty was concluded.

The rule is accordingly stated that a fundamental change of circumstances which has occurred with regard to circumstances existing at the time when the treaty was concluded and which had not been foreseen by the parties at that time may not be invoked as a ground for terminating or withdrawing from the treaty except in the following cases: (i) it must be shown that the circumstances in question formed the essential basis of the consent of the parties to be bound by the treaty and (ii) the change has the effect of radically transforming the extent of the obligation which was undertaken under the treaty which is yet to be performed thereunder.

Because of the controversy surrounding this subject under customary international law and at the insistence of the new States to which the subject is of special importance, boundary changes resulting from a treaty are excepted from the normal rule that a fundamental change of circumstances may be invoked as a ground for terminating or withdrawing from a treaty. If the treaty establishes a boundary, the rule does not apply. To avoid interminable disputes about changing frontiers, the vast majority of States at the UN General Assembly and at the Vienna Conference agreed upon this rule of exclusion in respect of treaties fixing boundaries.[22] It is often claimed in support of this that the exception maintains the integrity of treaties.

It is also agreed that a fundamental change of circumstances may not be invoked as a ground for terminating or withdrawing from a treaty where such a change is the result of a breach by the party invoking it either of an obligation under the treaty or of any other international obligation owed to any other party to the treaty. This principle whereby a party inducing the breach of a treaty is not permitted to invoke a fundamental change of circumstances as a ground for setting it aside will thus be seen as exactly the same principle as stated above in respect of supervening impossibility of performance. Both are two sides of the same coin. No party should be allowed to profit from its own breach, because this would be against the maxim of *pacta sunt servanda*.

Whenever a party may validly invoke a fundamental change of

circumstances, that party may do so whether it is for termination, suspension or withdrawal from, a treaty.[23]

Grounds of Invalidity of Treaties

These are so important that they should be treated as a separate section.

The termination, withdrawal from and suspension of the operation of treaties raise a number of problems of their own and details regulating such actions are provided in the Convention,[24] but it is not intended to highlight them in the present survey.

Functions of the Depositary of a Treaty

This branch of treaty law has been enriched and enlarged by the advent of the United Nations and its specialized agencies. By their treaty practice a considerable body of doctrine and procedures has developed and the Vienna Convention draws heavily upon these. The new States have inevitably followed the general practice of appointing depositaries for their treaties.

The practice is for the negotiating States to designate a depositary either in the treaty itself or in some other manner. The depositary many be one or more States, an international organization or the chief administrative officer of the organization. A depositary's functions are international in character and the depositary is required to act impartially in the performance of its duty. The depositary's functions continue whether or not the particular treaty has entered into force and also whether or not there is an existing dispute between a State and the depositary with respect to the discharge of the latter's functions.[25]

Among the functions of the depositary are the keeping of the custody of the original text of the treaty and of any full powers delivered to the depositary, the preparation of certified copies of the original texts, the receiving of signatures to the treaty and the receiving and keeping of related documents, the examination of the regularity of signatures and the bringing of any relevant matter to the attention of the States concerned, informing the States parties and others concerned of any relevant notifications and communications, registering the treaties with the UN Secretariat, and performing such other functions as may be specified in particular treaties or in the Vienna Convention itself.[26]

Registration

All treaties in force are required by the UN Charter to be registered or filed and recorded and published.[27] The mere designation of a depositary constitutes authorization for it to carry out any of the functions mentioned above.

We may now turn to a consideration of what is the most difficult part of the Vienna Convention on the Law of Treaties. This is the controversial Part V, which contains probably the most far-reaching elements of the progressive development of international law and its codification.

The Dynamic Character of Part V on Invalidity

There are six express grounds for holding a treaty invalid under Part V of the Vienna Convention, and these are apart from cases of invalidity arising from constitutional limitation of the authority of a State's representative to express the consent of a State to be bound by a treaty. Let us briefly deal with the specific grounds first: these are error, fraud, corruption of a State representative, coercion of a representative of a State, coercion of a State by the threat or use of force, and treaties conflicting with a peremptory norm of general international law (*jus cogens*).

Error: An error relating to a fact or situation assumed by a state to exist at the time of the conclusion of the treaty and forming an essential basis of its consent to be bound by the treaty may be invoked by that State as invalidating its consent to be bound by the treaty. But such a State is not entitled to claim that the error invalidates the treaty if it has contributed by its own conduct to the error or if the circumstances were such as to put that State on notice of a possible error. If the error relates only to the wording of the text, it does not affect the validity of the treaty, as it may be corrected in the usual way.[28]

Fraud: If the conclusion of a treaty has been induced by the fraudulent conduct of another negotiating State, the fraud may be invoked as invalidating a State's consent to be bound by such a treaty.[29]

It should be observed that "fraudulent conduct", and not "fraud" *simpliciter*, has been defined in Article 49. This is because the concept of *dolus* in Latin or of *dol*, its French synonym, is not considered wide enough in scope to embrace all the nuances of the moral turpitude which should invalidate a treaty induced by fraud. After all, it is not fraud in the abstract that is a vitiating element, but the intention manifesting itself in conduct of a kind regarded as reprehensible.

Corruption of a Representative of a State: If in the conclusion of a treaty, the expression of the consent of a State to be bound by it has been procured through the corruption of its representative directly or indirectly by another negotiating State, that consenting State may invoke such corruption as a ground for invalidation of the treaty.[30] This may seem a somewhat implausible ground, but examples are not unknown of cases in which a State representative may be corruptly induced to express the consent of his State to be bound by a treaty. What constitutes a legitimate or permissible gift to a State representative is not always discernible; mere presents, especially if moderate in cost and infrequent, may be innocuous enough, but gifts not ordinarily justified by the circumstances, either because they are extravagant or because they are otherwise inappropriate, may constitute forms of bribery or corruption.

In all these cases of incompetence to conclude treaties or restriction on authority to express consent, error, fraud and corruption of a State representative, a State may no longer invoke a ground of invalidating a treaty if, after becoming aware of the facts, it has expressly agreed that the treaty is valid or it must by reason of its conduct be considered to have acquiesced in the validity of the treaty.

Coercion: There are two distinct types of coercion; one is of a State representative, the other is of a State itself by the threat or use of force.

A treaty has no legal effect if the expression of the consent of a State to be bound by it has been procured by the coercion of its representative through acts or threats directed against him personally or against his family.

But a treaty is void if its conclusion has been procured by the threat or use of force in violation of the principles of international law embodied in the Charter of the United Nations.

Now, Article 2(4) of the UN Charter forbids member states from employing the threat or the use of force in the settlement of their disputes. At the Vienna Conference, as at the various meetings for the deliberation of the Principles of Peaceful Coexistence and Co-operation among States, there was a sharp division of opinion between the Western States and the Third World States (especially the Afro-Asian group) as to the interpretation of the term "force" — whether it means only military force or whether it embraces all forms of force, military, economic and moral. The West favor the former, while the Afro–Asian States insist that force means the latter.

After much heated controversy both inside the conference hall and in the corridors and after consultation among the leading representatives of the Western, Eastern, Latin-American and Afro-Asian groups during the breaks, the matter was resolved by adopting the rules stated in the preceding third paragraph under the present heading.[31] Its adoption was expressly made subject to the prior adoption of the Declaration on the Prohibition of Military, Political or Economic Coercion in the Conclusion of Treaties. This Declaration was adopted on the basis that it forms an integral part of the Vienna Convention on the Law of Treaties.[32] It was a wise concession to expediency.

Jus Cogens

The International Law Commission had, after long and heated debates in several sessions and after studying the reports of the UN General Assembly embodying the comments of member governments, come to terms with the controversial concept of *jus cogens* as a touchstone of the invalidity of any treaty inconsistent with it. The Third World, especially the Afro-Asian group, and the Eastern European group of States favoured the entrenchment of provisions on *jus cogens* in the Vienna Convention as a guarantee of the new international legal order, whereas the Western States were opposed to it on the ground that the concept was at best imprecise and at worst not sanctioned by State practice or doctrine. The Western States were also against the inclusion of provisions on *jus cogens*, even if an acceptable definition could be worked out, unless and until a satisfactory judicial settlement procedure was also included in the Convention.

The final form in which the *jus cogens* rule was cast is in Article 53 as follows:

> A treaty is void if, at the time of its conclusion, it conflicts with a peremptory norm of general international law. For the purposes of the present Convention, a peremptory norm of general international law is a norm accepted and recognized by the international community of States as a whole as a norm from which no derogation is permitted and which can be modified only by a subsequent norm of general international law having the same character.

To which we may add this addendum in Article 64 on the emergence of a new peremptory norm:

> If a new peremptory norm of general international law emerges, any existing treaty which is inconsistent with that norm becomes void and terminates.

It is quite clear that this safeguard is essential if international legal order is to be assured in the future as well as in the present. Any notion of *ordre public* assumed to exist within the international community is to be deemed subject to changes from time to time according to the prevailing ideas of international morality and social justice. If, therefore, what is permissible today according to existing norms should become outdated or no longer permissible, it should be possible to set it aside and replace it by a new universally adopted principle. After all, customary international law once recognized the validity of treaties between unequal parties, such as the various colonization arrangements made possible in the past.

As regards the procedure for judicial settlement of international disputes between the parties, a solution was also found, though not before the whole conference had been brought almost to the verge of collapse. The Western States would not conclude a treaty which included the various grounds of invalidity set out in Part V without the compulsory jurisdiction of the International Court of Justice being made the cornerstone for determining the invalidity of the particular ground invoked. A system which permitted the unilateral invocation of these grounds, including *jus cogens*, was utterly unacceptable to them. The new Third World States as well as the Eastern European group insisted on the retention of the conciliation and arbitration procedures submitted by the International Law Commission as part of the draft articles.

In the period between the two sessions of the conference, arguments raged between the warring factions, and several alternative proposals were canvassed. The second session was dominated by the consideration that, unless an acceptable solution was found to this problem, all the labors of two years at the conference and the twenty years preceding that time at the United Nations would have been in vain.

Then, on the last day, when it became almost certain that unless a last-minute formula could be found, the conference would end without a convention, the present writer submitted a proposal which was supported mainly by the Afro-Asian Group and which he presented to the entire conference as a "package deal". The proposal was to be voted on as a whole and not in parts. It is now to be found in Article 66 of the Convention and it reads:

> If, under paragraph 3 of article 65, no solution has been reached within a period of 12 months following the date on which the objection was raised, the following procedure shall be followed:
> (a) any one of the parties to a dispute concerning the application or the interpretation of article 53 or article 64 may, by a written application, submit

it to the International Court of Justice for a decision unless the parties, by common consent, agree to submit the dispute to arbitration;

(b) any one of the parties to a dispute concerning the application or the interpretation of any of the other articles in Part V of the present Convention may set in motion the procedure specified in the Annex to the Convention [which sets out detailed provisions concerning a Conciliation Commission] by submitting a request to that effect to the Secretary-General of the United Nations.

Both sides to the argument thus had a bit of what each wanted: "to each a crumb of right, to neither of them the whole loaf". Where the ground of invalidity invoked is *jus cogens*, then the dispute must go to the International Court of Justice. When any of the other grounds is invoked, the Conciliation Commission under the Secretary- General of the United Nations will settle the matter. The package deal was approved by an overwhelming majority, and the conference and the Vienna Convention were thereby saved for posterity.

Summary and Conclusion

At the time of the present writing, more than forty-seven States have signed the Vienna Convention, the last count being in 1975, but only twenty-three have so far ratified it; it is, therefore, short of a dozen ratifications to bring it into force. It is nevertheless true to say that it has already become widely accepted and referred to not only by the legal advisers of the foreign offices of many state governments, but also by the International Court of Justice in several judgments and advisory opinions given in recent years.[33] For example, the ICJ applied Article 60(3), (5) of the Vienna Convention in the *Namibia case*;[34] in the *Fisheries Jurisdiction (United Kingdom v. Iceland)*,[35] the Court applied Article 62 on Fundamental Change of Circumstances;[36] Fundamental Error was invoked before the Court in *Application for Review of Judgment No. 158 of the United Nations Administrative Tribunal*[37] which referred to Article 48 of the Convention as to whether the Tribunal had committed a fundamental error in procedure which had occasioned a failure of justice. It can thus be seen that both counsel and the Court have been dealing with the Vienna Convention as if it were already in force.[38]

It now remains to add that the Vienna Convention is very comprehensive and forward-looking, but as our definition and analysis of its scope have earlier indicated, it is not exhaustive of all the rules on treaty law. Apart from specific areas of treaty law not covered there are indications in certain provisions of the Convention that customary international law will continue to apply to situations not expressly excluded.[39]

It is nevertheless not too large a claim to make for the Vienna Convention on the Law of Treaties that it represents the most comprehensive body of law on treaties and certainly that it is so far the most authoritative and universal work of progressive development of international law and its codification yet achieved under the auspices of the United Nations.

NOTES

1. UN Doc. A/CN. 4/1, Nov. 5, 1948; also reissued as A/CN.4/1/Rev. 1, Feb. 10, 1949.

2. *Yearbook of the International Law Commission*, 1959, Vol. II, p. 91.

3. *Ibid.*, 1962, Vol. II, p. 160.

4. The present writer was the General Rapporteur for the two sessions.

5. Yearbook of the International Law Commission, 1966, Vol. II, pp. 173ff.

6. The first session lasted from March 26, to May 24, 1968 and was attended by representatives from 103 States, while the second session lasted from April 6, to May 22, 1969 and was attended by representatives from 110 States.

7. By Resolution 2501 (XXIV) of November 12, 1969 the General Assembly recommended to the Commission that it should study the question of treaties between States and international organizations or between two or more international organizations "as an important question".

8. For the purposes of the Convention, "treaty" means "an international agreement concluded between States in written form and governed by international law, whether embodied in a single instrument or in two or more related instruments and whatever its particular designation".

9. Miscellaneous provisions are to be found in Articles 73–75 reserving matters relating to succession of states, state responsibility, outbreak of hostilities, an aggressor state, severance or absence of diplomatic or consular relations and the conclusion of treaties.

10. E.g., succession of states in respect of treaties and "the most-favoured-nations clause" have been completed and submitted as draft articles to the UN General Assembly; state responsibility is at an advanced stage of preparation; relations between states and international organizations had been adopted by a plenipotentiary conference. Other related aspects on the whole topic are under study.

11. See UN Doc. A/CONF. 39/26.

12. See *The Work of the Asian–African Legal Consultative Committee*, 1975, pp. 33–35.

13. It may be added that Dr. M. K. Yasseen (Iraq) was the Chairman of the Drafting Committee of the Whole Conference.

14. It is to be noted that some of the rules on reservations in the Vienna Convention owed not a little to the questions formulated by the UN General Assembly as modified and applied in *Reservations to the Convention on the Prevention and Punishment of the Crime of Genocide*, Advisory Opinion, *I.C.J. Reports 1951*, p. 15.

15. See ss. 19–23 for the detailed rules on Reservations.

16. Ss. 28 and 29.

17. Article 30 spells out the details.

18. Article 31.

19. Article 26.

20. Article 27.

21. Article 61.

22. For example, the Charter of the Organization of African Unity provides for the maintenance of the boundaries of member states.

23. Article 62.

24. Articles 54–60.

25. Article 76.

26. Article 77.

27. Article 102(1) of the UN Charter.

28. Article 48.

29. Article 49.

30. Article 50.

31. This is Article 52 of the Convention,

32. See UN Doc. A/CONF. 39/26.

33. As Judge Ammoun observed in his separate opinion in the *Barcelona Traction case* (*I.C.J. Reports 1970*, p. 3) at page 313: "As is known, furthermore, a majority of States, through their representatives at the 1969 Vienna Conference on the Law of Treaties, pronounced in favour of a solution to the problem of *jus cogens* capable of giving definitive sanction to the principles of the Charter, regarded by them as imperative juridical norms." There is also a reference, on the same page, to Article 64 of the Vienna Convention.

34. On material breach of a treaty see *I.C.J. Reports 1971*, p. 16., paras. 94–96.

35. *I.C.J. Reports 1973*, p. 3, paras. 35–37. There is also this pronouncement of the Court in respect of Article 52 on Coercion: "There can be little doubt, as is implied in the Charter of the United Nations and recognized in Article 52 of the Vienna Convention on the Law of Treaties, that under contemporary international law an agreement concluded under the threat or use of force is void."

36. Articles 65 and 66 were also referred to in paragraph 44.

37. *I.C.J. Reports 1973*, p. 166.

38. The Convention have also attracted much literature of which we may mention the following: Elias, *The Modern Law of Treaties*, op cit., Sinclair, *The Vienna Convention on the Law of Treaties*, 1973; Rosenne, *The Law of Treaties; A Guide to the Legislative History of the Vienna Convention, 1970*; A.J.I.L. 161. 64, p. 508; Jacobs, "Innovation and Continuity in the Law of Treaties", 1970, *Modern Law Review*, Vol. 33, p. 508.

39. E.g. Articles 38 and 43.

Chapter 4

THE NEW LAW OF THE SEA — AN OUTLINE REPORT

Because the Fifth Session of the Third Law of the Sea Conference which lasted from August 2 to September 17, 1976, did not achieve the desired convention but only decided on holding yet another eight-week session from May 16 to July 1, 1977, we can only consider a progress report at the present conference (1977). Such a report should cover the main issues that engaged the delegates at the Fifth Session against the background of the Revised Single Negotiating Text presented to the Fourth Session, which was held from March 15 to May 7, 1976. This text was intended as a basis for negotiations for the conclusion of a convention at a future plenipotentiary conference.

It will be recalled that the text is in four parts: (a) Part I deals with the general principles for the implementation of the basic concept that the resources of the international sea-bed area beyond the limits of national jurisdiction are a common heritage of mankind; it seeks to establish an International Sea-bed Authority which would have the power to exploit the ocean-bed for its mineral wealth and also enter into contracts with States, corporations and other entities which might be permitted to participate in mining the ocean floor *pari passu* with the Sea-Bed Authority under its overall control; (b) Part II makes provisions on States' rights and duties within a twelve-mile territorial sea, a contiguous zone extending up to twenty-four miles from the shore, a 200-mile exclusive economic zone, the continental shelf underlying these three areas,[1] archipelagic waters (that is, those within States which consist of archipelagos), and the high seas; (c) Part III is concerned with marine environment and scientific research, including States' powers to enforce antipollution regulations and the promotion of the development and transfer of marine technology as well as the permission to foreign States to conduct research with other States in the economic zone and on the high seas; and (d) Part IV contains provisions dealing with compulsory disputes settlement, including references to a proposed Law of the Sea Tribunal, resort to the International Court of Justice, arbitral tribunals, conciliation commissions and a committee to settle technical disputes over fisheries, pollution, scientific research and navigation.

Let us summarize the basic issues and the main problems raised in each of the four groups of subjects just outlined. It will be convenient to consider them in the following order: (i) The Territorial Sea and other General Aspects of the Law of the Sea, (ii) Marine Environment, Scientific Research and Technology, (iii) the International Sea-bed Authority, and (iv) Settlement of Disputes.

The Territorial Sea and other General Aspects of the Law of the Sea

The Territorial Sea and other General Aspects of the Law of the Sea, as we all know, is a group of subjects which was assigned to the Second Committee of the main Conference but which for detailed discussion was committed to three Negotiating Groups. The first Negotiating Group dealt with the legal status of the Exclusive Economic Zone (EEZ) and the rights and duties of other States with respect to the living resources of that zone. It was the view of this Group, which was endorsed by the Whole Second Committee, that it was no longer debatable whether the EEZ was a zone of the High Seas or of the Territorial Sea; the EEZ is now generally accepted as a distinct zone by itself and 200 miles wide. It was also decided that there could no longer be any more radical amendment of Article 44 (rights of coastal States in the zone) and of Article 46 (rights of all States in the zone within the limits already agreed). The second Negotiating Group had a lively discussion. There were no radical modifications of the provisions dealing with rights of access of landlocked States and freedom of transit. As for the third Negotiating Group, its main concern was with the definition of the outer edge of the continental margin and the question of revenue-sharing with respect to the exploitation of the continental shelf beyond 200 miles. The small Group of 26 had approved the general structure of the revenue-sharing system. In addition to the three negotiating groups, two more new ones had been formed — one on straits used for international navigation and another on delimitation of sea areas between States adjacent to or facing one another.

There was general consensus on defining the continental shelf as extending to the outer edge of the continental margin, on the understanding that a realistic form of revenue-sharing in the area beyond 200 nautical miles from shore would be eventually adopted. Some delegations still opposed the extension of the continental shelf beyond 200 miles.

In the end, the chairman of the Second Committee reported that "no concrete results were achieved at this Session regarding any of the questions considered by the various negotiating groups".[2] Genuine efforts were, however, made to reach a compromise between those States that want coastal States to exercise the greatest measure of jurisdiction within the EEZ and those that want the EEZ treated as part of the high seas. The solution to a number of problems depends upon which position would be finally adopted by the Third Law of the Sea Conference.

As regards the delimitation of the sea areas, the Conference has yet to settle the question of whether or not the equidistance method is binding. The chairman's report stated that "some delegations felt that this method should be given primary importance, while others thought that the problem should be solved in accordance with equitable principles".[3]

Marine Environment, Scientific Research and Technology

The Third Committee's chairman's report stated that the Committee "made important progress towards the elaboration of draft articles on the three items allocated to the Committee, namely: the protection and preservation of the marine environment, marine scientific research, and the transfer of technology".[4]

There had been discussion of the future system for regulating marine scientific research in the exclusive economic zone and on the continental shelf. Also on the agenda were the subjects of the transfer of technology and the protection and preservation of the marine environment. But Article 60 of the Revised Negotiating Text[5] was the main focus of attention in regard to the proposed requirement that a coastal State must consent before marine scientific research is carried out in its economic zone. Many delegations also referred to the chairman's "test . . . . which was based on the principle that all types of marine research must fall under the jurisdiction proposal" on Article 60 of the coastal State, and insisted that there must be (a) express prior consent of the coastal State and (b) peaceful uses of the research in question. Some researching States had rejected the idea that there was no need to confer on the coastal State jurisdiction in the economic zone over matters which were not of an economic nature. There were also suggestions that Articles 64 and 65 should be amended to make them conform to Article 60 as revised.

On the whole, most delegations favored the so-called consent regime, in which the express as opposed to a tacit consent of the coastal State must first be obtained before any research could be carried out within the exclusive economic zone or on the continental shelf, since the researching State must have due regard for the security implications of such research for the coastal State. Most delegations did not favor any distinction between pure and applied (or resource-related) research such as is implicit in the chairman's text. Neither the proposed International Sea-bed Authority nor the jurisdiction granted to the coastal States would unduly hamper marine research if it were really undertaken in the interest of mankind as a whole. Making research in the international sea-bed area subject to the prior consent of the coastal States could not impinge upon the freedom of the seas; rather, provision for meaningful research for the benefit of mankind should be made part of the International Sea-bed regime and within its general competence.

Article 60 should be agreed upon independently of disputes settlement procedures. The suggestion by a delegation to the contrary would not solve the problem. Nor should "freedom of scientific research" be exaggerated into a claim that the exclusive economic zone is part of the high seas.

Some delegations, mainly of the European Communities, maintained that a satisfactory regime for fundamental research should provide for full information to, participation by and sharing of results with coastal State. They also accepted the necessity of giving the coastal States the right to give or refuse its consent in respect of any research which might bear upon the exploration and exploitation of living and non-living resources in the exclusive economic zone.

On the whole, the chairman's proposal would seem acceptable to the majority as a balanced and realistic basis for negotiation.

The subject of transfer of technology was not discussed, nor was that of marine environment, including pollution.

The International Sea-bed Authority

The report of the co-chairman of the First Committee of the Whole Conference[6] placed on record for the first time a detailed summary of the three working papers presented to its Workshop by the Group of 77 developing countries, the Soviet Union and the United States. The papers suggested differing systems by which the sea-bed should be mined under the new international regime being worked out by the Conference. The report indicated that the inconclusive discussion at this last session concentrated on the conditions under which States and corporations would have access to sea-bed resources, including criteria to be used by the proposed International Sea-bed Authority in selecting applicants for contracts to mine the sea-bed.

Many delegations thought that the Geneva text of 1975 was the only proper negotiating text, not the revised text submitted in May 1976. The various three proposals amounted to holding new debates, not the genuine negotiations which the stage of the work now required. The Group of 77 paper, which submitted the first report considered at the session, endorsed three principles: (a) that all sea-bed activities should be conducted by the international Sea-Bed Authority, either directly or through contracts, the authority being in full control; (b) that the Authority should have discretion in regard to contract applicants; and (c) that the sea-bed area must be administered by the Authority on behalf of mankind as a whole, so that the area of the sea-bed could not be divided or any zone reserved for multinational corporations to do whatever they liked in any part of the area of common heritage. It seemed as if agreement had been reached on the basic conditions for exploration as they stood in the Geneva text. There could be no question of a parallel or dual system of exploitation in the sea-bed area as laid down in the Revised Single Negotiating Text.[7] Both developed and developing countries (estimated at around 120) supported the paper of the Group of 77 and opposed the Workshop Papers 2 and 3 submitted respectively by the Soviet Union and the United States on the ground that "they ignored the principle that the international sea-bed was the common heritage of mankind".

It might have helped matters if the real positions of the United States, the European Economic Community and the Soviet Union had been examined on such points as the roles of the Assembly and the Council of the Sea-Bed Authority. Unfortunately, this last conference did not go into these matters. Delegations were advised instead to circulate any reviews they might have on them. There had been insufficient preparation for the August–September 1976 session, and much time had been wasted on procedural issues. The outstanding matters were primarily political and not technical.[8]

The great majority wanted the International Sea-Bed Authority to be comprehensive and preeminent in the sea-bed area; it must be a unitary as opposed to a parallel or dual system; and it must have access to financing and technology. Ultimately, the real questions are: (1) should a dual or parallel system be permitted?, which prompts the further question; (2) if a parallel system were adopted, would the Authority, on the one hand, and the States and other entities on the other, have coordinate and coeval powers?; and, further, (3) would the areas to be allocated be of the same extent or, if not, which should control how much space? The best solution ought to put the Sea-Bed Authority in overall control, subject to carefully worked-out safeguards with respect to allocation of resources, the granting of licenses and general operational management. All the detailed principles should be set out in the Law of the Sea Convention and the Authority charged with the responsibility of securing compliance with the plans of work and contracts approved by the Authority. Few delegations appeared to support an automatic assurance of access to the sea-bed resources. The great majority were in favor of discretion being granted to the Authority in nearly all these matters.

The most important consideration for the Sea-Bed Authority should be to avoid acting in such a manner as could be regarded as inconsistent or discriminatory. Several proposals, even from the developed States, however, stressed the need to give special consideration to the developing countries and to the particular requirements of the landlocked and the geographically-disadvantaged States.[9]

The report concluded on this note:

> Although this Session does not show any tangible results, the co-chairmen are of the opinion that the negotiating process is now under way. It is based on two important requirements: the need to have the real and effective participation of all delegations, and the need to have a thorough and detailed discussion of the issues involved. Only this kind of process can lead to the necessary appreciation of the various positions held and, finally, to durable results.

The developing countries, it now seems clear, must be guaranteed access to sea-bed technology, and States and other entities guaranteed a regulated access to sea-bed resources. The central question was rather how to exploit the common heritage. The underlying problem was the struggle between the maintenance of the *status quo* and the transformation of existing world economic system into a more equitable system. Neither the United States' emphasis on corporations' rights nor the Soviet Union's insistence on States' rights in the international sea-bed area could form the basis of an acceptable convention.[10] A middle way would have to be found between the coastal States' demand for greater independence in respect of the economic zone and their demand for greater interdependence with regard to the functioning of the International Sea-bed Authority.

Settlement of Disputes

It will be recalled that Mr. Amerasinghe, the President of the Third Law of the Sea Conference, had prepared and submitted the Revised Single Negotiating Text[11] to the Fourth Session of the Conference in May 1976. It was this document that the full Conference at this last session in August–September 1976 examined article by article in thirty-six "unofficial" sittings.[12]

In the end, the Conference President pointed out that the provisions concerning compulsory disputes settlement procedures had given rise to controversy, mainly as regards which of three bodies should be chosen by States: a Tribunal of the Law of the Sea, the International Court of Justice, or an arbitral tribunal. According to Mr. Amerasinghe, the provisions of the first six articles, laying down the principle that States are bound to settle by peaceful means any dispute concerning the interpretation or application of the Convention, did not provoke much controversy.

The main issues concerned the competence to be enjoyed by each judicial body, whether each should be empowered to indicate interim measures (in circumstances similar to those of the ICJ under Article 41 of its Statute), and the exclusivity of the compulsory settlement of disputes in respect of the rights of a coastal State in the exclusive economic zone.

A new, revised negotiating text on the settlement of disputes was promised by the President for distribution shortly after the end of the August–September Conference but it had not been received at the time this paper was submitted.

The Financial Problems of Exploitation

The First Committee, which at its 28th meeting requested the Secretary-General to prepare a preliminary note on "Alternative Means of Financing the Enterprise", received a Secretariat Report entitled "Financing Sea-bed Enterprise"[13] at its 32nd meeting held on September 7, 1976.[14] The report was based on the provisions of Part I of the Revised Single Negotiating Text, particularly the relevant section of annex II describing the Sea-Bed Enterprise as the operating arm of the Sea-Bed Authority in relation to the exploration and the exploitation of the sea-bed and the ocean floor beyond the limits of national jurisdiction. Some aspects concerning the acquisition of technology were taken into account.

The following four types of financial sources for the sea-bed part of the Authority are indicated:

  (i) Amounts determined from time to time by the General Assembly
      out of the Special Fund referred to in article 49;
 (ii) Voluntary contribution made by State Parties to the Law of the
      Sea Convention;
(iii) Amounts borrowed by the Sea-Bed Enterprise; and
 (iv) Other funds made available to the Enterprise, including charges
      to enable it to commence operations as soon as possible for
      carrying out its functions. (What the charges are and who would
      collect them are matters not yet clear.)

The report also sets out the estimated administrative costs of the
Enterprise as well as its operational costs, itemized as follows:

Exploration, research and development: U.S. dollars 75 to 150 million
(spread over three years).
  Capital investment: U.S. dollars 400 – 600 million (spread over four
                          years)
  Operating cost: U.S. dollars 120 –165 million (annually from
                          the seventh year).

The first year of commercial production from a 3-million-ton per year
project, could yield up to $300 million in revenue. It was envisaged
that the pre-production costs of the entire Enterprise could be
recovered after three to six years of commercial production.
     It must, however, be emphasized, that all these estimates are
provisional only, as the many gaps in our knowledge could be filled in
only in successive stages as the operation of the Sea-Bed Enterprise
might develop in accordance with a number of factors not all of which
could be foreseen at this stage.

Profits and Pollution

These topics were not dealt with at the conference the results of which
are now under review, but they are part and parcel of the new Law of
the Sea.
     Of the living resources of the sea, fish is the most important and
fairly reasonable sets of criteria have been included in the Revised
Single Negotiating Text.
     Pollution from ships, especially those carrying oil, is already
covered to a large extent by international regulations, and so is

dumping. The IMCO has detailed and technical regulations, but the general principles remain to be properly formulated by the present Conference on the Law of the Sea. It should be noted that the general principles adopted by the Stockholm Conference in 1972 should form a useful basis for codification of the law on marine pollution.[15]

It is the various types of marine pollution, which derive from land-based sources and which have been virtually neglected by the international community, that must receive great attention from the present Conference (1977), because they constitute the more dangerous forms of marine pollution.

The Latest Phase

When the Sixth Session of the Conference reconvened on May 13, 1977, for a seven- or eight-week period, it was clear that a good deal of fundamental consultations among the various negotiating groups had taken place, resulting in the crystallization of certain basic issues still dividing them. The most significant development has been the emergence of the so-called *parallel system*, according to which the exploitation of the mineral resources of the ocean-bed beyond national jurisdiction for the benefit of all mankind would be carried out simultaneously by the highly industrialized States and companies and firms on the one hand, and by the Sea-Bed Enterprise on behalf of the developing countries on the other. For this purpose the ocean floor would be divided into two roughly equal portions, each being the areas of exploitation assigned to each operating system.

There are, however, a number of unresolved problems. The first is to establish an International Sea-Bed Authority that could guarantee that the two parallel systems would always cooperate equitably and fairly in their mining operations, seeing that the industrialized countries, particularly the United States, with greatly advanced technology in this field, have a huge edge on their counterparts, the developing countries of the Third World. The parallelism envisaged, it must be remembered, is one that does not recognize a supranational authority which would have the power to regulate and control the entire operations under an all-embracing Sea-Bed Enterprise, which the Group of 77 clearly favor. The second problem, not unrelated to the first, is how, in the absence of such a central Sea-Bed Authority, the provision of the necessary quantity of technology and the rate of its provenance could be ensured to the developing countries in the actual operation of the two-sided project. Associated with this is the whole question of the transfer of the necessary technology from the industrialized States to the Third World. The unregulated system favoured by the United States and its allies is highly suspect in the eyes of the Group of 77 since the relationship that would exist between the two would place the developing countries too much at the mercy of the technologically-developed countries. Finally, there is a third problem which concerns the organization of an acceptable accounting mechanism, not only within each of the two parallel systems but also as between them, so as to ensure that the exploitation of the ocean sea-bed would really become "the common heritage of all mankind", based upon fair shares for all. It is this last concern that clearly shows the need for an overall International Sea-Bed Authority with power not only to allocate the available resources of the ocean bed to the various operating groups but also to establish a proper accounting system to make the whole enterprise worthwhile.

Dr. Henry Kissinger is known to have suggested the establishment of a development fund that would facilitate the bridging of the gap between the industrialized and the developing countries' two systems. Such a fund, however ample and generous, would fail of its purpose unless administered in such a way as to secure the confidence of the Third World countries as to the impartiality and fairness of its operation. In this respect it is difficult to see how such a fund would operate outside the framework of the International Sea-Bed Authority or of the UN Organization itself.

The whole problem, therefore, seems to hinge ultimately upon the setting up of a device or mechanism which must ensure, and be seen to ensure, the holding of the scales fairly between the understandable fears and apparently excessive precautions of the industrialized nations on the one hand and the equally understandable fears and apparently groundless scepticism of the developing nations. The former are afraid of numbers, as their experience of the United Nations and its agencies has shown that they cannot, except in the Security Council, always have their way in important political or economic matters. Most of the latter have too recent experiences of colonization or of the current North–South negotiations in Paris. And, yet, representation on the central Council of the proposed International Sea-Bed Authority has to reflect the preponderance of numbers of the developing States if the Authority is to have a chance of being acceptable to the majority of the world. A counterbalancing measure might have been the introduction of a form of veto, but this could not be granted only to certain representatives of the less numerous industrialized countries on anything like the Security Council arrangement. Nor is a weighted majority based on the relative economic strengths of members of the Sea-Bed Authority's

Council any less objectionable for the same reason.

It seems that a solution must nevertheless be found along something like the economic lines we have been considering. The industrialized countries and their mining companies or corporations might find it in their best interests and those of the Group of 77 to accept the proposed ratio of carefully balanced representations on the Sea-Bed Authority's Council as envisaged in the Revised Single Negotiating Text. After all, these fewer industrialized member States of the Authority would have two ultimate weapons in their hands if they should find the majority exercizing their majority powers in an unconscionable way in any particular situation during the operations under the Sea-Bed Enterprise. The first weapon is the possible control of the Enterprise Fund through the witholding of their contributions, and the second weapon is the potential restriction of the availability of technology, without which operations would be virtually impossible on any worthwhile scale. Both possibilities should deter irresponsible behavior within the Authority's Council. Finally, it would be a very long time in the future before the developing countries have overtaken the industrialized nations in both respects so as to make the latter afraid of continuing with the Enterprise. The key to the problem is really in the hands of the industrialized countries and whether they can be trusting and courageous enough to enter upon this adventure of the human spirit at this momentous stage in world history. The rumoured threats that the United States proposes to "go it alone" if the current session fails to reach an agreement on this issue will not do, as such an action would bring chaos to the public order of the oceans.

We must also not forget that all disputes are envisaged to be settled by a tribunal, the membership and calibre of which should reflect the same awareness of the delicate situation of all the parties to the Sea-Bed Enterprise and, indeed of the world, as the general operation of the International Sea-Bed Authority itself.

Whatever the structures adopted for the Tribunal, the best solution would be to link it in some way to the International Court of Justice at The Hague. The International Court possesses the knowledge and the experience necessary for dealing with all types of disputes of a legal nature that could possibly arise in this area of the Law of the Sea.

Now, if we look at the Informal Composite Negotiating Text,[16] we find the following choice of procedures provision in draft Article 287(1):

A State Party . . . . shall be free to choose, by means of a written declaration, one or more of the following means for the settlement of disputes relating to the

interpretation or application of the present Convention:
(a) The Law of the Sea Tribunal constituted in accordance with annex II;
(b) The International Court of Justice;
(c) The arbitral tribunal constituted in accordance with annex VI;
(d) A special arbitral tribunal constituted in accordance with annex VII for one
    or more of the categories of disputes specified therein.

Thus the International Court of Justice is offered as only one of the four alternative choices of procedure for the settlement of disputes relating to the interpretation or application of the proposed Law of the Sea Convention. As the International Court is "the principal judicial organ of the United Nations", it should have been given primacy in the matter of the interpretation and application of the constituent instrument of the sea-bed arrangements; the Law of the Sea Tribunal should rank next, followed by the various types of arbitral tribunal. It is appropriate that all the other tribunals be linked to the International Court of Justice by way of appeal in much the same way as the other specialized agencies of the United Nations like the ILO, UNESCO and the ICAO; advisory opinions should be sought from the International Court of Justice in like manner.

We may at this juncture ask the very important question as to the true legal status of the Sea-Bed Authority within the UN framework as a whole. For instance, is the Authority the eighth organ of the United Nations, or is it just another specialized agency, or is it midway between an organ and an agency? These questions are prompted by the studied attempt throughout the Draft Convention to equate the Law of the Sea Tribunal in particular with the International Court of Justice both in competence and authority.

If the Tribunal is not in fact and in law the equal of the International Court of Justice, there is no reason why the latter should not take precedence over the former in all legal disputes, especially those touching questions of the construction of the constituent instruments; all other disputes can equally well be referred to in the International Court of Justice or any of its Chambers, on the new procedures of which the Law of the Sea Tribunal and the arbitral tribunals seem to have been modelled. The International Court of Justice has had considerable experience and possesses high competence in dealing with Law of the Sea problems of practically all kinds during the past fifty years, as witness the cases it has dealt with both in its pre-1945 composition and since.[17]

NOTES

1. Cf. Article 1 of the Convention on the Continental Shelf, 1958, effective from June 10, 1964.

2. A/Conf./62/L.17, para. 60.

3. Ibid., para. 46 according to A/Conf. 62/WP.8/Rev. 1/Part II, para. 1 of Articles 62 and 71: "The delimitation of [the exclusive economic zone] [the continental shelf] between adjacent or opposite States shall be effected by agreement in accordance with equitable principles, employing, where appropriate, the median or equidistant line, and taking account of all the relevant circumstances".

4. A/Conf. 62/L.18, para. 2.

5. Doc. A/Conf. 62/WP.8/Rev. 1/Part III.

6. A/Conf.62/C.1/WR 5 and Add.1

7. See J. I. Charney's "The International Regime For the Deep Sea-bed: Past conflicts and Proposals For Progress", in *Harvard International Law Journal*, Vol. 17, No. 1, Winter 1976, pp. 1–50, for a detailed analysis of the problems.

8. That the current problems in the law of the sea should be evaluated by reference to both ideological and technological criteria is the theme of D. M. Johnston's "The New Equity in the Law of the Sea", in *the International Journal*, Vol. XXXI, No. 1, Winter, 1975–1976, pp. 79–99.

9. The Soviet Paper, which is No. 2, stated that the activities in the area should be conducted by States Parties and directly by the Sea-Bed Authority, and both should control an equal extent of the area. States Parties would operate on the basis of contracts with the Authority and would be under its effective financial and administrative supervision. States Parties might operate through State enterprises or juridical persons registered and sponsored by States which should ensure the latter's complying with the Law of the Sea Convention. The area would be free to all States irrespective of their geographical location, social system and level of industrial development. Consideration must also be given to the needs of developing countries, particularly landlocked and geographically-disadvantaged ones. The Authority should not be given a discretion as regards the rights of States to conduct exploration and exploitation activities, and the rights of States as juridical representatives of mankind under international law should be guaranteed in the Convention itself. The system of exploitation should have regard to the legitimate rights and interests of the socialist system. In short, the Authority should have only a secondary role.

The U.S. Paper, which is No. 3, favoured a parallel or dual access system. Enterprises and States Parties or other entities would carry out their activities directly by entering into contracts with the Sea-Bed Authority. Effective fiscal and administrative supervision over all activities in the area would be under the Authority, which must avoid discrimination in granting access and in implementing its powers and discharging its functions. All rights to the sea-bed area must not be impaired by the Authority which must safeguard those rights. In pursuance of provisions dealing with scientific research, technology transfer, and the distribution of revenues, the Authority should give special consideration to the interests and needs of developing countries, particularly the landlocked and the geographically-disadvantaged ones. Such special consideration would not be deemed to be discriminatory. Titles to the resources would be vested in the contractor at the moment the resources were recovered from the area according to the terms of the contract. All contractors should accept the Authority's supervision. In the case of applications received simultaneously, the Authority should make the award on a competitive basis. Contracts that satisfy the requirements laid down in the Convention or as stipulated by the Authority must not be refused. A number of delegations from developed countries supported this paper. In sum, they would deny the Authority the necessary discretionary powers.

10. Why the U.S. has not taken advantage of her extensive coastline and continental shelf to press for a coastal state regime with its attendant economic benefits will be found easy to understand by reading *New Era of Ocean Politics* by Ann L. Hollick and Robert E. Osgood, 1974, John Hopkins University Press.

11. Doc. A/Conf. 62/WP.9/Rev. 1.

12. Annex IA on Conciliation Procedures discussed
    Annex IB on Arbitration
    Annex IC on Statute of the Tribunal
    Annex IIA-D provides for Special Procedures dealing with disputes over Fisheries, Pollution, Scientific Research and Navigation.

13. A/Conf. 62/C.1/L.17.

14. See Press Release SEA/233 of 7/9/76.

15. See Chapters 8, 9 and 10 of *New Directions in the Law of the Sea*, Collected Papers — Volume III, edited by R. Churchill *et al.*, 1973, Oceana Publications.

16. A/Conf. 62/WP.10.

17. *The Lotus*. 1927, *P.C.I.J.* Series A, No. 9; Jurisdiction of European Commission of the Danube, 1927 *P.C.I.J.* Series B, No. 14; Territorial Jurisdiction of the International Commission of the River Od'er, 1929, *P.C.I.J.* Series A, No. 23; Access to, or Anchorage in, the Port of Danzig, 1931 *P.C.I.J.* Series A/B No. 43, p. 128; Delimitation of the Territorial Waters Between the Island of Castellorizo and the Coast of Anatolia, 1933, *P.C.I.J.* Series A/B, No. 51, p. 4; Lighthouses Case Between France and Greece, 1934 *P.C.I.J.* Series A/B No. 62, p. 4; Diversion of Water from the Muese, 1937 *P.C.I.J.* Series A/B No. 70, p. 4; Lighthouses in Crete and Samos, 1937 *P.C.I.J.* Series A/B, No. 71, p. 94; Corfu Channel, *I.C.J. Reports 1949*, p. 4; Fisheries, *I.C.J. Reports 1951*, p. 116; Minquiers and Ecrehos, *I.C.J. Reports 1953*, p. 47; Antarctica -*U.K.* v. *Argentina*) *I.C.J. Reports 1956*, p. 12; Antarctica (*United Kingdom* v. *Chile*) *I.C.J. Reports 1956*, p. 15; North Sea Continental Shelf, *I.C.J. Reports 1969*, p. 3; Fisheries Jurisdiction (*United Kingdom* v. *Iceland*) *I.C.J. Reports 1973*, p. 3; Fisheries Jurisdiction (*Federal Republic of Germany* v. *Iceland*) *I.C.J. Reports 1973*, p. 49; Fisheries Jurisdiction (*United Kingdom* v. *Iceland*) *I.C.J. Reports 1974*, p. 3; Fisheries Jurisdiction (*Federal Republic of Germany* v. *Iceland*) *I.C.J. Reports 1974*, p. 175; Aegean Sea Continental Shelf, *I.C.J. Reports 1976*, p. 3.

PART II

The ICJ and the Judicial Process

Chapter 5

THE INTERNATIONAL COURT OF JUSTICE: PRESENT TRENDS AND FUTURE PROSPECTS*

I

The present composition of the International Court of Justice is laid down in Article 2 of its Statute as follows:

> The Court shall be composed of a body of independent judges, elected regardless of their nationality from among persons of high moral character, who possess the qualifications required in their respective countries for appointment to the highest judicial offices, or are jurisconsults of recognized competence in international law.

There are thus four main elements in this provision that require comments: that the judges must be independent, that their election should not necessarily depend upon their nationality, that they should have high moral character in addition to their normal competence for the highest judicial offices in their own countries, and that, barring such competence, they could be jurists with recognized competence in international law. Let us now consider each element in turn.

The requirement that the judges of the Court should be independent is one commonly acknowledged, at least in theory, in nearly all legal systems in the world today. Practice varies from State to State, however, depending upon particular constitutional arrangements and the notions of administration of justice accepted by the relevant societies. What is required in the present context is that judges of the Court, once elected, must remain their own masters in the performance of their judicial functions, untrammelled by any consideration as to national origin or interests or by partial affections towards one party or the other in the award of their verdicts. In other words, they must not only do justice but must also let it be seen that justice is being done. To this end, Article 20 provides:

> Every member of the Court shall, before taking up his duties, make a solemn declaration in open court that he will exercise his powers impartially and conscientiously.

*Reprinted from *Judicial Settlement of International Disputes — An International Symposium* (Max Planck-Institute for Comparative Public Law and International Law), 1974, Heidelberg and New York.

The independence of the judges is further secured by the requirement in Article 16 that no judge may exercise any political or administrative function or engage in any other professional occupation; nor are they permitted, under Article 17, to act as agent, counsel or advocate in any case, or to participate in the decision of any case in which they have previously acted in any such capacity or in which they have acted as members of a national or international court or of a commission of inquiry or in any other capacity. Article 18(1) is of particular significance in this regard. It provides as follows:

> No member of the Court can be dismissed unless, in the unanimous opinion of the other members, he has ceased to fulfil the required conditions.

This constitutes a real safeguard for the judges' security of tenure, as the issue of removability is nearly always and everywhere regarded as the main test of judicial independence. While it is true that the mode of appointment[1] is also considered to be of vital importance — preference is sometimes given to appointment by a Judicial Service Commission over that by the Executive — there can be no doubt that the real test lies in the extent to which judges are dismissible and by whom. The Statute of the Court clearly specifies in Article 18(1) that a judge may be removed only by the unanimous verdict of his peers arrived at on the basis of the prescribed conditions. Fellow judges are not likely to dismiss one of their number lightly. Where the charge is well-founded and the guilt unanimously established, a notification to the Secretary-General to that effect under Article 16(2) and (3) is sufficient to vacate the guilty judge's post. As it is equally important that judges should feel absolutely free to dispense justice without fear or favour, they are also guaranteed certain privileges and immunities with regard to things done or words spoken in the course of their judicial functions. In the case of judges of the Court, Article 19 provides that "when engaged on the business of the Court", Court members enjoy diplomatic privileges and immunities, in respect of which they are each issued a *laissez-passer*. Before we conclude this aspect of the matter of judicial independence, we should note that judges of the Court have, under Article 32(5), their salaries, allowance, and compensation fixed by the General Assembly and these may not be decreased during their term of office.

In order to ensure that the judges attain this high level of juristic integrity, they must not be elected on the mere basis that they belong to particular nationalities, whatever the reputation of their nations or countries of origin for legal development or the dispensation of justice. The judges must stand on their own merit as professional men of the law, and not as Englishmen, Frenchmen, Nigerians or Swedes. The one limiting factor is that, under Article 3(1) of the Statute, no two of the fifteen judges may be nationals of the same State. It can be claimed that this is intended to prevent any one nationality being over-represented on the Court, possibly on the ground that that nationality has a better claim than any other. It is further provided in Article 3(2) that, if a candidate possesses dual nationality, he will be deemed to be "a national of the one in which he ordinarily exercises civil and political rights". This must be regarded as the State with which the candidate has, on the principle of the *Nottebohm case*,[2] the most real connection as a citizen. To strengthen the rule against electing two nationals of the same State, Article 10(3) provides that, where more than one national of the same State obtains an absolute majority of the votes cast by both the General Assembly and the Security Council, only the eldest is considered as elected. Finally, in the discharge of their functions, Article 31 permits judges of the nationality of each of the parties to retain their right to sit in the case before the Court and, if a judge of the nationality of one of the parties is on the Bench, any other party may appoint an additional judge. In any case, parties to a case may, if the Bench does not include judges of their own nationality, choose additional judges to sit upon the case. Such judges take part in the proceedings on terms of complete equality with their colleagues on the Bench. ▪

Let us now turn to a consideration of the third element of the provision of Article 2 on the composition of the Court, namely, the requirement that the judges should have "high moral character" as well as "qualifications required in their respective countries for appointment to the highest judicial offices". No legal system worthy of the name would tolerate the elevation to any post on its Bench of a knave, however brilliant or gifted he might be as a lawyer. It would be true to say that almost all modern legal systems would hesitate to appoint to its highest judicial offices lawyers that are depraved or of doubtful virtue, if only because they and the State would otherwise be embarrassed by their very presence on the Bench. When the court in question is "the principal judicial organ of the United Nations", it is but fair to demand a reasonable measure of moral probity on the part of candidates for the Bench. It is to be noted that the Court's Statute does not exact the highest moral character in the same way that it stipulates for the candidate that he must attain the qualifications requisite for the highest judicial office in his own country; it only asks for high moral character, that is, more or less the equivalent of unimpeachable conduct as a public figure; in other words, the candidate need not be an angel, though he must not be only a little better than a rascal. The test may be a subjective one insofar as his

State of origin is concerned, but the candidate's character is to be judged objectively by the international community — which may have to rely on the nominating national groups. With regard to the requirement that the candidate's qualifications should entitle him to the highest judicial office in his own country, it appears that he need be competent only in his municipal legal system, although he may happen to be competent also in other municipal systems or, indeed, in international law, if that be a stipulation in his own municipal law. All that is required is that the candidate should be highly competent in his own municipal law.

That this is so, is emphasized by the alternative contained in the fourth element of the omnibus provision of Article 2 of the Statute. The candidate, if he is not qualified for appointment to the highest judicial office, may be a jurisconsult of recognized competence in international law.[3] The question is: Who is a jurisconsult? Is he a university teacher of international law, or an independent legal practitioner of international law normally hired to act as an agent, counsel or advocate before the International Court of Justice or any other tribunal? Would a mere publicist or text-writer in international law qualify as a jurisconsult? Since the use of the term is something of an anachronism, we can only understand it in this context — not in its pristine Roman law usage, but in its general sense of a jurist, a specialist, in international law. The presence on the Bench of such a person, if he also qualifies as possessing recognized competence in international law, could only redound to its credit by reinforcing the objectivity of the Court's deliberations and, possibly, its decisions. It may be recalled in this connection that one of the sources of law which, under Article 38, the Court is enjoined to apply is "the teachings of the most highly qualified publicists of the various nations, as subsidiary means for the determination of rules of law".

II

In considering the foregoing issues arising out of the composition of the Court, we must take cognizance of this overriding provision of article 9 of the Statute:

> At every election, the electors shall bear in mind not only that the persons to be elected should individually possess the qualifications required, but also that in the body as a whole the representation of the main forms of civilization and of the principal legal systems of the world should be assured.

The electors referred to here are the members of the UN General

Assembly and those of the Security Council, the two bodies proceeding independently of one another to elect the members of the Court (Article 8); in this connection, it must be borne in mind that the vote of the Security Council is taken without any distinction between permanent and non-permanent members of the Council (Article 110(2)). The importance of Article 9 lies in the fact that it provides a fundamental guideline of action when the United Nations is about to constitute the Court, whether initially or from time to time. It enjoins two prerequisites: (a) that the main forms of civilizations, and (b) that the principal legal systems of the world, should be assured. The two expressions "civilization" and "legal system" are not coterminous, but are intended to represent the divergent ways of political thought and social action as well as the diverse juridical ideas in the world of today. The United Nations has by its hitherto vigorous policy of decolonization, especially in Asia and Africa, succeeded in replacing the two previously dominant Anglo–American and Civil Law political and legal hegemonies with a plethora of independent and increasingly separate ones of the newly independent States and has encouraged the increased articulateness of the Third World as a whole.

This new thinking on the part of the United Nations will be found to be reflected in Article 8 of the Statute of the International Law Commission with precisely the same wording as that of Article 9 of the Statute of the Court. One of the principal effects, at any rate in the case of the Court, has been the widening in recent years of the membership of the Court without any express amendment either of the Charter of the United Nations or of the Statute of the Court. Whereas the Permanent Court of International Justice included only one Asian and one African (UAR) up to its demise in 1946, and whereas the International Court of Justice numbered among its members only one African (UAR) and two Asians up to 1963,[4] the present Court consisted on February 1, 1971 of three Africans (Nigeria, Dahomey and Senegal), three Asians (Pakistan, Lebanon and the Phillipines), two Latin Americans (Mexico and Uruguay), five Western Europeans (the United Kingdom, France, Spain, Sweden and the United States) and two Eastern Europeans (the Soviet Union and Poland). The changes that have taken place within the last decade or so have been as fundamental as they have been epoch-making. The membership of the Court, which formerly consisted mainly of representatives of Western States and their European allies, with sometimes up to five Latin American States at a time, is now made up of one-third Latin American, Western and European States. The increased African and Asian membership would seem to have come about at the expense of the Latin American States, while the Eastern European States may be said to have done slightly better than hitherto, not so much perhaps in numbers as in stature and influence.

As we have seen, neither the UN Charter nor the International Court's Statute contains any stipulation that, in respect of membership of the Court, due regard be paid to "equitable geographical distribution", as is to be found, for instance, in Article 23 of the Charter in relation to the election of the non-permanent members of the Security Council. The enlargement of the Afro-Asian representation on the Court must be seen, therefore, as part of the general pattern of according increased membership to the new States in such organs as the Economic and Social Council, the Trusteeship Council, the Security Council, the UNESCO and a number of others. The General Assembly itself has risen in membership from the founding fifty at San Francisco in 1945 to the 127 in New York in 1971. This single development may be seen as being largely responsible for the recent change in the composition of the Court.

III

It will be noticed that nationality looms large in the selection of the members of the Court. Many have criticized the basis of election which in Article 4 requires that members must be elected by the General Assembly and by the Security Council from a list of persons nominated by their Governments. The fear has been expressed that this requirement that candidates for election to the Bench of the Court should be Government nominees implied the risk that each judge would tend more often than not to see his task primarily as that of the protector and defender of his country's interests. These interests might induce a national or a regional bias in a judge or a group of judges in the consideration of issues before the Court. Thus, Western European States could be led into taking positions on certain questions as against their East European counterparts, or ex-colonial powers might feel their positions threatened by certain of the claims and pressures on the part of the newly independent States and their collaborators.

One or two recent illustrations may be cited. In *Certain Expenses of the United Nations*,[5] the Western European judges of the Court and their associates would seem to have adopted a teleological or even a hyperteleological interpretation of the relevant provisions of the Charter in order to establish the liability of both the Soviet Union and

France to contribute their quotas to the cost of maintaining the UN forces in the Middle East and the Congo (Kinshasa). They argued that peace-keeping, being one of the cornerstones of the purposes and principles for which the UN Organization was founded, must necessarily come within the competence of the General Assembly that adopted the original Uniting for Peace resolution, and that it was immaterial that the Charter contains no express provision on the subject. The French and the Soviet judges, on the other hand, insisted on the application of a restricted rule of interpretation which would favor their case against liability: on a strict treaty interpretation of the UN Charter as a multilateral treaty, the General Assembly lacked the competence to assume the role of an insurer of international peace and security because there is no express grant of such power in the Charter. In the end, the Western European judges, except the French one, won their point by applying a constitutional, flexible interpretation, an approach that might have appealed to the French judge had France's political attitude on the subject not dictated otherwise. The national interest appears to have prevailed over the regional interest in this case.

The second illustration occurs in the *South-West Africa* cases[6] between Ethiopia and Liberia on the one hand, and the Republic of South Africa on the other. In their 1962 interim judgment, the Court had held that it had jurisdiction to hear the case but, in its 1966 judgment, it ruled that the complaints had no *locus standi* to maintain the action. The Western European and the Soviet judges clearly reversed their former roles in the *Certain Expenses* case, the only exception being Mr. Philip Jessup of the United States, who had maintained a consistently teleological approach.[7] In these *South-West Africa* cases, the Western European judges insisted on a restrictive interpretation of the League Covenant and of the UN Charter, in both of which they failed to find any ground for the complaints made by the two African States against South Africa in respect of its mandate over South-West Africa (Namibia). Although the issue of interests had been little canvassed in the pleadings and the oral arguments before the Court, the Western judges nevertheless preferred to stick to a narrow view of the matter which resulted in their having missed a good opportunity to deal with questions of absorbing legal and sociological interests in international law — respect for and application of human rights in Namibia, the legality of apartheid, the mandates system, and the future of Namibia and its people. The Soviet judge, for his part, favoured a teleological interpretation of the legal predicament with which the United Nations in particular and the world in general was faced in respect of

South Africa's administration over Namibia.[8]

One obvious lesson to be learnt from these illustrations is that the international law being developed by the Court on the basis of the shifting stances of its judges, who seem to be serving mainly the national or group interests of the States that elected them, is not likely to inspire confidence in the Court as a dynamic instrument to maintain the right balance between stability and change, and between the strong and the weak States. Edward McWhinney has warned that if judges of the Court act only as mirrors of the various political views of their individual States, no reliance should be placed on the judgments of the Court as an exposition of international law since there would be no consistency in its approach to the legal problems coming before it.

We may now consider the extent to which the existing provisions of the Statute which places an emphasis on nationality and Government sponsorship of candidates for the International Court is mitigated somewhat by another provision of the Statute. Article 13(1) provides for an arrangement by which five of the fifteen judges retire every three years, thus leading to a reasonably quick change of membership. In 1967, five new judges were elected and, in 1970, five more were elected in November to replace those who retired in February of that year.[9] Given the new impetus from the Third World, there does not appear to be any likelihood of a return to the old order in which Europe dominated the Bench. This is not to say that Western Europe would in future be under-represented but rather that Western European candidates in the future would stand a far better chance of being elected if they had or were thought to have liberal or progressive views vis-à-vis the problems of the Third World.

One of the results of the International Court's judgment in the *South-West Africa case* was the failure of Sir Kenneth Bailey, an able lawyer, to secure election in 1966, partly on the ground that he was considered to be narrow and conservative and partly because he was of the same Australian nationality as Sir Percy Spender — who had given the decisive casting vote against the complainants. Another result has been that, in order to avoid Western European dominance on the Bench of the Court, the objective of electing only candidates with real competence in international law and possessing professional integrity may be impossible in the future. The three-yearly elections often involved a good deal of horse-trading at the best of times; henceforth, this has become accentuated, leading to a situation in which candidates have been and will in future be likely to be elected more on a consideration as to how they might vote on certain delicate issues coming before the Court than on whether they would or could render objectively valid judicial opinions in all cases and at all times. It has been suggested that, instead of the existing system of electing from a list of Government nominees who continue to be their countries' representatives on the Bench, judges of the Court should be elected on the same principles and by the same procedures as are members of the International Law Commission of the United Nations. The Commission's Statute requires in Article 2 that its twenty-five members must be "persons of recognized competence in international law" and that "no two members of the Commission shall be nationals of the same State". Each Member State of the United Nations may, under Article 4, nominate for election not more that four candidates, of whom two may be nationals of other States. This method seems preferable to the one by which candidates for the Court are at present nominated; it diffuses loyalty by encouraging States to go beyond their immediate frontiers to acknowledge merit wherever it may be found. Once due regard is had to the principle of equitable geographical distribution, this system could, if properly utilized, promote the election of judges of the Court on the basis of personal competence and intellectual distinction regardless of nationality.

It is well-known that members of the International Law Commission, once elected, represent only themselves as legal scientists and not as individual representatives of the Governments of the countries from which they happen to hail. The result has been to make the Commission behave more often as a group of jurists than as a group of statesmen intent on ensuring the maintenance of the "vital interests" of their several countries. There are occasional lapses from grace, but the end products are often better than they might have been under the system of nomination and election at present employed for the International Court. It may be objected, on this score, that the functions of the two bodies — the Commission and the Court — are so dissimilar that their membership composition cannot be the same; and that the exercise of codification of rules generates less heat than does the process of adjudication of disputes. There is, however, a strong case for assimilating the method of elevation to the Bench of the World Court to that of election of members of the International Law Commission, if only because the latter is, on the whole, more conducive to the achievement of consensus on major world issues, be they legal or judicial.

We may ask, in conclusion, whether the Court's membership should be increased from fifteen to twenty-five, as has happened with the International Law Commission? There are no doubt pros and cons on the subject, but the point does not appear to be the most urgent facing the Court today. It would seem right to maintain the present strength of fifteen members, at least for the time being.

IV

Another problem is the question whether regional or special chambers of the Court should be established for certain categories of disputes. The power to form chambers consisting of three or more judges for dealing with particular categories of cases is expressly granted to the Court by Article 26(1), the examples of such cases mentioned in the section are labor cases and cases relating to transit and communications. But it is clear from paragraph 2 of the same section that other subjects may from time to time be assigned to other chambers similarly established and that their constitution may be determined by the Court with the parties' approval. In any case, the parties are, under Article 27, free to request that their dispute be heard and determined by any of such chambers rather than by the full Court itself; but any judgment given by a chamber is considered to be a judgment of the Court. We must not lose sight of the provision of Article 28 to the effect that any chamber can sit and exercise its functions elsewhere than at The Hague.

Also, to ensure speedy dispatch of its business, the Court is enjoined under Article 29 to form an annual chamber consisting of five judges for the purpose of hearing and determining cases by summary procedure, if the parties so request. For the replacement of judges who find it impossible to sit, two additional judges must be selected. The Court can establish its own rules of procedure and organize its business as it may deem fit; according to Article 30, it may provide by its rules of procedure for the appointment of assessors to sit with the Court or with any of its chambers, but without the right to vote. An assessor, be it noted, is not an *ad hoc* judge who has a voting right (Article 31(6)). It is important to observe that this annual chamber of five judges may sit and exercise its functions elsewhere that at The Hague. It is thus possible for the Court to constitute one such chamber for a particular region of the world to deal with disputes arising from that area if and when the need arises. There does not, however, appear to be an immediate prospect of bringing into force the provision of Article 29, seeing that the cases coming before the Court itself are at the moment few and far between. We should nevertheless not discount such a possibility if the employment of such a procedure in any particular case would be more acceptable to the parties concerned than a recourse to the full Court. The summary nature of its procedure and, no doubt, of its jurisdiction may well be an additional factor to recommend the use of such a chamber to the parties.

The real issue is, however, whether the establishment of regional or special chambers would be conducive to the maintenance and preservation of the unity of international law and its progressive development. There is risk of different chambers in course of time laying down differing rules of international customary law or of interpretation of international conventions and codes. Such divergencies could arise *either* out of the normal operation of the judicial process, as when several high courts of a State give divergent judgments involving a legal rule of that State, *or* the divergencies could arise out of the fact that certain regional legal attitudes have to be taken into account by the Bench of five judges sitting in the particular region and hearing counsel's argument based upon such a regional approach, as for example, the Latin American view of what constitutes "exhaustion of local remedies" on Tanzania's doctrine regarding succession of States and governments. Not to take judicial notice of such regional peculiarities where these exist would be to detract from the value of such regional chambers of the Court if not to denigrate them in the estimation of the requesting parties. Such a development would be likely to damn the Court still further in the eyes of those for whom the establishment of regional or special chambers have largely been designed in the first place.

The situation is scarcely improved by the superimposition of a system of appeal to plenary proceedings. This would certainly increase the cost of litigation, in addition to involving more delays. Then there is the question of what the full International Court sitting in an appellate capacity can or should do when faced with the findings of a regional or special chamber which of itself has heard and studied the evidence at first hand. The full Court would almost certainly find itself on the horns of a dilemma if the regional chamber's judgment appealed from should prove to turn on an application of a regional legal rule of international law. If it were to uphold the lower court, its own ruling might become suspect. If, on the other hand, it should overrule its chamber, the International Court might begin to lose internal cohesion and juristic objectivity. In sum, the unity of international law and its progressive development would suffer a set-back.

V

It remains to consider how, if at all possible, the proceedings of the Court can be speeded up. Various suggestions have been put forward. It has, for instance, been suggested that the Court should abandon oral hearings by adopting a procedure of dealing with certain categories of cases in chambers, somewhat along the lines of the procedure followed by the Supreme Court of the United States whereby many appeal cases are assigned to individual judges for summary judgments, especially in between Court sessions. This is clearly not apt, since, unless the International Court of Justice is sitting on appeal from one of its chambers, it normally sits as a court of first instance. Nevertheless, a limited use of this procedure is recommended, if only as an experiment. Again, the Court should, it has been argued, alter its present rules of procedure to provide for written memoranda and other pleadings to be kept within stated limits as regards bulk and complexity. Article 42 would need an amendment. This should facilitate a somewhat more rapid assimilation of the essential data on the part of both judges of the Court and counsel on the other side. *Pari passu* with this should be a Rule of Court which limits the length of oral statements before the Court to a stated period — say, one or two hours at the most. This is within the provisions of Article 48 of the Statute of the Court. The Court would, of course, have a discretion to grant an extension of time in exceptional circumstances.

One of the possibilities for speeding up the Court's processes is that more frequent use should be made of the summary proceedings discussed in Part IV above. The view has also been expressed that itinerant chambers of the Court be constituted for giving advisory opinions requested by parties to a dispute. This is open to the same objections as we have advanced above against regional or special chambers, the only difference being that advisory opinions are less binding on the parties whatever their juristic value in other respects.

The Rules of Court regulating the examination of preliminary questions would appear to require little change. It is certainly in consonance with the principle of natural justice that questions, such as the refusal of one or more of the judges of the Court who is about to sit on a case, or the interpretation of its rules, should be for the Court to determine. The Registrar of the International Court of Justice should be given rather wider powers than he has under existing rules to settle the records with agents and counsel on both sides, in order to limit, as far as practicable, the bulk of the case records. He should be given powers analogous to those of the Registrar of the Privy Council in England.

It has been said that the giving by individual judges of separate opinions in addition to the main opinion of the Court with which the judges agree should be discontinued. Here, caution is needed. It should be sufficient for the President to indicate to his colleagues by an unwritten law certain criteria limiting the probable length of separate opinions; the President should have the right to refer an unduly expansive separate opinion back to its author for necessary curtailment, on pain of its being rejected for failure to comply. Dissenting opinions are, however, in a different category. Their authors should be allowed to express themselves as freely and as fully as possible, although certain dissenting opinions in recent rulings of the Court have been distressingly rendered at inordinate length. There must be a way of bringing it home to writers of such opinions that the international legal profession does frown upon them.

Let us end up by considering very briefly the problem of costs of litigation before the International Court of Justice. It makes little difference whether the case is a contentious suit or one requiring an advisory opinion, the costs are comparable and frequently too high. One means of reducing costs, is of course, to limit the size of written pleadings and the length of oral statements. Agents, counsel and advocates of parties to disputes before the Court should be implored to enact a self-denying ordinance so that fees charged for services rendered to relatively impecunious clients or in respect of disputes not involving complicated commercial and industrial enterprises could be kept within reasonable bounds. The idea of introducing a legal aid scheme for developing countries, which some have advocated in recent years, should be discountenanced, as these countries would view with suspicion and even resentment any offer of financial assistance or charity in the prosecution of their claim for redress before an international tribunal.

Additional Comments

In presenting his report, Mr. Elias made the following explanatory statements:

Referring to the present composition of the International Court of Justice he pointed out that in his opinion there was a gap in Article 2 of its Statute, since qualification for the highest judicial body of a State did not necessarily entail qualification in international law. On the other hand, a specialist in international law lacking experience in judicial procedure would probably quickly catch up with the questions of the Court's competence and procedure.

Furthermore Mr. Elias wished to construe Article 9 of the Statute as not emphasizing the principal legal "systems" in the traditional sense, but rather the distinctive legal "cultures" which had grown beyond the range of civil law and common law systems. These clearly distinguishable cultures that had been developing within Latin America, Asia and Africa should be given as fair representation as possible.

Referring to the procedure of appointment of the members of the Court, he briefly mentioned the recommendations of the Institut de Droit International and the United States' suggestions in reply to the Secretary-General. The plan to set up a committee of the General Assembly examining the list of candidates prepared by the Secretary-General might help to guarantee that future members of the Court possessed a reasonable standard of knowledge of international law. In Mr. Elias' opinion, qualification in international law was a greater safeguard for independence than any conceivable method of selection.

Turning to the question of regional and special chambers, Mr. Elias pointed to the amendment of the Rules of Procedure of May 1972, which in his opinion made it possible to consult parties on their preferences for candidates to be included in a particular chamber, without, of course, requiring the Court to abandon the requirement of secret ballot and of being finally responsible for the selection of the judges.

In general, he continued, the establishment of regional chambers was not very likely to help the cause of international law. The argument that regional chambers would exhibit a certain affinity to the respective geographical, or rather political backgrounds and their legal cultures which might diminish the reluctance of States to submit their cases to adjudication was losing much of its force. The International Law Commission, by broadening its basis, had greatly improved the situation in the sense that now representatives of the main forms of civilization and legal systems are participating in the codification and progressive development of international law. Also the law of other international bodies, like UNCTAD was increasingly universal. Thus regional particularities would in due course be ironed out.

Finally, Mr. Elias turned to some questions of the Court's procedure. He wondered whether, in the vast majority of cases, the parties would not reject the alternative of a summary procedure. Considering the lengthy engagement of the International Court of Justice in preliminary issues on questions relating to jurisdiction, he pointed to the *Namibia case*, in which the Court — as opposed to its attitude in the *South-West Africa* decisions in 1962 and 1966 and the

Barcelona Traction case — had shown remarkable flexibility and adaptability.

Delays, he pointed out, were often the fault of the parties, and in the *Namibia case* the Court has rightly set a time limit. Both the practice of exchanging memorials and counter-memorials and the methods of oral pleadings might be subjected to substantial modifications. In this the procedure of the US Supreme Court and that of the United Kingdom's Privy Council aimed at concentrating party statements might serve as examples. Both courts were admittedly courts of appeal, yet valuable as guiding models.

One reform might be to establish a bureau under the Chief Registrar, who, in consultation with the President or in association with the Vice-President, would discuss with the representatives of the parties possibilities of delimiting forthcoming cases, while at the same time establishing guidelines for the concentration of memorials and indicating points of specific interest which should be elaborated. Lengthy oral statements to the Court, repeating the contents of the memorials, should in any event be eliminated.

The costs were doubtless a factor deterring States — especially younger ones, whose resources were limited — from making use of the Court. Still, these States, anxious not to be ostracized as poor, would also shy away from any possible legal aid fund. A workable solution might be the reduction of the costs of litigation, leaving to the parties only the expenses of documents and counsel.

NOTES

1. Judges of the Court are elected by the UN General Assembly and the Security Council from a list of persons nominated by the national groups in the Permanent Court of Arbitration or, in the case of Member States not represented on the Permanent Court of Arbitration, from a list of persons nominated by national groups appointed for the purpose by their governments. Article 6 requires that extensive consultations must be held by the national groups with various shades of opinion before they make their nominations. The Secretary-General submits such lists to the two UN organs, which then proceed independently of one another to elect the Court members. (See articles 4–12 of the Statute.)

2. *International Court of Justice Yearbook 1954–1955*, pp. 76–80.

3. The Indian Constitution provides, for example, that a distinguished jurist is eligible for direct appointment to the Supreme Court, even though he may not otherwise qualify via appointments to the lower Benches (see s. 124[3] [c] of the Constitution of India).

4. As at May 1, 1968, the Court was made up as follows:
Africa — Nigeria and Senegal (2); *Asia* — Japan, Pakistan, Lebanon and Phillipines

(4); *Latin America* — Peru and Mexico (2); *Eastern Europe* — U.S.S.R. and Poland (2); and *Western Europe and others* — United Kingdom, United States, France, Italy and Sweden (5).

5. *I.C.J. Reports 1962*, p. 151.

6. *I.C.J. Reports 1966*, p. 3. See also D. H. N. Johnson, "Recent Developments in the International Court of Justice", *Modern Law Review*, Vol. 33, No. 1, 1970, pp. 53–62.

7. See *I.C.J. Reports 1966*, pp. 323ff. for his dissenting opinion in which he criticized the majority view.

8. For a perceptive analysis of the whole problem, see E. McWhinney, "The Changing United Nations Constitutionalism. New Arenas and New Techniques for International Law-Making", *The Canadian Yearbook of International Law*, Vol. 5, pp. 68–83, 1967.

9. According to the *International Court of Justice Yearbook*, 1968–1969: On July 31, 1969, 126 States were members of the United Nations and *ipso facto* parties to the Statute of the Court. Three States, not Members of the United Nations, were parties to the Statute — Liechtenstein, San Marino and Switzerland. Under Articles 35(2) of the Statute, the Court is open to certain States not parties to the Statute; these were the Federal Republic of Germany and the Republic of Vietnam.

Chapter 6

THE INTERNATIONAL COURT OF JUSTICE AND
JUDICIAL REVIEW

One of the rapidly evolving new fields of international law since the Second World War is what may be termed International Constitutional Law, a logical development from the proliferation of international organizations, both universal and regional, with constitutions and charters specifying their functions and competences. The United Nations itself and its specialized agencies furnish examples of the universal type, while the Council of Europe, the Organization of American States, the Organization of African Unity and the Arab League are instances of the regional type. There is, allied to this new International Constitutional Law, a complementary area of International Administrative Law dealing mainly with the internal regulation of matters such as staff conditions and budgeting.[1]

In this paper, however, we are not concerned with the whole field of international law, but only with the question of judicial review which the interpretation of the charters and constitutions of the various international organizations inevitably entail. It should be stated that the present study is concerned primarily with examining the issue of the interpretation of the UN Charter by the International Court of Justice as "the principal judicial organ of the United Nations".

Although judicial interpretation of treaties and other international agreements is not new even under the League of Nations system in that the reports of the Permanent Court of International Justice are replete with judgments and advisory opinions touching the subject, there would seem to have been no known case of judicial *review* of a provision of the League Covenant concerning the analysis, functions and competences of the principal organs — the Council and the Assembly. The reason is not hard to find. It is that, even though the Statute of the International Court of Justice is almost a carbon copy of that of the Permanent Court of International Justice, there was never any organic link between the League and the Permanent Court[2] as there is between the United Nations and the International

Court of Justice, the Statute of which is an integral part of the UN Charter. The loose arrangement which thus existed between the League and the Permanent Court made it unthinkable that the latter should deign to review the structures and competences of the League Council and the League Assembly if such questions were ever referred to it. The International Court of Justice, despite the organic relationship between it and the United Nations, is faced with immense problems regarding its power, if any, to review the political actions of the General Assembly and the Security Council. It is to a consideration of this issue that we shall now turn.

We may begin with the main conclusions reached at the San Francisco Conference on the subject of interpretation of the UN Charter. Among the proposals submitted at the Conference was that of the Belgian delegation that the Security Council be authorized to request from the Court an advisory opinion on the interpretation or application of a provision of the Charter and then itself decide the dispute on the basis of that opinion or refer the opinion to the General Assembly for determination. It was further suggested that, in case of any disagreement between the two principal organs as to the interpretation of a provision of the Charter, the matter should be referred to the Court. In the result, the Committee IV/2 adopted a statement in which were set out several modes of interpreting the UN Charter.[3] The Security Council, the General Assembly and the International Court of Justice could, as organs functioning within the framework of the Charter, interpret such parts of it as are applicable to its functions. There was no need to include express provisions in the Charter "either authorizing or approving the normal operation of this principle", since differences of interpretation are bound to arise as to the correct interpretation of certain provisions of the Charter in the common, everyday use of the document by these organs. The statement also noted: "Under unitary forms of national government the final determination of such a question may be vested in the highest court or in some other national authority. However, the nature of the Organization and of its operation would not seem to be such as to invite the inclusion in the Charter of any provision of this nature". Any two States disagreeing as to the correct interpretation of a provision of the Charter could go to the International Court of Justice "as in the case of any other treaty". Similarly, the General Assembly and the Security Council might ask the Court for an advisory opinion concerning the meaning of a provision of the Charter, or might set up an *ad hoc* committee of international jurists to examine the matter and report thereon, or refer the issue to a joint conference for determination. The statement made it clear that interpretations of the Charter arrived at in any of these ways would, of course, have no binding force, and that for any interpretation to become authoritative it must be incorporated as a result of an amendment of the Charter carried out in accordance with the normal procedure therein laid down in Articles 108 and 109 of the Charter.[4]

This summary of the conclusions contained in the statement of Committee IV/2 of the San Francisco Conference in 1945 deserves attention because it contains the germ of the idea underlying our present consideration of the problem of judicial review by the International Court of Justice. Each of the principal UN organs — the Security Council, the General Assembly and, presumably, the Secretariat under the Secretary-General and his permanent staff — can make political reviews of its powers and functions in the light of those provisions of the Charter that apertain to their activities and also the International Court of Justice can make a judicial review of its own powers and determine its jurisdiction. As regards the powers of the Court to make a judicial determination of the competences and functions of these other organs, the procedure must be by way of an advisory opinion sought specifically for that purpose. There was no specific decision made at the San Francisco Conference, and there is no specific clause in the UN Charter, empowering the International Court of Justice to declare a provision of the Charter invalid, or void, in the way that federal and some unitary constitutions expressly empower their supreme courts to do. In the Charter there is no provision "authorizing or approving the normal operation of this principle" of judicial review, and the power of making a final determination of such a vital question has not been given to the Court because "the nature of the organization and of its operation would not seem to be such as to invite the inclusion in the Charter of any provision of this nature". It is submitted that, apart therefore from the power to knock down any provision of the Charter as invalid or void, the International Court of Justice should, to the extent of its limited power of review, be able to say whether or not one of the principal organs has acted *ultra vires* in any given case, albeit by way of an advisory opinion only. It at least has a specific power granted to it by both the UN Charter (Article 96(1)) and by its own Statute (Article 65(1) an integral part of the Charter) to offer advisory opinions when requested to do so. This point is very important and would seem to be often overlooked by those opposed to the Court's exercise of its judicial review, as we shall see later.

II

We begin with the fundamental question as to whether the Court, in the exercise of its function of judicial review, possesses the power to declare a resolution of either the General Assembly or the Security Council invalid or void for any reason whatsoever. Given the division of powers under the UN Charter as between the Security Council, the General Assembly and the Court as sovereign each in its own sphere, and remembering also the lack of any express power to that effect being granted in the Charter, it is clear that, for a smooth functioning of the UN Organization none of these three organs has any supremacy over the others in the sense that one can quash the decision of the others if such a decision is within its sphere of competence. The analogy between the arrangement under the Charter and that within a State as to the division of competences among the executive, the legislative and the judicial branches of government is an attractive one which can furnish a number of useful parallels. It is as much the duty of the International Court to apply the Charter as it is that of a State's courts to enforce the constitution. In order to achieve this juridical aim certain rules apply. Thus there is a rebuttable presumption in favour of the constitutionality or the validity of UN resolutions in a manner similar to State statutes. There is also a presumption that prescribed formalities for the passing of the Resolutions or the Statutes have been observed and the conditions laid down by the law fulfilled, and it is up to the challenger to establish the contrary. Again, one golden rule of the application or the interpretation of the basic law and of the acts claimed to have been carried out in pursuance of it is the principle of respect by the judiciary for the determinations of the principal organs of the United Nations or of the State legislative body in matters involving the policy or desirability of the resolutions or measures and their expediency. It is not for the court of law to sit in judgment on the wisdom or otherwise of the measure taken; the proper business of the Court is to apply or interpret the relevant measure.[5] It is equally an established principle that courts of law must show a healthy respect for long-standing practices of decision-making or rule-making organs which are proved to be well-founded, because such respect may reinforce the presumption in favor of the constitutional validity of the measure in question. Finally, by way of summary of the guiding principles of interpretation in the process of judicial review, it may be mentioned that there are certain situations in which a court of law merely takes judicial notice of the determinations of decision-making or rule-making bodies — in our case, the Security Council and the General

Assembly — of matters within the bounds of those bodies or organs.[6] In such cases a court does not question the determinations once it is satisfied that the bodies concerned have the necessary competence to deal with such matters and that the relevant formalities have been observed.

There are three main types of limitation on the power of judicial review which a court is expected to observe in the exercise of its function in this regard. There may be a constitutional limitation in the form of a restriction contained in the constitutive instrument by which the court is established providing either that it may not review certain matters at all or that it may review only to a certain, specified extent. The International Court of Justice falls, as we have seen, into the latter category in that it may apply or interpret the Charter in the exercise of its advisory jurisdiction, but it cannot strike down a provision of the Charter as invalid or void. Many municipal constitutions do, on the other hand, grant to the States' highest courts the power to declare invalid not only the organic laws but also the constitutional provisions themselves. When a court declares a provision of the State constitution invalid, the executive government may through the legislature, amend as directed by the court or it may even take the extreme step of overruling the court's decision and set it at nought, although the occasions for so doing must be very rare indeed if orderly government is to be assured.

Another form of limitation on the court's power of judicial review may not be extrinsic to the constitutive instrument establishing it. An instrinsic limitation occurs where the court is not expressly forbidden to review but it is of the nature of the institutions with which the sovereign powers are shared by the court that it should not sit in judgment over them to the extent of modifying or even abrogating them by judicial review. Thus it is a rule that English courts may not declare an act of Parliament invalid or void.

Self-imposed limitations are such as all courts of law find it necessary to observe in the exercise of their judicial functions *as* courts of law. Judicial caution takes many forms. It may occur where a court decides that it has no jurisdiction or declines to exercise jurisdiction in a case brought before it. It also occurs where a court decides to limit itself to the consideration of only such aspects of a case as the court believes to be relevant to the disposal of the matter in litigation before it. But judicial caution must not be carried as far as to permit a court to declare a *non-liquet*, that is to say, to declare that it cannot judge the case before it, either on the ground that there is no applicable rule of law or on any other ground than the want of a plaintiff or of a dispute between parties.

III

It may not be inappropriate to begin our analysis with an examination of what the Court said in its advisory opinion in the *Namibia case*.[7] We shall, no doubt, examine other cases both before and after this case in order to see how the Court has fulfilled its function of judicial review, but the justification for commencing with *Namibia* is that here the issue of judicial review was first raised in an acute form. During the debate preceding the making of the request, not less than five members of the Security Council denied the Court's power to pass upon the validity or otherwise of the various resolutions of the General Assembly and of the Security Council, which formed the basis of the decision to request the advisory opinion. The request itself is as follows:

> What are the legal consequences for States of the continued presence of South Africa in Namibia (South West Africa) notwithstanding Security Council resolution 276 (1970)?

In reply the Court was of the opinion, by thirteen votes to two, "that the continued presence of South Africa is under obligation to withdraw its administration from Namibia immediately and thus put an end to its occupation of the Territory"; by eleven votes to four, "that States Members of the United Nations are under obligation to recognize the illegality of South Africa's presence in Namibia, and the invalidity of its acts on behalf of or concerning Namibia, and to refrain from any acts and in particular any dealings with the Government of South Africa implying recognition of the legality of or lending support or assistance to, such presence and administration"; also by eleven votes to four, "that it is incumbent upon States which are not Members of the United Nations to give assistance, within the scope of sub-paragraph (2) above, in the action which has been taken by the United Nations with regard to Namibia".

It is, therefore, clear that the Court did not make any direct reference to nor pass upon the validity of the General Assembly and the Security Council resolutions in the operative paragraphs of the advisory opinion, although it reviewed them in detail in the course of its analysis and reasoning leading to the reply to the request.

Let us examine three representative opinions of some of the judges that supported the advisory opinion. In his separate opinion, for example, Judge Petrén observed:

> In other words, a political organ is entitled to take a decision upon grounds which are admittedly of a legal nature, but the validity of which cannot be examined by

the Court once the political organ has taken its decision within its proper sphere of competence.

I, therefore, consider that in the present case the Court should have confined itself to the finding that resolution 2145 (XXI) is valid without examining the correctness of the assessment of the facts upon which that resolution is based. To embark upon such an enquiry, as the Court has done in the present Opinion, amounts to implying that the Court could possibly have reached conclusions different from those of the General Assembly and could therefore have declared the resolution invalid. But, in the light of the foregoing, I consider that to be out of the question.[8]

Judge Onyeama, who took the opposite view that the Court should examine the validity of General Assembly and Security Council resolutions, put the matter thus:

The Court's powers are clearly defined by the Statute, and do not include powers to review decisions of other organs of the United Nations; but when, as in the present proceedings, such decisions bear upon a case properly before the Court, and a correct judgment or opinion could not be rendered without determining the validity of such decisions, the Court could not possibly avoid such a determination without abdicating its role of a judicial organ.

The question put to the Court does not, in terms, ask the Court to give an opinion on whether General Assembly resolution 2145 (XXI) is valid, but the "legal consequences" which the Court is requested to define, are postulated upon its validity. Were the Court to accept this postulate without examination, it would run the risk of rendering an opinion based on a false premise. The question itself has not expressly excluded examination of the validity of this and other related resolutions . . . .; it would require the clearest inhibiting words to establish that such a limitation of the scope of the Court's consideration was intended.[9]

Judge Onyeama concluded his argument with these words: "The matter is, in my view, concluded by the principle stated by the Court in the *Certain Expenses of the United Nations case* (*I.C.J. Reports 1962*, p. 151–157) as follows:

. . . the Court must have full liberty to consider *all relevant data available to it in forming an opinion on a question posed to it for an advisory opinion* (italics added).[10]

A third view of the matter would seem to be that of Judge Dillard who expressed the opinion that "the greatest deference must be given to resolutions adopted by the organs of the United Nations. There is, of course, nothing in the Charter which compels these organs to ask for an advisory opinion or which gives this Court (as in many domestic arenas) a power of review to be triggered by those who may feel their interests unlawfully invaded".

Judge Dillard then added:

But when these organs do see fit to ask for an advisory opinion they must expect the Court to act in strict accordance with its judicial function. This function precludes it from *accepting without any enquiry whatever*, a legal conclusion which itself conditions the nature and scope of the legal consequences flowing from it. It would be otherwise if the resolutions requesting an opinion were legally neutral as in the three previous requests for advisory opinions bearing on the Mandate.[11]

Five "other considerations" were mentioned (but not discussed) by Judge Dillard in support of his position: that his view was "compatible" with the Court's own jurisprudence as revealed, especially in the *Certain Expenses case* (*I.C.J. Reports 1962*, pp. 156, 157, 216 and 217) that only five States opposed the Court's passing upon the validity of the relevant resolutions; that the representative of the Secretary-General retracted in the course of argument from a dogmatic assertion that the Court could not examine the issue of validity of the resolutions; that, "as a sheer practical matter, had the Court refrained from such an enquiry and had a strongly reasoned dissent cast grave doubt on the validity of the resolutions, then the probative value of the advisory opinion would have been weakened": and, "finally, it may not be presumptuous to suggest that as a political matter, it is not in the long range interest of the United Nations to appear to be reluctant to have its resolutions stand the test of legal validity when it calls upon a court to determine issues to which this validity is related.[12]

If we may deal with Judge Dillard's view first, we note that it is almost on all fours with Judge Onyeama's, in that he too regards the present request as warranting a review and that it is only after such a review that the legal consequences could be drawn by the Court. But it would appear that Judge Dillard understood the necessary "review" in a somewhat different sense from that expected by Judge Onyeama. Judge Dillard would seem to be satisfied that the Court had carried out the review by examining the various resolutions of the General Assembly and of the Security Council, since, according to him, although the Court was not asked to call into question the validity of Resolution 276 or 2145 the "Court has not felt justified in attaching this limited scope to its enquiry". The question is: has the Court in fact done this? That Judge Dillard did seem to have assumed that the Court had passed upon the validity of the resolutions would appear to follow becomes evident from one of his "other considerations", this to the effect that "as a sheer practical matter, had the Court refrained from such an enquiry and had a strongly reasoned dissent cast grave doubt on the validity of the resolutions, then the probative value of the Advisory Opinion would have been weakened". Judge Onyeama, on the other hand, thought that the Court had assumed, as had the Security Council, the validity of the relevant resolutions and accepted their correctness without examination. After stating the Court's view, he observed: "I do not think that this approach to the question of the Court's competence to examine and pass upon decisions and resolutions of the General Assembly and the Security Council which touch upon issues before it leads to a sufficiently definitive answer".[13] In other words, Judge Onyeama would not have wished Judge Dillard to appear to have assumed that the Court had implicitly held the relevant resolutions valid; the Court should have said so *expressly*. It is thought that Judge Dillard's position could in a sense be defended, and the point will be made a little later.

How did the Court see its role in this matter? On the one hand it was faced with the argument that, though the request was not directed to the question of the validity of the relevant resolutions, the Court was not precluded from making such an enquiry. On the other hand, the Court was not authorized by the request to go into the validity of the resolutions; and "the Court should not assume powers of judicial review of the action taken by the other principal organs of the United Nations without specific request to that effect, nor act as a court of appeal from their decisions".[14] More specifically the Court stated its position thus:

> Undoubtedly, the Court does not possess powers of judicial review or appeal in respect of the decisions taken by the United Nations organs concerned. The question of the validity or conformity with the Charter of General Assembly resolution 2145 (XXI) or of related Security Council resolutions does not form the subject of the request for advisory opinion. However, in the exercise of its judicial function and since objections have been advanced the Court, in the course of its reasoning, will consider these objections before determining any legal consequences arising from those resolutions.[15]

The Court accordingly embarked upon a systematic examination and analysis of the relevant resolutions and came to the conclusion that the subject-matter of the request, the occupation by the South African Government of the mandated or Trust Territory of Namibia, was within the competence of the General Assembly which had rightly determined the said occupation in accordance with the Charter; that the issue of self-determination of peoples as a principle of contemporary international law was peculiarly within the province of the General Assembly which had developed it, that South Africa's policy of *apartheid* is contrary to the UN Charter and that South Africa's illegal occupation should cease forthwith. It seems that the Court could be deemed to have applied the constitutional principles of judicial review, namely, the presumption of legality of official acts of UN organs, the rebuttable presumption in favour of the constitutionality of what had been done by both organs within their legitimate sphere of competence, which must be regarded as reinforced by long-standing practice within both organs as borne out by the evidence of the various resolutions, and the established principle that a court takes judicial notice of determinations of the two organs on matters within the bounds of their competence.[16]

With regard to Judge Onyeama's citation from the *Certain Expenses case* to the effect that the Court must have full liberty to consider all relevant data available to it in forming an opinion on a question posed to it for an advisory opinion, the Court's answer is that the question of validity or conformity of the resolutions with the Charter does not form the subject of the request for advisory opinion. It is true that in the *Certain Expenses case* there was a specific request made to the Court to determine the question of the validity of the resolution in the light of the Charter. There, the Court was asked to say whether the expenditure had been validly authorized by a series of General Assembly resolutions as the "expenses of the Organization within the meaning of Article 17, paragraph 2, of the Charter of the United Nations".[17] It has been suggested that the Security Council did not, in Resolution 284, question the validity of Resolution 276 (1970) and that the Court was not bound to consider that question in order to answer the request submitted to it. The Court considered the validity of Security Council Resolution 276 (1970) and General Assembly Resolution 2145 (XXI) only insofar as it was deemed necessary to remove doubts in respect of matters preliminary to answering the question asked by the Court.[18]

Judge Gros, in his dissenting opinion, observed that the Court had deviated from the line of its case law when it "hesitated to examine the lawfulness of the legal step which gave rise to the question upon which the Court is asked to pronounce, i.e. General Assembly Resolution 2145 (XXI)". He disagreed with the Court that the question of validity did not form the subject of the request for advisory opinion: "It used not to be the Court's habit to take for granted the premises of a legal situation, the consequences of which it has been asked to state ".[19] Like Judges Onyeama and Dillard, he cited the *Certain Expenses case* and insisted that the situation in the two cases is "parallel". But, as we have just seen, it is not. Judge Gros insisted that Resolution 2145 (XXI) was invalid and the Court should have said so; the Court should also have made an analysis "based on a judicial finding that there had been a breach of the obligation to transform the Mandate by negotiation as the 1950 opinion prescribed".

In other words Judge Gros agreed with those who hold that the Court should have made a definitive pronouncement as to the invalidity of the relevant resolutions. He said: "In the present case, in which the Court has based its opinion on an interpretation of Articles 24 and 25 of the Charter as to powers of the Security Council, and on an interpretation of the legal nature of the powers of the General Assembly, it would have seemed particularly appropriate to have exercised unambiguously the Court's power to interpret the Charter, which the General Assembly itself, in Resolution 171 (II) of 14 November 1947, formally recognized that it possessed. That resolution recommends the reference to the Court of points of law relating to the interpretation of the Charter".[20] No one now doubts that the International Court of Justice possesses the power of review of the UN Charter; what is in question is whether that power extends to the declaration of invalidity of the resolutions of the two principal organs, the Security Council and the General Assembly.

In the *Namibia case*, the Court would seem to state or assume two conditions for the exercise of its power of judicial review: (a) Where the request put to the Court so expressly demands as, for instance, in *Certain Expenses of the United Nations*, when an opinion is requested for an interpretation of the Charter concerning the consistency of the organs' resolutions therewith; and (b) where the request must be deemed to imply a limited kind of review, in the normal exercise of the judicial function, as seems to be the case in *Namibia*.[21] But how far the Court can go in (b) is the bone of contention. Should the review go as far as Judges Onyeama, Dillard and Gros would want, so that the Court should *proprio motu* declare resolutions of the General Assembly and of the Security Council invalid and void in all appropriate cases? Or should it merely review the request in the light of all its relevant antecedents, without passing expressly upon the validity of the resolutions as a necessary condition of replying to the request itself, as the Court did in *Namibia*? The principle of self-imposed limitation which judicial caution demands may be pleaded in justification of the latter course taken by the Court. Does such a course necessarily hamper the normal exercise of the judicial function, in the absence of express constitutional limitation upon the powers of the Court to carry out judicial review to that extent?

In the present state of international law, and having regard to the existing law of the United Nations, the sovereignty of States and the Charter would not make it easy for the Court to declare invalid the resolutions of the two principal UN organs without express demand for this in the relevant request to the Court. The San Francisco Accord, on which the relevant provisions are founded, would be against it. Those asking the Court to "go the whole hog" might be thinking of the probably unprecedented initiative which the U.S.

Supreme Court took in *Marbury* v. *Maddison*[22] when Chief Justice Marshall declared a provision of the Constitution invalid, although the U.S. Constitution did not (and still does *not*) contain any express granting of such power. This bold assertion of the power of judicial review has since remained the law and practice of the U.S. Constitution and of its courts. Later federal constitutions like those of Canada, Australia, India and Nigeria have, however, made express provisions for the granting of power of judicial review to their supreme courts. Despite this express grant, conflict is occasioned even between the court on the one hand and the executive and the legislature on the other. Both these latter bodies tend to resent what they characterize as judicial supremacy or even as usurpation of their powers.[23] Echoes of the same cry against the International Court of Justice are still heard from time to time.[24] As it is highly improbable that the UN Charter could be reviewed so as to provide express grant of power of judicial review to the Court to enable it to declare the resolutions of UN principal organs invalid, one hopes that practice within the framework of the UN Organization might later develop to such a stage as to permit the Court to assume such power, without express request by the United Nations, as is being demanded of it in *Namibia*. That happened in the United States in 1803, but it is yet to happen within the United Nations framework.

IV

We may now turn to an examination of other cases in which the International Court of Justice has exercised its power of judicial review in the sense of a constitutional interpretation or application of the UN Charter, whether in relation to the two principal organs themselves or to the member states of the UN Organization. It is not intended to discuss in the present study, as has been made clear from the beginning, cases concerning the interpretation or application of the constitutional instruments of the specialized agencies and other subordinate organs of the United Nations or cases involving mere treaty interpretation *per se*.

The first case in which a request for an advisory opinion on an interpretation of a provision of the UN Charter was made to the International Court of Justice is *Conditions of Admission of a State to Membership in the United Nations (Article 4 of the Charter)*.[25] The questions requested are as follows:

Is a Member of the United Nations which is called upon, in virtue of Article 4 of the Charter, to pronounce itself by its vote, either in the Security Council or in the

General Assembly, on the admission of a State to membership in the United Nations, juridically entitled to make its consent to the admission dependent on conditions not expressly provided by paragraph 1 of the said Article? In particular, can such a Member, while it recognizes the conditions set forth in that provision to be fulfilled by the State concerned, subject its affirmative vote to the additional condition that other States be admitted to membership in the United Nations together with that State?

The Court recalled that the General Assembly Resolution 171 of November 17, 1947[26] did not require the Court "either to define the meaning and scope of the conditions on which admission is made dependent, or to specify the elements which may serve in a concrete case to verify the existence of the requisite conditions". It was not an invitation to the Court to say "whether the views thus referred to are well-founded or otherwise. The abstract form in which the question is stated precludes such an interpretation".The Court rejected the contention that it should regard the question put to it as a political one which fell outside its jurisdiction, that it should not deal with a question couched in abstract terms, and that "the Court cannot reply to the question put because it involves an interpretation of the Charter". This attempt to deny the Court's competence to interpret the UN Charter is the most critical submission, to which the Court replied:[27]

> Nowhere is any provision to be found, forbidding the Court "the principal judicial organ of the United Nations", to exercise in regard to Article 4 of the Charter, a multilateral treaty, an interpretative function which falls within the normal exercise of its judicial powers. Accordingly, the Court holds that it is competent, on the basis of Article 96 of the Charter and Article 65 of the Statute, and considers that there are no reasons why it should decline to answer the question put to it.

On the other hand, the Court rejected an argument based on Article 24 of the Charter claiming that the Security Council as well as the General Assembly had "complete freedom of appreciation in connection with the admission of new Members". The Court pointed out that "Article 24, owing to the very general nature of its terms, cannot, in the absence of any provision, affect the special rules for admission which emerge from Article 4. The foregoing considerations establish the exhaustive character of the conditions prescribed in Article 4". It is important to note how the Court refused to accept the somewhat large claims made for the two principal organs by those who ascribe to them powers based on their political responsibilities. The operative rule of *ultra vires* which the Court would observe in such cases is stated thus:

> The political character of an organ cannot release it from the observance of the treaty provisions established by the Charter when they constitute limitations on its powers or criteria for its judgment. To ascertain whether an organ has freedom of choice for its decisions reference must be made to the terms of its constitution.

The reply of the Court to both questions was accordingly in the negative.

In *Reparation of Injuries Suffered in the Service of the United Nations*,[28] a series of important legal questions were put to the Court by the General Assembly. The replies were (a) that if an agent of the United Nations in the performance of its duties suffers injury in circumstances involving the responsibility of a State, whether a member or a non-member, the United Nations as an organization has the capacity to bring an international claim against the responsible *de jure* or *de facto* government with a view to obtaining the reparation due in respect of the damage caused to the United Nations and to the victim or to persons entitled through him; and (b) that, when the Organization is bringing such a claim for the reparation of damage caused to its agent, it can only do so by basing its claim upon a breach of obligations due to itself, in order thereby to prevent a conflict between the action of the United Nations and such rights as the agent's national State may possess. In reaching these conclusions, a number of interesting legal findings were made — e.g. that the United Nations *as* an international organization possesses an international juridical personality enabling it in that behalf to sue and be sued like all other corporate bodies as a matter of legal theory; and that it is not only States *qua* States that are entitled to sue and be sued before the International Court of Justice, whatever view one might take of the position in the past under customary international law.[29] Thus the Court declared:

> In the opinion of the Court, the Organization was intended to exercise and enjoy, and is in fact exercising and enjoying, functions and rights which can only be explained on the basis of the possession of a large measure of international personality and the capacity to operate upon an international plane. It is at present the supreme type of international organization, and it could carry out the intentions of its founders if it was devoid of international personality. It must be acknowledged that its Members, by entrusting certain functions to it, with the attendant duties and responsibilities, have clothed it with the competence required to enable those functions to be effectively discharged.[30]

The Court, however, emphasized:

> That is not the same thing as saying that it is a State, which it certainly is not, or that its legal personality and rights and duties are the same as those of a State. Still less is it the same as saying that it is a 'super-State', whatever that expression may mean . . . What it does mean is that it is a subject of international law and capable

of possessing international rights and duties, and that it has capacity to maintain its rights by bringing international claims.[31]

The Court reviewed some Articles of the Charter to enable it to deduce the nature of the characteristics of the UN Organization based largely upon its functions and purposes. It concluded in these words: "Under international law, the Organization must be deemed to have those powers which, though not expressly provided in the Charter, are conferred upon it by necessary implication as being essential to the performance of its duties".[32]

Article 4, paragraph 2 of the UN Charter came to be considered in the *Competence of the General Assembly for the Admission of a State to the United Nations*,[33] in which the General Assembly requested an advisory opinion from the Court as to whether the admission of a State to membership of the United Nations, pursuant to Article 4, paragraph 2, could be effected by a decision of the General Assembly when the Security Council has made no recommendation for admission because the candidate in question had failed to obtain the requisite majority or had received the negative vote of a permanent member upon a resolution so to recommend. There were two objections made to the Court's replying to the request: one was that the Court was not competent to interpret the provisions of the Charter, and the other was that the question was political and not legal. The Court met the first objection by pointing out that it had declared in the *Admissions case*[34] that, according to Article 96 of the Charter and Article 65 of the Statute, it was competent to give an opinion on any legal question, there being "no provision which prohibits it from exercising, in regard to Article 4 of the Charter, a multilateral treaty, an interpretative function falling within the normal exercise of its judicial powers".[35] As to the second objection. the Court said that it "cannot attribute a political character to a request which, framed in abstract terms, invites it to undertake an essentially judicial task, the interpretation of a treaty provision".[36] The Court, accordingly, held that the General Assembly is not competent to decide to admit the candidate in the absence of a prior recommendation by the Security Council as required by Article 4, paragraph 1, of the UN Charter. It took the view that "nowhere has the General Assembly received the power to change, to the point of reversing, the meaning of a vote of the Security Council".[37] Paragraph 2 of Article 4 requires that the Security Council's "recommendation" must precede the General Assembly's "decision" before there can be an admission of a candidate to the United Nations. What happened in the Security Council as to the voting procedure is not the point; the fact was that the Council had failed to submit a recommendation to the General

Assembly. Since the Court found no difficulty in ascertaining the natural and ordinary meaning of the words of Article 4, paragraph 1, and no difficulty in giving effect to them, it refused to admit the *travaux preparatoires* of the UN Charter in interpreting the provision in question.

In *International Status of South West Africa*,[38] the Court was asked for an advisory opinion as to whether the Territory of South West Africa had an international status, what obligations the Union of South Africa had towards it under the Mandate, whether the provisions of Chapter XII applied to the Territory and whether the Union of South Africa was competent to modify the international status and, if not, who had the power to do so. The replies were that the Territory has international mandate assumed by the Union Government, that the latter was under both the international obligation stated in Article 22 of the League Covenant and the treaty obligations to transmit petitions from the inhabitants and to be subject to the supervisory functions to be exercised by the United Nations, that Chapter XII (Trusteeship System) still applied to the Territory even though there was no obligation on South Africa to place it under the Trusteeship System, and that "the competence to determine and modify the international status of the Territory rested with the Union of South Africa acting with the consent of the United Nations".

The competence of the General Assembly to receive reports from and to supervise the Territory was, so the Court held, derived from Article 10 of the Charter.[39] Another important advisory opinion dealing with aspects of the competence of the General Assembly is *Effect of Awards of Compensation Made by the United Nations Administrative Tribunal*.[40] The request was whether, having regard to the Statute of the UN Administrative Tribunal and to any other relevant instruments and to the relevant records, the General Assembly had the right on any grounds to refuse to give effect to an award of compensation made by that Tribunal in favour of a staff member of the United Nations whose contract of service had been terminated without his consent. The Court's answer was that the General Assembly has no right on any grounds to do so. A number of grounds why the General Assembly could be held by the Court as having the right were advanced: one was that the General Assembly could not be bound by the awards of a tribunal established by itself — a subordinate organ — to do justice as between the Organization and the staff members appointed by the Secretary-General under the Charter. The Court held: "Capacity to do this arises by necessary intendment out of the Charter"; it added that in national systems, legislatures do establish courts that have power to make decisions binding even upon themselves. A second contention was that, even where an implied power is assumed, and, "implied power to impose legal limitations upon the General Assembly's express Charter powers is not legally admissible", because it would amount to the Assembly divesting itself of the power conferrred by paragraph 1 of Article 17 of the Charter which reads: "The General Assembly shall consider and approve the budget of the Organization". The short answer by the Court to this was that Article 17 comes under the section of Chapter IV, entitled "Functions and Powers" of the Assembly, being devolved upon the tribunal for necessary discharge; a singular argument that the Tribunal was being allowed to intervene in matters falling within the province of the Secretary-General was dismissed, as were some other pettifogging objections.

We may now turn to an extended consideration of *Certain Expenses of the United Nations* (Article 17, paragraph 2, of the Charter,[41] which we referred to in our earlier discussion of the *Namibia case*. The question put to the Court was whether certain expenditures authorized by the General Assembly to cover the costs of the UN operations in the Congo (ONUC) and of the operations of the UN Emergency Force in the Middle East (UNEF) "constitute expenses of the Organization within the meaning of Article 17, paragraph 2, of the Charter of the United Nations". A French amendment to the resolution requesting the advisory opinion would have asked the Court to give an opinion on the question whether the expenditures relating to the operations were "decided on in conformity with the provisions of the Charter", and only if the Court's answer had been in the affirmative could the question which was in fact posed be put to the Court for an advisory opinion. The amendment was rejected by the Assembly. As the Court was quick to observe, the suggested amendment did not propose to ask the Court whether the resolutions *in pursuance of which the operations in the Congo and in the Middle East were undertaken* were adopted in conformity with the Charter, but only whether the resolutions *authorizing the expenditures* were decided in conformity with the Charter. The Court refused to "expound the extent to which the proceedings of the General Assembly, antecedent to the adoption of a resolution, should be taken into account in interpreting that resolution", and did not agree to the submission that the rejection of the French amendment in any way hampered the Court in the exercise of its judicial functions since the Court would construe Article 17 within the context of the whole Charter.

The Court recalled that on previous occasions when it had had to interpret the Charter it had "followed the principles and rules applicable in general to the interpretation of treaties, since it has recognized that the Charter is a multilateral treaty, albeit a treaty having certain special characteristics". It went further:

> In interpreting Article 4 of the Charter, the Court was led tó consider "the structure of the Charter" and the relations established by it between the General Assembly and the Security Council; a comparable problem confronts the Court in the instant matter. The Court sustained its interpretation of Article 4 by considering the manner in which the organs concerned "have consistently interpreted the text" in their practice (*Competence of the General Assembly for the Admission of a State to the United Nations*, Advisory Opinion, *I.C.J. Reports 1950*, pp. 8–9).

After carefully examining Article 17, paragraph 1, in the light of the United Nations practice over the years in budgetary matters, the Court concluded that there was no justification for reading into the text any limiting or qualifying word like "administrative" or "operational" before the word "budget". Also, it found that "expenses of the Organization" means "all the expenses and not just certain types of expenses which might be referred to as "regular expenses", as had been suggested in relation to Article 4, paragraph 2. It, therefore, concluded:

> The Court does not perceive any basis for challenging the legality of the settled practice of including such expenses as these in the budgetary amounts which the General Assembly apportions among the Members in accordance with the authority which is given to it by Article 17, paragraph 1.[42]

Judged on the basis of the objects and purposes of the United Nations as set out in Article 1 of the Charter, the expenses were properly incurred in the discharge of the functions assigned to the General Assembly. The Court said:

> But when the Organization takes action which warrants the assertion that it was appropriate for the fulfillment of one of the stated purposes of the United Nations the presumption is that such action is not *ultra vires* the Organization".[43]

An important question of constitutional interpretation decided by the Court on the issue of *ultra vires* is that if one of two principal organs acted *ultra vires* its own granted powers, the Organization as a whole would still be liable for all the expenses incurred so long as they were undertaken in the discharge of its purposes. Said the Court:

> If the action was taken by the wrong organ, it was irregular as a matter of that internal structure, but this would not necessarily mean that the expense incurred was not an expense of the Organization. Both national and international law contemplate cases in which the body corporate or politic may be bound, as to third parties, by an *ultra vires* act of an agent.[44]

The objections that expenses resulting from the operations for the maintenance of international peace and security are not "expenses of the Organization" within the meaning of Article 17, paragraph 2 since they fall to be dealt with by the Security Council in the special sphere of which they fell, was next considered. This led to "an examination of the respective functions of the General Assembly and of the Security Council under the Charter, particularly with respect to the maintenance of international peace and security". The Court closely analyzed various relevant provisions of the Charter dealing with the respective powers granted to both the Assembly and to the Council and came to this conclusion:

> The provisions of the Charter which distribute functions and powers to the Security Council and to the General Assembly give no support to the view that such distribution excludes from the powers of the General Assembly the power to provide for the financing of measures designed to maintain peace and security.[45]

Far from regarding Articles 11(2) and 14 as limiting the powers of the General Assembly regarding the enforcement of "coercive action", a proper appraisal of the design of the Charter provisions, considered as a whole, would lead to this conclusion reached by the Court: ". . . there is a close collaboration between the two organs.[46] Both in respect of ONUC and of UNEF, the Secretary-General's actions were authorized by reiterated resolutions which did not always specify under which particular Articles of the Charter the expenditures were to be incurred; all the expenses thus incurred by the Secretary-General in pursuance of the resolutions of both the Security Council and the General Assembly constituted obligations of the Organization for which the two principal organs were entitled to make provisions under the authority of Article 17, paragraph 2.

It is to be noted that in both the present case (*Certain Expenses*) and in the *Conditions of Admission* case there have been shifts of responsibilities as between the two principal organs, shifts recognized even by the Court itself. Thr necessities of each case probably made these inevitable. It must nevertheless be recognized also that the executive authority of the Security Council must not be eroded in all proper cases, and that there are checks on any attempted transfer of power from the Security Council to the General Assembly since no such shift can in fact be effected without the support of the major powers. The Court itself showed how militant it has always been in delimiting the respective competences of both organs when, in the *Certain Expenses case*, it pointed out:

> Thus while it is the Security Council which, exclusively, may order coercive action, the functions and powers conferred by the Charter on the General

> Assembly are not confined to discussion, consideration, the initiation of studies, the making of recommendations; they are not merely hortatory.[47]

A little later on, the Court added:

> "These 'decisions' do indeed include certain recommendations, but others have dispositive force and effect".[48]

We have said at the outset of our consideration of this advisory opinion that the French amendment demanding a pronouncement by the Court on the validity of the resolutions upon which the UNEF and ONUC operations were based was rejected by the General Assembly. The rejection was justified by, *inter alia*, Judge Spiropoulos who, while agreeing with the majority, said in his declaration that he felt bound to refrain from pronouncing on the validity of the relevant resolutions because it seemed to him that "it was natural, indeed, that the General Assembly should not have wished that the Court should pronounce on the validity of resolutions which have been applied for several years".[49] Judge Spender did not, in his separate opinion, consider that a conclusion as to the validity or regularity of the relevant resolutions would not affect the answer required by the request put to the Court.[50] Judge Sir Gerald Fitzmaurice, in his separate opinion, raised a point of interest with which, however, the Court did not deal. It is this. On the issue of the validity of the expenditures, the Court had said that "each organ must, *in the first place at least*, determine its own jurisdiction". While it is true that any doubt as to the validity of the exercise should first be decided therein, would the ruling or resolution be regarded as final? In the particular instance Judge Fitzmaurice said he could not accept the view that the mere fact that certain expenditures had been actually apportioned by the General Assembly was conclusive as to their validity; his reason is that, so to hold would make a resolution improperly or irregularly adopted to be binding upon *all* Member States. There are arguments for and against this view but, as the Judge himself said that "it is not necessary to express any final view about these points" (this being one of them) and as it was not necessary to the answer given in the opinion with which he otherwise agreed, we shall not pursue the matter here.[51] The Court is clearly logical to have answered the request which concerns the validity of the *expenditures* and to have omitted to answer what was not asked about, namely, the validity of the resolutions. But as we have earlier indicated, the general question remains as to whether the Court can, without a specific request to that effect, declare invalid a resolution of either the General Assembly or the Security Council.

V

The Charter gives the International Court of Justice the power to interpret or apply its provisions when requested either in contentious or in advisory cases but gives the Court no express power to declare the Charter invalid in whole or in part. The San Francisco Conference settled that point in the statement on the subject to which we have referred at the beginning of this paper. This limiting factor has since then been dogging all the footsteps taken by the Court whenever it has had to deal with the issue involving judicial review.

Accordingly, in the exercise of its judicial function, the Court has claimed the power to declare unconstitutional a resolution of the General Assembly or of the Security Council only when expressly asked to do so as in the *Expenses case*, or, it would seem, when by necessary implication obliged to do so in order to discharge its official duty in any particular case: it is plausible to deduce this from the *Namibia case*. Apart from this, the Court may one day be in a position to assume a *general* power of judicial review *ex necessitate* and, probably, by consensus, as we have seen the U.S. Supreme Court do in *Marbury* v. *Maddison*; but it would seem uncertain that it would ever do so without any express amendment of the Charter or an adoption of a resolution to that effect. Any premature assumption by the Court of a general judicial power might, however, either be acquiesced in, or might provoke an amendment of the Charter or a resolution by one or both organs.

Within the present limits of its judicial power of review, however, the Court has, from the early days of the UN Organization, asserted power to interpret and construe the Charter, despite opposition to its exercising the power,[52] and also despite the General Assembly Resolution 171 (II) of November 14, 1947, to which we have also referred earlier. Nevertheless, short of declaring the Charter or any of its provisions invalid, the Court has used the power to interpret and apply the various provisions of the Charter in a dynamic manner in order to achieve what it has considered to be the true aim and purpose of the Charter in establishing the UN Organization.[53] In the process, it has sometimes been criticized as having adopted a *teleological* interpretation of the Charter and, at least in the *Expenses case*, to have thereby equated the General Assembly with the Security Council by ascribing powers to them in a manner not regarded by the critics as those assigned to them by the Charter.[54] Our analysis has, however, shown that this is not the case at all and that, far from claiming over-large powers for each of the two principal organs, the Court has not hesitated to "cut each down to size" as and when it has considered the occasion had warranted it. Let us take, for example, the Court's denial of power to the General Assembly when it sought to assert in the *Admissions case* the prerogative of exercising power of admission without having satisfied the Charter stipulation that the prior "recommendation" of the Security Council is a *sine qua non* to its "decision"; or, again, when the Court disallowed the attempt in the *Conditions of Admission case* to engraft upon Article 4 of the Charter the additional but impermissible condition that certain Member States could exercise their voting rights to admit a candidate only if other Member States would also admit their own candidates.

No doubt the Court sometimes adopted a policy-orientated approach in its dealing with particular types of matter brought before it, as when the majority in the preliminary judgment in the *South West Africa* cases[55] showed a leaning towards the policy-objective of the UN Organization while the minority, including Judges Spender and Fitzmaurice, adopted the analytical (some would say static) approach. It seems that the Court, conscious of its responsibilities as 'the principal judicial organ' of the United Nations, was ever anxious to give efficacy and purposive direction to the functioning of the UN Organization to the end that it should achieve its aim. Thus, in the *Injuries case*[56] the international personality of the UN Organization was put by the Court upon a secure and firm foundation while at the same time it was held to be able not only to sue but also to be sued in all appropriate cases like every corporate entity. In the circumstances, the interests of the UN Organization and the requirements of social justice demand no less.

There is probably no need to repeat that the present study is confined to judicial review in respect of the United Nations Charter vis-à-vis the two principal organs, and that it does not take into account what in a sense is judicial review of administrative action[57] at the international law level, namely, the judicial interpretation or application of the Charters and constitutions of the United Nations Specialized and related Agencies. We may refer in parenthesis to the *Convention of the Maritime Safety Committee of the Inter-Governmental Maritime Consultative Organization*,[58] the first case in which the International Court of Justice held the action of an international institution unconstitutional and invalid. The request made of the Court for an advisory opinion was:

> Is the Maritime Safety Committee of the Inter-Governmental Maritime Consultative Organization, which was elected on 15 January 1959, constituted in accordance with the Convention for the Establishment of the Organization?

The Court, after a careful analysis of the relevant provisions of the constitutive instruments, gave a negative reply.[59] It is clear that three factors are present here: firstly, the organization concerned is a subordinate organ; secondly, the request was a direct invitation to the Court by the requesting organ to pronounce on the validity of the constitutional instrument on which the body in question was established; and, thirdly, the request for the advisory opinion was based upon a unanimous resolution. The third factor, it is fair to point out, is not an obligatory condition, though it is a useful one. Otherwise the situation is analogous to that in the *Expenses case* and the Court answered the request (as to the validity of the expenditures in question) in the affirmative, since a decision on the validity of the antecedent resolutions was not necessary to the reply demanded and, indeed, given.

It remains for us to speculate as to what might have happened in the *Namibia case* had the Court gone on to make a specific pronouncement on the validity of the various General Assembly and Security Council resolutions before stating the legal consequences demanded of it. Both organs might have repudiated such pronouncements without also repudiating the statement of legal consequences which was in fact favorable to the Organization. Suppose that the Court's reply to the request had been negative either on the issue of validity of the resolutions or on that of the legality of the consequences or on both, it is not inconceivable that the UN Organization might have taken steps, such as by adopting a resolution, to nullify the Court's advisory opinion in its entirety.[60] On the other hand, the Court, finding itself in the position that it must pronounce on the validity of the resolution as a necessary condition of advising on the legality of South Africa's continued occupation of the Territory, could have done one of two things: *either* to have refused at that point to render any advisory opinion at all, which it is as a matter of law entitled to do; *or* to have gone ahead and declared the resolutions null, invalid and *ultra vires* the UN Organization, with the result that South Africa's continued occupation would have had to be declared valid. In either event, the Court would have found itself on the horns of a dilemma.

Given the existing limitations upon its power of judicial review in the fullest sense, the International Court of Justice has to await any express amendment of the Charter, an invitation to pronounce on the validity of resolutions or other forms of decision-making on the part of either of the two principal UN organs, or an assumption of the power to declare invalidity *suo motu* if and when the Court judges the situation to be opportune.

In view of the somewhat conflicting views expressed by a number of judges in the separate as well as dissenting opinions in the *Namibia* case, it is not absolutely clear whether the Court was regarded (1) by some as possessing the general power of judicial review which it could in principle exercise when it should see fit, or (2) enjoying a limited power of survey or review before going on to take judicial notice of what the two principal organs had done, or was regarded by others, (perhaps the majority) as (3) having no power to declare the two organs' acts unconstitutional unless when expressly or by necessary implication called upon so to pronounce by the request in question.

NOTES

1. For a seminal study of the subject, see W. Friedmann's *The Changing Structure of International Law* pp. 152–162, Stevens and Sons Ltd., London, 1964.

2. The Statute of the Permanent Court was established in pursuance of Article 14 of the League Covenant, of which it was, however, entirely independent. Also, States Members of the League were not associated with the Statute of the Permanent Court. (There was no equivalent of Article 35 of the Statute of the ICJ in the Statute of the PCIJ.)

3. See UNC/0, Vol. 13, p. 703, at p. 709; Final Report of Committee IV/2, Doc. 933, IV/2/42/2, pp. 7–8.

4. For a study of the whole question of the UN Charter and the San Francisco Conference see Djura Niucic's *The Problem of Sovereignty in the Charter and in the Practice of the United Nations*, especially Chapter XVI on "The Interpretation of the Charter and the Sovereignty of States", 1970, M. Nijhoff.

5. In municipal constitutional theory, this is often expressed as meaning that courts are not concerned with the *need* for a particular piece of legislation which it is called upon to construe (see *McCullock* v. *Maryland* (1819) 4 Wh. 316, at p. 421), nor with the *best means* of achieving the object of the legislation in question (see e.g. *Chicago Railways Co.* v. *McGuire* (1911) 219 U.S. 549 at p. 569).

6. E.g. it was held in *Bradlaugh* v. *Gossett* (1884) 12QBD271 that the Court must take judicial notice of a resolution of the British House of Commons ordering an MP not to take his seat in Parliament and that the Court could not make a declaration that the order of the House was invalid or void.

7. Legal Consequences for States of the Continued Presence of South Africa in Namibia (South West Africa), notwithstanding Security Council Resolution 276 (1970), Advisory Opinion, *I.C.J. Reports 1971*, p. 16.

8. Legal Consequences for States of the Continued Presence of South Africa in Namibia (South West Africa), notwithstanding Security Council Resolution 276 (1970), Advisory Opinion, *I.C.J. Reports 1971*, pp. 132–133.

9. *Ibid.*, pp. 143–144.

10. Judge Onyeama was further of the view that when the question put to the Court is such that it "could not properly perform its judicial function of a thorough consideration of all relevant data or where for any other reason the Court is not permitted the full liberty it is entitled to in considering a question posed to it, the

Court's discretion to render or without an opinion would protect the Court from the danger of rendering an opinion based on, conceivably, false assumptions or incomplete data" (pp. 144–145).

11. Emphasis is the author's own. This seems to imply that *some* enquiry at least might be sufficient.

12. *Legal Consequences . . . Namibia case*, pp. 151–152.

13. Ibid., p. 143.

14. *Namibia case*, para. 88.

15. Ibid., para. 89.

16. In this connection it may be recalled that the Court made the following findings: "For it would not be correct to assume that, because the General Assembly is in principle vested with recommendatory powers, it is debarred from adopting, in specific cases within the framework of its competence, resolutions which make determinations or have operative design" (para. 105).

Again, the Court (para. 117) observed: "A binding determination made by a competent organ of the United Nations to the effect that a situation is illegal cannot remain without consequence".

17. *I.C.J. Reports 1962*, p. 152.

18. See Judge de Castro's Separate Opinion, *I.C.J. Reports 1971*, pp. 185–188. It was Judge de Castro's view that the Court had done the same in the *Certain Expenses of the United Nations case* (pp. 155–181).

19. *I.C.J. Reports 1971*, p. 331, para. 18.

20. *I.C.J. Reports 1971*, p. 332, para. 19.

21. But, here, there is need for caution. In the case itself, the Court made it clear that it did not "possess power of judicial review or appeal in respect of the decisions taken by the United Nations organs concerned" (*I.C.J. Reports 1971*, p. 45). Before then, the Court had stated in the case concerning the *Northern Cameroons*, (*I.C.J. Reports 1963*, p. 15 at p. 33), as follows: "The role of the Court is not the same as that of the General Assembly. The decisions of the General Assembly would not be reversed by the judgment of the Court".

22. (1803) 1 Cr. 137. The theory was that "it is as much the duty of the Courts to apply the law as it is to enforce the constitution".

23. Justice Holmes in *Blodgett* v. *Holden* (1927) U.S. 142, at p. 147 and Sastri C. J. (of India) in *State of Madras* v. *Row* (1952) S.C.R. 597 both described power of judicial review as usurpation.

24. See, for example, in the *Certain Expenses case, I.C.J. Reports 1962*, p. 151; *Reparation for Injuries case, I.C.J. Reports 1949*, p. 174.

25. *I.C.J. Reports 1948*, p. 57.

26. This was the same resolution cited earlier by Judge Gros to support his contention in the *Namibia case* that the Court should exercise its granted power of judicial review to pass upon the validity of the relevant resolutions in that case.

27. *I.C.J. Reports 1948*, pp. 61–62.

28. Advisory Opinion, *I.C.J. Reports 1949*, p. 174.

29. As the Court pointed out (p. 182): "The Court is here faced with a new situation. The questions to which it gives rise can only be solved by realizing that the situation is dominated by the provisions of the Charter considered in the light of the principles of international law".

30. Ibid., p. 179.

31. Idem.

32. Idem, p. 182.

33. Advisory Opinion, *I.C.J. Reports 1950*, p. 4.

34. *I.C.J. Reports 1947*, p. 57.

35. Ibid., p. 61.

36. *I.C.J. Reports 1950*, pp. 6–7.

37. *I.C.J. Reports 1950*, pp. 6–7.

38. Advisory Opinion, *I.C.J. Reports 1950*, p. 128.

39. Advisory Opinion, *I.C.J. Reports 1950*, p. 137.

40. Advisory Opinion, *I.C.J. Reports 1954*, p. 47.

41. Advisory Opinion of July 20, 1962, *I.C.J. Reports 1962*, p. 151.

42. Ibid., p. 162.

43. Ibid., p. 168.

44. Idem. The Court observed: "In the legal systems of States, there is often some procedure for determining the validity of even a legislature or governmental act, but no analogous procedure is to be found in the structure of the United Nations".

45. Ibid., p. 164.

46. Ibid., p. 163.

47. *I.C.J. Reports 1962*, p. 163

48. Idem.

49. Ibid., p. 181.

50. Ibid., p. 182.

51. Ibid., p. 204ff.

52. See the *Conditions of Admission case*, *I.C.J. Reports 1948*, pp. 61–62.

53. There has been understandable reaction on the part of the Court against certain attempts by some States to give the Organization a restricted power of competence, as when in the *Petitioners case* (1956) *I.C.J. Reports 1956*, p. 23, South Africa sought to interpret the 1950 Opinion of the Court as having limited the General Assembly's supervisory powers over the Mandate. The Court held, however, that there is nothing in the League Covenant, the UN Charter or any other document, which so restricts the authority of the General Assembly. See also *Namibia*, *I.C.J. Reports 1971*, pp. 33–37, where the Court held Article 10 to be the operative provision.

54. But the Court recognizes in the *Namibia case* the very wide competence which the Security Council had to deal with the issue of self-determination by virtue of its "primary responsibility for the maintenance of international peace and security" (Article 24, para. 1). It pointed out that the duties imposed upon the Security Council by Article 24, paragraph 2 are derived from the powers granted to it under Chapters VI, VII, VIII and XII. The Court even said, in *I.C.J. Reports 1971*, p. 52, that the "only limitation on that authority are the fundamental principles and purposes found in Chapter I of the Charter".

55. *I.C.J. Reports 1962*, p. 319.

56. *I.C.J. Reports 1949*, p. 174 where the Court acknowledged the United Nations' assertion of stature.

57. See S.A. de Smith's *Judicial Review of Administrative Action*, 1975 (3rd edition).

58. Advisory Opinion, *I.C.J. Reports 1960*, p. 150.

59. The real question was whether, in not electing Liberia and Panama to the Maritime Safety Committee, the Assembly complied with the provision of Article 28 (a) of the Convention which established the UN Organization, in spite of the fact that both Member States, on the basis of the registered tonnage, were included among the eight largest ship-owning nations.

60. It may be recalled that the General Assembly must have been induced to adopt Resolution 2145 (XXI) in the belief, widely shared at the time, that the Court would seem to have abdicated at least part of its responsibilities in its 1966 Judgment in the *South West Africa, Second Phase case*, (*I.C.J. Reports 1966*, p. 6.).

Chapter 7

THE ROLE OF THE INTERNATIONAL COURT OF JUSTICE IN THE SEARCH FOR PEACE

On November 12, 1974, the General Assembly of the United Nations adopted Resolution 3232 (XXIX) on the Review of the Role of the International Court of Justice (see Appendix II). After recalling that the Court is the principal judicial organ of the UN Organization, the Resolution recites the role of the Court which, in conformity with Article 10 of the United Nations Charter, remains an appropriate matter for the attention of the world assembly, and recalls that, in accordance with Article 2, paragraph 3 of the Charter, all Member States shall settle their international disputes by peaceful means in such a manner that international peace and security and justice are not endangered. The Resolution takes note of the views expressed by Member States during the debates in the Sixth Committee on the question of the review of the role of the International Court of Justice in the preceding four years and the consequent exchange of communications between the Secretary-General and the President of the Court culminating in the amended Rules of Court with a view to facilitating recourse to the Court for the judicial settlement of disputes by the creation of *ad hoc* chambers. The resolution further recalls the increasing development and codification of international law in conventions open for universal participation and the consequent need for their uniform interpretation and application, and recognizes that the development of international law may be reflected *inter alia* by declarations and resolutions of the General Assembly which may to that extent be taken into consideration by the Court. The Resolution finally recalls the opportunities afforded by the power of the Court, under Article 38, paragraph 2, of its statute, to decide a case *ex aequo et bono* if the parties agree thereto. After asking States to make as few reservations as possible in accepting the compulsory jurisdiction of the Court, drawing their attention to the advantage of inserting in their treaties clauses for the submission to the Court of disputes which may arise from the interpretation or application of such treaties, calling upon States to keep under review the possibility of identifying cases in which use can be made of the Court, including the use of chambers

115

for particular categories of cases, and recommending that the duly-authorized UN organs and specialized agencies should from time to time refer legal questions to the Court for advisory opinions, the Resolution finally reaffirms the important principle that recourse to judicial settlement of legal disputes, particularly their reference to the Court, should not be considered as an unfriendly act between States.

The theme of the 1974 Resolution is, therefore, a useful basis for the study of our subject in that it is a clarion call by the world body for a review of the role of the International Court of Justice in the search for justice — in other words, an analysis of the dynamics of the operation of the Court in the administration of justice within the United Nations framework. Although it is not the only tribunal to which Member States may entrust the solution of their differences by virtue of agreements already in existence or to be made in the future,[1] it is nevertheless the principal judicial organ of the United Nations[2] capable of applying the same body of law, including the uniform interpretation and application of the numerous multilateral conventions by which the development and codification of international law are being steadily enhanced.

The Applicable Law

When a dispute is submitted to the Court, Article 38 of its Statute provides as follows:

> 1. The Court, whose function is to decide in accordance with international law such disputes as are submitted to it shall apply:
> (a) international conventions, whether general or particular, establishing rules expressly recognized by the contesting States;
> (b) international custom, as evidence of a general practice accepted as law;
> (c) the general principles of law recognized by civilized nations;
> (d) subject to the provisions of Article 59, (which prescribes that the Court's decision has no binding force except between the parties and in respect of that particular case, judicial decisions and the teachings of the most highly qualified publicists of the various nations, as subsidiary means for the determination of rules of law.
> 2. This provision shall not prejudice the power of the Court to decide a case *ex aequo et bono*, if the parties agree thereto.

In its attempt to settle disputes between two or more States, the Court is required to have recourse to those sources of law as enumerated above — which must, however, be regarded as given in an outline form only. Thus the term "international conventions" must be taken to relate to both bilateral and multilateral treaties and agreements in the sense of Article 2 of the Vienna Convention on The Law of Treaties.[3] One has only to look at the list of the United Nations Treaties In Force to realize how greatly international conventions have increased in scope and variety under the auspices of the world body within the last quarter of a century, thereby widening the area of the Court's conventional law, particularly in the sphere of treaty interpretation and application to an ever-increasing complexity of situations in all parts of the world. This is certainly the most prolific source of law for the Court in the exercise of its judicial functions since the great bulk is based on it.

As for international custom as evidence of a general practice accepted as law, there is no doubt that the Court has been the principal agent of clarification of this sometimes elusive expression. While international custom is more commonly referred to on some occasions as "international customary law" and on others as "customary international law", it is not always easy to distinguish between custom and practice in the developing international jurisprudence of recent years. The Court has had occasion to lay down certain helpful criteria for the recognition of certain practices as international custom. For present purposes it is sufficient to refer to the Court's observation in the *North Sea Continental Shelf Cases* in these words: "Not only must the acts concerned amount to a settled practice, but they must also be such or be carried out in such a way, as to be evidence of a belief that this practice is rendered obligatory by the existence of a rule of law requiring it".[4]

The third source of law which the Court is required to apply in appropriate cases is the one entitled "General Principles of Law Recognized by Civilized Nations" and it is the most controversial in contemporary international law. Without entering here upon any learned disquisition on the history and the provenance of the term "civilized nations", it seems sufficient to say that in the practice of the United Nations a different and more intelligent formula has been always adopted. For instance, Article 9 of the Statute of the International Court of Justice requires that candidates for election to the Court should individually possess legal and moral qualifications and "also that in the body as a whole the representation of the main forms of civilization and of the principal legal systems of the world should be assured." The same expression is also used in Article 6 of the Statute of the International Law Commission for the purpose of delimiting the scope and character of its members and of the law they are called upon to draft for the Organization. Even the International Court of Justice itself has hardly ever made any express recourse to the use of the expression "general principles of law recognized by civilized nations" by reference to Article 38(3) of the Statute which had been taken over at the San Francisco Conference in 1945 from the Covenant of the League of Nations in a somewhat uncritical exercise of borrowing from the earlier institution. Whenever the Court has had occasion to refer to general principles of law, it seems to have employed only such expressions as "the principle universally accepted by international tribunals",[5] "general and well-recognized principles",[6] and "well-established and generally-recognized principle of law".[7] The Court, therefore, has not allowed itself to be hampered in its search for peace by a resort to the antiquated jargon of the 1920 Commission of Jurists connoted to the qualification of general principles of law to be applied by the Court as only those "recognized by civilized nations"; it has rightly and wisely contented itself with the notion that the general principles to be resorted to must be such as are common to national legal systems and international law.[8] This is in consonance with the principle of universality and unity of the membership and of the aspirations of the world body in which there is no such distinction as that between civilized and uncivilized nations as members.

The fourth "source" to which the International Court of Justice may have recourse under Article 38 of the Statute is made up of "judicial decisions and the writings of the most highly qualified publicists of the various nations". Accordingly, the decisions of municipal courts and of mixed courts like arbitral tribunals may be resorted to by the Court and so may the opinions of the most respected authors; but both these categories are subsidiary means for the determination of rules of law. While international conventions, customary international law and general principles of law seem to be coordinate as sources of law which the Court may invoke in the settlement of disputes before it, judicial decisions and the legal opinions of learned jurists are not in themselves norms of law but are only bases upon which rules of law may be founded. The Court is, therefore, given a discretion as to the choice of decisions or opinions it will use in its judicial function in a particular case depending upon the authority of the national court or the arbitral tribunal or upon the legal standing of the jurist concerned. The opportunity to fashion new rules, especially where there are gaps in the law or where new initiatives are called for in the modification of existing law, will thus present itself in the application of this subsidiary means for the determination of rules of law. It must be borne in mind, however, that the judicial decisions that may be resorted to are expressly made subject to Article 59, which prescribes that the Court's judgments have no binding force except between the parties and in respect of that particular case. This means that the decisions of both the permanent Court of International Justice and the International Court of Justice are subject to this limitation and are referred to only as subsidiary means for the determination of rules of law, thus emphasizing indirectly that such decisions are not entitled to the high status which judicial precedents enjoy in Anglo-Saxon systems of law.[9] In practice, however, the nature of the judicial process is such that, without in any way regarding itself as bound by any doctrine of judicial precedent, the Court sometimes asserts that it is in certain cases obliged to "adhere to its own jurisprudence". Thus, in the *Namibia* (Advisory Opinion) Case,[10] the Court said: "*the failure of South Africa to comply with the obligation to submit to* supervision and to render reports, as essential part of the Mandate, cannot be disputed in the light of determinations made by this Court on more occasions than one. In relying on these as on their findings of the Court in previous proceedings concerning South-West Africa the Court adheres to its own jurisprudence". It is worthy of note to refer in this connection to Lauterpacht's observation: "They state what the law is, their decisions are evidence of the existing rule of law. That does not mean that they do not in fact constitute a source of international law. For the distinction between the evidence and the source of many a rule of law is more speculative and less rigid than is commonly supposed . . . . insofar as they show what are the rules of international law they are largely identical with it".[11]

Finally, Article 38(2) contains a supplementary provision to the effect that, if the parties agree, the Court may settle the dispute *ex aequo et bono*, that is to say, by the application of principles of fairness and justice that the particular circumstances of the case may require. The *ex aequo et bono* principle should not be confused with law or equity in the strict legal sense, but it should be applied to the solution of a problem when no conventional rules, whether customary law or general principles of law, seem directly applicable to the case in hand, nor is the *ex aequo* principle a factor to be invoked for the purpose of making a judicial decision of a municipal or international tribunal suit the settlement of a particular dispute. It is to be employed as an autonomous agency in aid of a judicial settlement. There is no recorded case in the history of the Court's jurisprudence in which this source or recourse has so far been made use of in the settlement of any dispute before the Court. It is a principle which is intended as a last resort in the judicial process of the Court when all other means cannot supply a solution or remedy; it is, in the final analysis, to prevent the Court from entering a *non liquet*. It is included in Article 38 probably not so much to be employed as an independent source of power or aid as a catalytic agent in the chemical reaction which the judicial process connotes. Its presence rather induces the other "sources" enumerated in the first paragraph of the Article to come alive and, separately or together, to supply a solution, so long as the Court acts judicially and with due regard to justice; the *ex aequo et bono* power is a necessary *vade mecum* to the Court in the exercise of its judicial function. We must not overlook the appeal made in the final preambular paragraph of Resolution 3232 (XXIX) of November 12, 1974 regarding the need to make use of "the opportunities afforded by the power of the International Court of Justice under Article 38 paragraph 2, of its Statute, to decide a case *ex aequo et bono* if the parties agree thereto", to which we referred at the beginning of the present study.

To that reminder we must add the reference in the same resolution to "the increasing development and codification of international law in conventions open for universal participation and the consequent need for their uniform interpretation and application". Since, as we have already pointed out, by far the bulk of the judicial work of the Court concerns the interpretation and application of international conventions and agreements of various kinds from all parts of the world, the importance of the Court cannot be over-emphasized as the one unique means of ensuring uniformity and, indeed unity, in the developing international law of today. There is also the need to recognize as does the following preambular paragraph of the Resolution that development of international law may be reflected, *inter alia*, by declarations and resolutions whenever deemed appropriate, in addition to the international conventions mentioned in Article 38(1) of the Statute even if only as subsidiary means for the determination of rules of law.

It is needless to say that, in its search for peace and justice through the judicial settlement of disputes, the International Court of Justice has had to employ at one stage or another those sources of the law which we have already outlined. It remains to examine the use the Court has made of them in a number of cases which may illustrate the manner and effectiveness of its operation in the quest for justice. It is proposed to classify the main groups under these six headings:

(1) Questions of Sovereignty
(2) Private Law Issues in Public International law,
(3) Diplomatic Law and Nationality Problems,
(4) The Law of the Sea,
(5) Mandate and Trusteeship, and
(6) Humanitarian Law.

Questions of Sovereignty

We may well begin our study by previewing the role played by the International Court of Justice in the search for peace by considering cases in which the principal questions of political sovereignty of States as the normal subjects of international law have been agitated within the past twenty-five years. The earliest case to come before the court is *Minquiers and Ecrehos*,[12] in which the United Kingdom and France asked the Court to determine which of them had produced the more convincing evidence of title to *Minquiers and Ecrehos*, two groups of islets situated between the British island of Jersey and the French Coast. As a result of the Norman Conquest of England in 1066, these islets became part of the Union between England and Normandy and remained so until Philip Augustus of France, although conquering Normandy in 1204, did not, however, occupy the two islets — which continued under British administration. The United Kingdom proved that this position was confirmed by subsequent treaties between her and France. On her part, France claimed that the two groups of islets came under her control after 1204 and relied on the same treaties as those invoked by the United Kingdom. The matter became one of fact and of treaty interpretation, and the Court was of the view that, as the treaties did not specify which of the two parties to the dispute had sovereignty over the two groups of islets, direct evidence of possession and the actual exercise of sovereignty must prevail over the presumptions on which French claims had been based.[13] The sovereignty over the *Minquiers and Ecrehos* was accordingly awarded to the United Kingdom which had established satisfactory evidence of continuous occupation and exclusive control over the groups of islets.[14]

In the *Right of Passage Over Indian Territory*,[15] in which Portugal claimed a right of passage to two enclaves, Dadra and Nagar-Aveli, which formed part of the Portuguese possessions in India, it seems that, subject to its overall control, India had up to July 1954 permitted the Portuguese this right in the exercise of its authority over the possessions in question. It would appear that India had, however, begun to forbid the Portuguese the further use of this right after establishing an autonomous local administration over the area. Portugal brought an action before the Court to make India restore the right, but India, *inter alia*, challenged the jurisdiction of the Court to hear the case. The Court, having overruled India's objections on this and some other grounds, held that Portugal's claim to the right of passage in 1954 was well founded, but that the right in question did not extend to the passage of Portuguese armed forces, armed police, arms and ammunition. The Court also held that, in thus restricting Portugal's exercise of its right of passage, India had not in any way exceeded her legitimate sovereign rights over its territory, including the two enclaves of Dadra and Nagar-Aveli.

Another case involving the enclaves belonging to one State within the territory of another was decided in *Sovereignty Over Certain Frontier Land*.[16] There, two plots of land situated in an area with unusual features at the frontier between Holland and Belgium was the subject of a dispute as to sovereignty, the Netherlands' communes of Baarle-Nassau adjoined the Belgium commune of Baerle-Duc, Belgium and the Netherlands asked the Court to settle the dispute. A Descriptive Minute and map annexed to the Boundary Convention of 1843 attributed the plots to Baerle-Duc, but a Communal Minute drawn up between 1836 and 1841 attributed them to Baarle-Nassau. The Government of the Netherlands contended that the Boundary Convention recognized the existence of the *status quo* in accordance with the Communual Minute that the provision of the Convention attributing the two parcels of land to each State had been vitiated by a fundamental error, and that, despite the provision, the Netherlands had since 1843 been exercising acts of sovereignty over the disputed territories. The Court was satisfied, after carefully examining the evidence adduced in support of the Dutch claim that Belgium was entitled to sovereignty over the two plots. It is to be noted that, whereas the treaties relied upon by both the United Kingdom and France in the *Minquiers and Ecrehos case* were inconclusive as to the respective rights claimed by the parties and the Court was therefore obliged to fall back on the evidence of possession and occupation in determining sovereignty, in the instant case it disregarded such evidence in favour of a treaty provision the strict and the logical interpretation of which made it clear which State had true sovereignty over the disputed territories. The attempt to invoke the plea of error as vitiating the treaty provisions did not seem to have convinced the Court.[17]

The issue of sovereignty raised in the *Temple of Preah Vihear*[18] is a simple one, though in an unusual context. The ruins of the Temple of Preah Vihear were surrounded by a piece of Cambodian territory used as a place of worship and pilgrimage for Cambodians. Thailand had, since 1954, stationed an armed detachment in the temple. Cambodia asked the Court to declare that the temple was under its sovereignty and that Thailand should withdraw her armed forces therefrom. After a careful examination, the Court rejected Thailand's objection to its jurisdiction and ruled that the temple was situated on Cambodian territory from which Thailand must withdraw her military or police force. The Court also held that Thailand should restore all the objects which had been removed from the ruins since 1954 when her armed detachment was first stationed there.

It is thus clear that the Court has not had the opportunity to consider other aspects of the concept and the exercise of sovereignty in the types of disputes which have so far come before it.[19]

Private Law Issues in Public International Law

Here, the intention is not to consider the traditional relationship between municipal law and international law from either a monistic or dualistic standpoint, but mainly to draw attention to the extent to which the International Court of Justice has been increasingly constrained to resort to concepts normally or originally evolved within national legal systems in the application of international law to disputes between States. In the emerging era of transnational law and multinational corporations, the Court has had perforce to show an awareness of this relatively recent phenomenon.

An illustration of the type of these problems is provided by the *Ambatielos case*.[20] In that case a Greek shipowner called Ambatielos had, in 1919, entered into a contract with the United Kingdom Government for the purchase of ships. When that government failed to execute the terms of the contract, he brought an action in the English Courts for damages for breach of the contract, but the judgment went against him on the basis of the English constitutional law rule, which, *inter alia*, forbids the bringing of an action against a successor United Kingdom Government in respect of a contract made with a predecessor. Ambatielos claimed that this English municipal Court judgment involved a violation of international law. The government of Greece took up the case of Ambatielos as its national and invoked the terms of certain treaties concluded between the United Kingdom and Greece in 1886 and 1926 respectively, according to which the United Kingdom Government was alleged by Greece to be under an obligation to submit the dispute to arbitration. An objection to the jurisdiction of the Court filed by the United Kingdom was overruled in 1952, and the Court finally decided in 1953 that, under the two treaties invoked by Greece, the United Kingdom was under a duty to submit the dispute to arbitration. The Court, however, held that it was without jurisdiction to pronounce on the merits of the claims put forward by Ambatielos since the questions involved related to private law issues outside the Court's competence.

The issue in the *Anglo-Iranian Oil Company case*[21] was a concessionary

contract between the Anglo-Iranian Oil Company and the government of Iran which was the subject of an agreement made in 1933.
The immediate cause of the dispute was, however, the enactment of a
law by the Iranian government for the nationalization of the oil
industry. As in the *Ambatielos case*, the United Kingdom Government
took up the case of its national, the Anglo-Iranian Oil Company,
before the Court. The Court upheld the submission of the United
Kingdom that it had no jurisdiction to entertain the dispute on the
ground that the Iranian declaration accepting the Court's compulsory jurisdiction under Article 36(2) of the Statute of the Court which
had been ratified in 1932, concerned only any dispute arising out of
treaties entered into after that date, whereas the United Kingdom's
claim arose out of treaties entered into before that date. The Court
also repudiated the Iranian government's contention that the 1933
agreement was a concessionary contract between itself and the oil
company as well as an international treaty between the United
Kingdom and Iran; while the 1933 agreement constituted a contract
between Iran and the oil company, it could not at the same time be
an international treaty between Iran and the United Kingdom
because the latter was not a party to the contract even though it was
negotiated through the good offices of the Council of the League of
Nations. The Court accordingly granted the application of the
United Kingdom Government for a request for the indication of
interim measures of protection of the rights of either party pending
the final judgment in the case. In the event that happened, the Court
rescinded the order when it was found that a peaceful settlement of
the dispute had meanwhile been achieved between both sides.

In *Barcelona Traction Light and Power Company Limited*,[22] the issues of
municipal and transnational laws involved were more complicated.
The Barcelona company had been formed in Toronto, Canada, in
1911 and, in 1948, had been adjudicated bankrupt in Spain under
Spanish law. In 1958, Belgium thereupon instituted proceedings
against Spain because of this bankruptcy adjudication. Belgium
claimed in its application that, despite the incorporation of the
Barcelona company in Canada, Belgian nationals owned the bulk of
the company's share capital, and that the acts of the organs of the
Spanish State in declaring the company bankrupt and liquidated
engaged the responsibility of the Spanish State for the damage
resulting to the company, the cause of which Belgium was espousing
by the institution of these proceedings. Spain must therefore be
deemed to have incurred responsibility under international law
requiring it either to make reparation or to pay compensation for the
assets thus liquidated. Spain challenged the jurisdiction of the Court

but, before any further steps had been taken, Belgium gave notice of withdrawal from the suit because certain steps were being taken to settle the matter out of Court. That was in 1961. In the middle of 1962, on the breakdown of negotiations, Belgium brought a new application. Spain filed a number of preliminary objections, stating, *inter alia*, that the Belgian claims on its nationals were inadmissible or unfounded in law. After examining the legal character of share-holding, control and incorporation of limited liability companies under certain municipal laws, the Court held that Belgium had no *locus standi* to exercise diplomatic protection of Belgian shareholders in a Canadian company with regard to Spanish municipal law as applied to the company under Spanish lawful jurisdiction. The fact that the majority of the shareholders of the company incorporated in Canada under Canadian law were Belgians did not affect the legal character of the company as a Canadian Company. In reaching the conclusion that the Belgian claims were not well-founded, the Court examined at considerable length various municipal laws on the subject of the limited liability company, a phenomenon that was comparatively little known to international law up to that time. Because of the application of "general principles of law" in this case, we may refer to this significant passage in the Court's judgment:

> If the Court were to decide in disregard of the relevant institutions of municipal law it would, without justification, invite serious legal difficulties. It would lose touch with reality, for there are no corresponding institutions of international law to which the Court could resort. Thus the Court has, as indicated, not only to take cognizance of municipal law but also to refer to it. It is to rules generally by municipal legal systems which recognize the limited company whose capital is represented by shares, and not to the municipal law of a particular State, that international law refers. In referring to such rules, the Court cannot modify, still less deform them.[23]

In this dictum is contained a summary of how the Court deals with cases in which private law issues are entangled with public international law.

Diplomatic Law and Nationality Problems

In the sphere of diplomatic and consular law there has been a good deal of conventional law-making within the last fifteen years or so.[24] Some of this has inspired, and been inspired by, judicial decisions emanating from the Court and its predecessor. We are not here concerned with an examination of the various conventions and agreements on the subject, and we shall only refer to them as and when we discuss the relevant case-law.

It sometimes happens that the role of the Court in the settlement of disputes has an indirect effect on the attitude of the parties. For instance, the reference of the dispute to the Court was often sufficient to induce one or more of the parties to seek a settlement out of Court. Thus in the *Protection of French Nationals and Protected Persons in Egypt*,[25] the Egyptian Government enacted certain laws which would affect the persons and property of certain French nationals and protected persons in Egypt. The French government promptly instituted proceedings invoking the provisions of the Montreaux Convention of 1935 by which the institution of *capitulations*[26] in Egypt had been abrogated. The government of Egypt therefore decided not to proceed with the proposed measures and, by mutual agreement between the two governments, the Court made an order removing the case from the Court's list. Although this illustration is from diplomatic law, there are other examples from other areas of public international law where the Court has rendered a similar service.[27]

In the *Asylum case*,[28] the question of diplomatic immunity as well as of extradition was raised. Mr. Haya de la Torre, a Peruvian national who was a political leader, was accused of having instigated a military rebellion; he sought asylum in the Colombian Embassy in Lima, Peru. The Peruvian government demanded his surrender from the embassy but Colombia refused. Although under the *Pan-American Havana Convention on Asylum* (1928) asylum was in certain cases to be granted in a foreign embassy to a political offender who was a national of the territorial State, the issue, however, was to decide whether the offense allegedly committed by Haya was a political offense or a common crime so that if it were the latter, he could be surrendered. Colombia, as the asylum-granting State, claimed to be entitled unilaterally to "qualify" the offense which the refugee committed; it also demanded an assurance that, in the event of its agreeing to surrender or extradite, Peru would guarantee Haya's personal safety in leaving the country. The Court held that both requests by Colombia could not be granted as a matter of international law, since Peru had yet to prove that Haya was a common criminal and not a political offender. The Court further decided that Colombia's grant of asylum to Haya undoubtedly violated the 1928 Havana Convention. Soon after this decision the Court was asked by Colombia to interpret the judgment, especially as to whether it implied an obligation on its part to surrender Haya to Peru. The Court refused the request for interpretation as inadmissible. Colombia, thereafter, filed a fresh application in consequence of its refusal to surrender Haya to Peru.[29] The Court held that neither its earlier decision nor the 1928 Havana Convention obliged Colombia to surrender Haya to Peru, particularly as the Convention only required the surrender of a common criminal. The Court pointed out, however, that Peru was entitled to demand the termination of the asylum granted by Colombia to Haya since the grant was irregular, but that Colombia was under no obligation to surrender him. The Court saw no contradiction between these two conclusions since there were ways by which the irregular asylum in the Colombia embassy could be terminated other than by surrendering Haya.

A Court case involving the consular jurisdiction of the United States in Morocco is *Rights of Nationals of the United States in Morocco*.[30] In 1948, when France was still the administering authority of the Moroccan Protectorate, a decree was promulgated establishing a system of licence control in respect of imports not involving an official allocation of currency but limited to products absolutely essential to the local economy. The US Government challenged this law as contrary to its consular jurisdiction under the General Act of Algeciras of 1906 and certain treaties between it and Morocco which disallowed the application to US citizens of any Moroccan laws and regulations within its domain without prior US consent. The United States further contended that its consular jurisdiction covered cases in which only the defendant was a citizen or protégé of the United States. The Court rejected both these submissions, pointing out that the United States' consent was required only where the intervention of its consular courts was necessary for the strict enforcement of such laws and regulations in their application to US citizens. Similarly rejected by the Court was the US counter-claim that its nationals in Morocco were entitled to immunity from local taxation. On the other hand, the Court ruled in favour of two US contentions: first, that the import control imposed by the French authorities was contrary to the General Act of Algeciras and the 1836 Treaty between the United States and Morocco as the laws and regulations in question amounted to discrimination against the United States in favour of France; secondly, with regard to the extent of US consular jurisdiction in Morocco, that the United States was entitled to exercise such jurisdiction in the French zone in all disputes, whether civil or criminal, between US citizens or persons protected by the United States. It will, therefore, be seen how meticulous the Court was in disentangling the complicated web of claims and counter-claims in this case in order to arrive at a just settlement of a dispute involving diplomatic and nationality issues in a protectorate.

Of particular interest in such matters as those just considered is the

Nottebohm case[31] between Liechtenstein and Guatemala. In 1905, Mr. Nottebohm, who was then a German national, had settled in Guatemala and continued to reside there until October 1939 when, after the outbreak of the First World War, he visited Europe and there obtained Liechtenstein nationality, returning to Guatemala in 1940 to resume his residence and general business activities. In 1943, Guatemalan authorities interned him as an enemy alien. Liechtenstein instituted an action on the ground of Nottebohm's acquired nationality of 1939, claiming restitution and compensation from Guatemala for the international wrong done to him by the latter. Guatemala's objection to the Court's jurisdiction was, however, overruled and, in a final judgment, the Court held that the Liechtenstein claim was inadmissible on the ground of nationality. At international law, a State is entitled to institute proceedings on behalf of its national for the redress of a wrong done to him by another State only if a genuine bond of nationality exists between the claimant State and the national concerned. In the circumstances of this case, however, the acquisition of nationality could not be recognized by other States since it was not based on any genuine connection between Nottebohm and Liechtenstein. Mere residence by Nottebohm in Guatemala, for however long a period, did not by itself confer Guatemalan nationality on him, nor did it deprive him of his German nationality, which he acquired at birth and which had not been subsequently altered by an effective legal act. A fleeting sojourn in Liechtenstein during a European visit after some thirty-four years in Guatemala was held by the Court to be insufficient to confer the nationality claimed on his behalf, the real object of the nationalization which he hurriedly obtained being only to enable him acquire the status of a neutral national in Guatemala in time of war. The Court accordingly held that Liechtenstein's claim against Guatemala on behalf of Nottebohm was not well-founded since this was not the normal case of a State instituting proceedings on behalf of its national against another State for reparation and compensation for an internationally wrongful act committed against that national.

The Law of the Sea

This subject is of contemporary relevance and it is instructive to summarize briefly here the various aspects of this branch of the law with which the Court has so far had occasion to deal. Some of these decisions have made contributions to the international conventions and agreements since adopted or concluded under the auspices of the United Nations.

We may well begin our consideration with the first reported decision by the Court in the well-known *Corfu Channel case*.[32] In 1946, that is, shortly after the Second World War, the Allied naval authorities carried out mine-clearing operations in the Corfu Channel. Certain British warships suffered damage and members of their crew were killed as a result of explosions of mines which occurred while passing through an area previously swept. The United Kingdom thereupon accused Albania of having laid or allowed a third party to lay the mines afterwards. The complaint which the United Kingdom laid before the United Nations was then referred to the Court on the recommendation of the Security Council. After overruling Albania's objection to the jurisdiction of the Court, the Court held that Albania was responsible under international law not only for the explosions that had occurred in the Albanian waters but also for the consequent damage to the ships and the loss of lives. The Court was of the opinion that, while Albania did not itself lay the mines, the mines which did the damage could not have been laid without the knowledge of the Albanian Government. For its part, Albania accused the United Kingdom of a violation of its sovereignty by sending warships into Albanian territorial waters and also of carrying out mine-sweeping operations in Albanian waters after the explosions. The Court upheld the second of Albania's complaints that the United Kingdom's mine-sweeping operations after the explosions constituted a violation of Albanian sovereignty, in that they were carried out without the consent of Albania. On the question of the United Kingdom sending warships through Albanian territorial waters, however, the Court rejected Albania's complaint, holding that the United Kingdom was merely exercising thereby its right of innocent passage through an international strait as permitted under customary international law. The Court later assessed and ordered the payment of the amount of reparation which Albania should make to the United Kingdom Government.[33]

From right of innocent passage through straits, we turn to the establishment of fisheries zones by maritime States. In the *Fisheries case*,[34] Norway enacted in 1935 a decree reserving certain fishing grounds off its northern coast for the exclusive use of its own fishermen. The bone of contention between the United Kingdom and Norway was the validity in international law of this decree which prescribed a method for drawing the baselines from which the width of the territorial waters of Norway should be calculated. The point was that the Norwegian coastlines were highly irregular and delicate by reason of the many fjords, bays, islands, islets and reefs which feature them. After careful consideration, the Court held that the

Norwegian decree was in accordance with customary international law both as to the method it had laid down and as to the actual lines drawn for the fisheries zones.

The matter was taken a stage further in the *Fisheries Jurisdiction cases*[35] between the United Kingdom and Iceland on the one hand, and the Federal Republic of Germany and Iceland on the other. Early in 1972, Iceland made certain regulations extending the limits of its exclusive fisheries jurisdiction from a distance of twelve to one of fifty nautical miles with effect from September 1, 1972. Both the United Kingdom and the Federal Republic of Germany instituted separate proceedings against Iceland which, however, challenged the Court's jurisdiction and refused to take any part in the proceedings. Both applicant States requested the Court to grant interim measures of protection against Iceland so that it be ordered to refrain from implementing the new regulations for the extension of the Icelandic fishery zone insofar as their vessels were concerned, and the annual catch of their vessels be limited to certain maxima. The Court granted both requests. In a later judgment the Court held that it had jurisdiction to entertain the suits. In its final judgments in both cases in 1974, the Court decided that the Icelandic regulations, though amounting to unilateral extension of exclusive fishing rights to a limit of fifty nautical miles, were not opposable to either the United Kingdom or the Federal Republic of Germany, that Icelend was not entitled unilaterally to exclude their fishing vessels from the disputed area, and that the parties were under mutual obligations to enter into negotiations in good faith for the equitable solution of their differences, not by resort to an *ex aequo et bono* principle, but by recourse to requirements of fairness and justice. In the event that followed this decision, the parties undertook negotiations and settled the disputes between them amicably.

In this area of the law, the Court has also been fortunate to have had the opportunity of pronouncing on so topical an aspect of the law of the sea as the continental shelf. In the *North Sea Continental Shelf cases*[36] between the Federal Republic of Germany and Denmark on the one hand, and the Federal Republic of Germany and the Netherlands on the other, the Court had occasion to deal with (a) the application of the Geneva Convention on the Continental Shelf of 1958, (b) the issue of when a rule of customary international law should be deemed to have crystallized, and (c) a case where the jurisdiction of the Court was accepted by all the three parties as a basis for their application to the Court for adjudication, thus resembling a request for an advisory opinion by the States concerned. In asking the Court to state the principles and rules of international law applicable to the determination of the continental shelf of the North Sea, they also undertook thereafter to carry out the delimitation in accordance with the Court's guidelines. As the Court found the Netherlands and Denmark to be in the same interest, it joined the two proceedings together. It then decided that the boundary-lines in question should be drawn by agreement between the parties and in accordance with equitable principles in such a way as to leave each party those areas of the continental shelf which constituted the natural prolongation of its land territory under the sea; it further indicated certain factors to be taken into consideration for that purpose. It had been contended that the delimitations in question should be carried out in accordance with the principle of equidistance as defined in the 1958 Geneva Convention on the Continental Shelf, but the Court rejected the argument. Insofar as the Federal Republic of Germany had not ratified the Convention, the Court held that the principle of equidistance was not inherent in the basic concept of rights in the continental shelf and that, at any rate, the principle has not yet acquired the status of a rule of customary international law. The Federal Republic of Germany was accordingly not bound by the equidistance principle nor by the 1958 Convention, which it has not yet ratified.

The whole judgment is no doubt one of the most seminal delivered by the Court in recent years. It shows the Court at its high-water mark in the search for peace and equity. In doing so, it clarifies an area of the law that was in need of elucidation, namely, when an international custom becomes law.

Mandate and Trusteeship

In the era of decolonization and self-determination, it is not surprising that the Court was, during the first two decades of its functioning, very much preoccupied with adjudication of disputes touching these questions in various forms.

In the *Northern Cameroons case*[37] the Republic of Cameroons instituted proceedings against the United Kingdom Government contending that the latter had violated the Trusteeship Agreement for the Territory of the Cameroons under British administration by making it possible for the Trusteeship to become attached to Nigeria instead of to the Republic of Cameroons. The Court saw that there was no point in its adjudicating on the merits because, as the Republic of Cameroons had itself recognized, any judgment it might give would not alter the earlier decision of the General Assembly that, in accordance with the results of a plebiscite conducted and supervised by the United Nations, the Cameroons should be attached to Nigeria. The Court accordingly decided that it had no power to entertain the claim of the Cameroons Republic.

South-West Africa, later re-named as Namibia at the United Nations, provided, however, the widest platform for the Court's exercise of its judicial function in this sphere of the law. No less than six cases were dealt with by the International Court of Justice within the relatively long span of some twenty years, that is, from 1950 to 1971. Four of these cases were advisory opinions given by the Court in replies to questions requesting it to determine legal issues in connection with the Trusteeship System and its predecessor, the Mandate.

The first problem that was brought before the Court was the determination of the legal status of the Territory in the case of the *International Status of South-West Africa.*[38] In 1950, the General Assembly requested the Court for an advisory opinion on the legal position concerning the administration of the Territory which, after the First World War, was placed by the League of Nations under the mandate of the Union of South Africa. On the demise of the League, its supervisory functions lapsed and no provision was made in the Charter of the United Nations for the continuation of the supervision or for the mandate to come under United Nations Trusteeship. The Court held that the dissolution of the League did not entail the lapse of the mandate; that the mandatory Power continued to be under an obligation to give an account of its administration to the United Nations, which had the authority to continue the supervisory functions of the League; that the mandatory Power was not obliged to place the Territory under Trusteeship, but that it had no power unilaterally to modify the international status of South-West Africa. Some four years later, the General Assembly followed up this Court decision with another request for an advisory opinion in *Voting Procedure on Questions Relating to Reports and Petitions Concerning The Territory of South-West Africa.*[39] The Court held that the special rule, adopted by the General Assembly on voting procedure in taking decisions on questions relating to reports and petitions concerning the Territory by a two-thirds majority of those present and voting, was a correct application of its earlier advisory opinion. That rule was in accord with the degree of supervision which the United Nations could reasonably be expected to assume as a successor to the League in this respect. As a sequel to the 1950 opinion of the Court, the General Assembly requested the Court to say whether the Assembly was competent to set up the Committee on South-West Africa and empower it to grant oral hearings to petitioners on matters relating to the Territory. The Court held that the General Assembly was qualified to do so in the exercise of its supervisory powers which the League itself would have had. It took the view that the hearing of petitions by the Committee on South-West Africa might enhance the efficacy of the mandate system.

After these three advisory opinions, Ethiopia and Liberia instituted separate proceedings against the Union Government of South Africa as the mandatory power, asking the Court to declare that South-West Africa remained a mandated Territory and not part of the territory of South Africa, that the latter had been in breach of its obligations under the mandate and that the mandate and therefore, the mandatory authority, were subject to United Nations supervision. Having found Ethiopia and Liberia to be in the same interest, the Court joined the two proceedings, and overruled the four preliminary objections to the jurisdiction of the Court which South Africa had filed. After protracted public hearings, the Court held that Ethiopia and Liberia could not be considered to have established any *locus standi* to institute the proceedings. This strange conclusion had been reached by the casting vote of the President of the Court, prior to which the vote had been equally divided 7 to 7. In the estimation of the great majority of the members of the United Nations and in the international legal community generally, by this decision, the reputation of the Court touched its nadir. Far from contributing to the search for peace, the Court took the contemporary world back to the Middle Ages by a process of legal reasoning which would have baffled the Schoolmen.

This judgment of the Court in 1966 caused so much dissatisfaction in UN circles that the General Assembly passed a number of resolutions which had the effect of denouncing it and reasserting the authority of the United Nations over Namibia; indeed, a resolution expressly terminated South Africa's mandate and required South Africa to withdraw immediately from Namibia. The Security Council, having passed similar resolutions, adopted the one requesting the Court to say what the legal effects were of the termination of the mandate. In *Legal Consequences for States of Continued Presence of South Africa in Namibia (South West Africa) notwithstanding Security Council Resolution 276(1970)*,[40] the General Assembly had adopted Resolution 2145(XXI) in October 1966 terminating the mandate of South Africa over Namibia and declaring that South Africa had no other right to administer it. Some three years later, in 1969, the Security Council declared in Resolution 276 that the continued presence of South Africa in the Territory was illegal, that all acts taken or done by that government on behalf or in respect of Namibia since the termination of the mandate were equally illegal and invalid, and that all States should refrain from any dealings with South Africa which were incompatible with that declaration by the Security Council. In July 1970, the Security Council submitted a request to the Court for an advisory opinion. After public hearings at which appeared the legal representatives of the UN Secretary-General, the Organization of African Unity[41] and some other UN Member States and the South African Government, the Court held in its opinion of June 1971 that the continued presence of South Africa was illegal; that South Africa was under an obligation to withdraw its administration immediately therefrom; that Member States of the United Nations were under an obligation to recognize the illegality of South Africa's presence in Namibia and the invalidity of its acts on behalf of or concerning Namibia; and that all Member States should refrain from any acts implying recognition of the legality of, or lending support or assistance to, South Africa's presence in and administration of the Territory. The Court held further that non-Member States were bound to give assistance in the action taken by the United Nations in regard to Namibia.[42]

Thus was brought to an end a legal as well as a judicial tussle that, but for the unhappy interlude of 1962–1966, might have been regarded as part of the agonizing search for social justice in recent years. The 1971 judgment did much to restore some of the image of the Court in its role of arbiter for peace by putting a seal upon the principle of self-determination as a recognized right of nations under contemporary international law. After a glorious period of evolution from being a political concept and later an aspiration of the human mind, self-determination was nurtured and reared by the General Assembly of the United Nations until it became an accepted reality as a legal right of peoples the world over.

Human Rights and Humanitarian Law

Under this heading we may briefly consider the Court's exercise of its judicial function in the administration of justice on a humanitarian basis. There is no doubt that the actual development in what is now called Humanitarian Law has taken place in the field of declarations, resolutions and other forms of lawmaking mostly under the auspices of the United Nations, beginning with the Universal Declaration of Human Rights in 1948, and supplemented by a number of subsequent covenants and conventions on economic, political, social and cultural rights.[43] The idea of an International Court of Human Rights to apply and interpret these formal rules has become a reality only in Europe and not yet within the UN framework; it is not thought feasible for a separate court to be set up now or in the near future. It is thus left, to the International Court of Justice to play the role, albeit indirect, of injecting humanitarian principles and ideals into those of its judicial decisions that might call for them from time to time.[44]

The Court would appear to have found its advisory opinions the more convenient vehicle for serving this purpose than its decisions in contentious cases. There is no reason why the Court should not deal with the Human Rights declarations, covenants and conventions in the discharge of its function under Article 38(1) of its Statute.

In *Reparation for Injuries Suffered in the Service of the United Nations*[45] the Court, in reply to a series of requests to that effect, held that the United Nations has the international legal personality to institute proceedings for reparation for the injuries suffered by Count Bernadotte and other members of the United Nations mission to Palestine who were assassinated there. The diplomatic protection which should enable their own States to bring actions on behalf of these UN civil servants notwithstanding, the United Nations was entitled to sue on their behalf in this case, although any possible competition could be eliminated by means of a convention or agreement. The Court found that the customary law empowering only States to institute such actions must also recognize the new legal situation of the international personality of the UN Organization as an employer of labor which imposes an obligation upon it to seek redress from the State responsible for the assassination of its agents and servants and those entitled to claim through them. The Court was able to achieve this humanitarian end by embarking upon a measure of progressive development of existing customary international law.

Similarly, in *Certain Expenses of the United Nations*, the Court gave an advisory opinion which enabled the United Nations to continue to maintain its peace-keeping operations in the Middle East (and the Congo) against the strenuous contentions of France and the Soviet Union that neither the General Assembly nor the Secretary-General had the necessary competence under the Charter to incur the expenses requisite for their undertaking. The Court saw the need to give judicial support to the Organization in its worthwhile efforts to maintain international peace and security — the main purpose and indeed, the *raison d'être* of the establishment of the Organization. If the Security Council would or could not act in such emergencies as were created in the Congo or the Middle East where human lives and valuable resources were in imminent danger, the Court took the view that action taken by the General Assembly on behalf of the Organization for one of the purposes stated in the Charter must be regarded as valid and the expenditure as having been properly incurred: all Member States are under an obligation to make their allotted shares of the contribution.

One of the most important advisory opinions in the humanitarian field is the Court's judgment in *Reservations to the Convention on the Prevention and Punishment of the Crime of Genocide.*[46] Without concerning ourselves here with the three abstract questions asked of the Court in that case on the issue of reservations to a multilateral treaty, we find the reasoning of the Court instructive by its elucidation of the principles which should govern the worldwide concern for the international crime of genocide: failure of a State to sign the Genocide Convention does not preclude another State party from being affected by the operation of the Convention.

We may close this section of our study with a reference to three awards of administrative tribunals touching the rights of certain international civil servants whose employment has been brought to an end in circumstances calling for review. In the earliest of these cases, *Effect of Awards of Compensation Made by the United Nations Administrative Tribunal,*[47] the UN Administrative Tribunal, which was established by the General Assembly for dealing with applications complaining against breaches of the terms of contracts or of contracts of employment of staff members of the Secretariat, held that a staff member had been wrongly dismissed. On a reference to the Court for an advisory opinion, the Court held that the United Nations and, *a fortiori*, the General Assembly, were bound to accept the decision of the Tribunal, even though it was a subordinate body set up by the General Assembly. The Tribunal possessed judicial independence and enjoyed the power to pronounce final judgments without appeal; it was not a merely advisory body to the General Assembly.[48]

Some eighteen years later, in 1972, the Tribunal gave a ruling on a complaint by another staff member that his fixed-term contract of employment had not been renewed. The complainant applied for the review of this ruling to the Committee on Application for Review of Administrative Tribunal Judgments, an appeal body set up in consequence of the Court's advisory opinion of 1954. The Committee found that the complainant's application had a sufficient basis for a review and, as an organ entitled to request an advisory opinion, requested the Court to say whether, according to the applicant's contention, the Tribunal had failed to exercise the jurisdiction vested in it or had committed a fundamental error in procedure which had occasioned a failure of justice. In 1973, the Court held that the Tribunal had been right on both questions.

It can, therefore, be seen that the Court appears to be as concerned about the rights and interests of the individual in the limited area in which it is allowed to function as it is in deciding disputes between States. In this important sphere, the Court has shown particular concern for humanitarian considerations and equity as between the organization and the complaining individual.

Conclusions

Among the principal aims and objects set out in the UN Charter is the determination "to establish conditions under which justice and respect for the obligations arising from treaties and other sources of international law can be maintained." We have seen that the Statute of the International Court of Justice seeks to fulfil this aspiration by the provision in its Article 38 that the Court is to apply to the settlement of disputes international conventions, rules of customary international law, generally accepted principles of law, judicial decisions and the writings of acknowledged publicists of the various nations. In order to avoid the possibility of a lacuna in the sources upon which the Court may draw, there is also the provision that the Court may resort to the exercise of an *ex aequo et bono* power, which is really more administrative than judicial. Our preceding analysis shows that all these sources, except the *ex aequo et bono* provision, have been applied in the judicial process of the Court as and when necessary, and that by far the largest source is the interpretation and application of treaties and other international agreements having relevance to particular disputes before the Court.

Whether the Court has been exercising its jurisdiction in contentious cases or in advisory proceedings, it seems that the occasions have been few when it has consciously departed from its role as a judicial organ charged with the responsibility of deciding a case other than by the application of juridical technique and *"scientifique recherche"*. In a few cases involving elements of political controversy, such as the *Certain Expenses case*, the Court found itself having to supply a solution that might be regarded by the States affected as a teleological interpretation of the Charter when it decided that the General Assembly resolutions authorizing peace-keeping operations of the United Nations were essential for the fulfilment of the purposes of the Charter, even though the Charter assigns primary responsibility for international peace and security to the Security Council. If, as a result of an inexplicable paralysis, the Security Council could not or would not act in situations threatening world peace and security, the General Assembly stepped in and did what the majority of the members of the United Nations expected of it, the Court certainly did right to settle the dispute among the Great Powers by upholding the validity of the General Assembly resolutions which authorized the necessary expenditures for the maintenance of the United Nations forces in the Congo and the Middle East, notwithstanding the refusal of France and the Soviet Union to pay their shares of the total expenditure.

There is no doubt that the Court has occasionally arrived at what resulted in disappointing conclusions as, for example, happened in the series of sterile juridical disputations in the *South-West Africa cases* between 1962 and 1966, especially in the matter of preliminary questions of admissibility, jurisdiction and *jus standi*. The general expectations of the 1966 decisions were disappointed. Even though carried by the very narrow majority of one, the decision in the 1966 case was without a doubt too much influenced by excessive analytical positions in which the International Court of Justice ought not to indulge in its delicate task of administration of justice and ensuring world order. By 1971, however, the *Namibia* Advisory Opinion restored somewhat the image of the Court as not being the reactionary body that it was judged to be in the preceding decade or so. This is probably because the General Assembly had by that time worked out more fully and more perspicaciously the principle of self-determination as an acceptable norm of contemporary international law.

A type of negative result similar to that of 1966 was achieved recently in the *Nuclear Tests cases*[49] between France and Australia on the one hand, and France and New Zealand on the other. After granting Australia's and New Zealand's requests for interim measures of protection against France, which had been carrying out a series of nuclear tests in the atmosphere in the Pacific Ocean for some years, the Court eventually decided that it could neither go into the pending issue of jurisdiction nor pronounce on the merits of the complaints filed by Australia and New Zealand because, in the Court's view, the whole case no longer had any object. France had from the beginning refused to accept the jurisdiction of the Court and, therefore, did not take part in the proceedings. France had, however, made some declarations through high functionaries that she would carry out no more atmospheric nuclear tests in the Pacific, and this was accepted by the majority of the Court as sufficient for it not to proceed with the case any further.

The role of the Court may also be seen as having a more or less indirect effect on the promotion of world peace and security. We have referred to some cases in which the very fact of the institution of proceedings sometimes resulted in the parties changing their minds and withdrawing their case from the Court in order to settle their disputes out of Court. Such was the case, for instance, in the *Trial of Pakistani Prisoners of War*.[50] a situation that might have got out of hand but for the timely decision of the parties to settle their dispute out of Court.

The existence of the Court as a forum for the ventilation of genuine inter-State grievances may also be considered as a form of indirect contribution to peace. A situation which in former times would have called for the use of force for the redress of wrongs, real or imaginary, might more often than not be now dealt with by reference to the Court in one way or another, thus providing an opportunity "to let off steam" and permit tempers to cool down. This happened quite recently when Greece filed an application with the Court asking it to indicate measures of protection to both itself and Turkey in respect of their dispute in the *Aegean Sea Continental Shelf case*.[51] Greece simultaneously placed the complaint before the Security Council, mainly, it claimed, from the point of view of the likely breach of peace and security in the Aegean Sea area. The Security Council heard both sides and finally adopted a resolution appealing to both States to do nothing to endanger the peace and to enter into negotiation with a view to finding an amicable settlement of their disputes. In those circumstances the Court felt that it could not indicate any provisional measure of protection in accordance with Article 41 of the Statute of the Court.[52]

We may once more draw attention to Resolution 3232 (XXIX) of November 12, 1974 on Review of the Role of the International Court of Justice which ends with the reaffirmation "that recourse to judicial settlement of legal disputes, particularly referral to the International Court of Justice, should not be considered as an unfriendly act between States". This very important note of warning is salutary at this time when States not only fight shy of the Court but also tend to regard reference to the Court as part of the reason why they would not even resume negotiations unless the party that has filed an application with the Court would first withdraw it. An instance occurred in the *Aegean Sea Continental Shelf case*.

The internalization of disputes which the institution of proceedings in the Court implies has the positive value of educating the international community as to the causes and nature of inter-State conflicts and frictions, and it may also show other States how not to do things.[53] By the time each case is ended, international law will have been better understood and probably strengthened as a consequence of the exchange of arguments for and against the opposing points of view and, in the case of advisory opinions, the world will have benefited from the Court's wise counsel, coming as it necessarily does after the United Nations' prolonged debate and the careful reappraisal of the legal issues put before the Court by all the parties concerned.[54]

Granted the limited role that both the Charter of the United Nations and the Statute of the Court have permitted it, the Court has tried to cope as best it could, although it would have done a good deal more (a) if its jurisdiction were not subjected to the niggling inhibitions of the so-called Optical Clause, making it dependent upon the consent of States parties to a dispute before the Court, and (b) if its jurisdiction were made available to a wider range of would-be litigants. The emergence of transnational law, the growing activities of the multinational corporations and the expanding frontiers of humanitarian law are making it ever more necessary for these two developments to be introduced into contemporary international law.

Meanwhile, in order to make its role more dynamic and, therefore, more effective, the Court must be ready and will be more responsive to the needs and aspirations of the present-day international community. In short, the Court must set its gaze towards new horizons.

NOTES

1. See Article 95.

2. Article 92.

3. Accordingly, "Treaty" means "an international agreement concluded between States in written form and governed by international law, whether embodied in a single instrument or in two or more related instruments and whatever its particular designation." See also Elias *Modern Law of Treaties*, p. 13.

4. *I.C.J. Reports 1969*, p. 3. Compare Article 24 of the Statute of the International Law Commission: "The Commission shall consider ways and means for making the evidence of customary international law more readily available, such as the collection and publication of documents concerning state practice and of the decisions of national and international courts on questions of international law, and shall make a report to the General Assembly on this matter." Since this guide relates to the material which the Commission is required to employ when codifying and progressively developing international law, the Court is hereby being assisted in what law it should apply when dealing with cases before it.

5. *Electricity Company of Sofia and Bulgaria*, Series A/B, No. 79 (1939) p. 199.

6. *Corfu Channel Case, I.C.J. Reports 1949*, p. 22.

7. *Effect of Awards of the United Nations Administrative Tribunals, I.C.J. Reports 1954*, p. 53.

8. For a brief discussion of the problems, see Sir Hersch Lauterpacht's *The Development of International Law by the International Court*, 1958, pp. 167–168. See also G. I. Tunkin's *Theory of International Law*, pp. 190–203.

9. For a spirited analysis of this whole question see C. W. Jenks: *The Prospects of International Adjudication*. 1962, pp. 237–238.

10. I.C.J. Reports 1971, p. 16 at p. 50 para. 104. The emphasis is the author's.

11. Op. Cit., p. 21. A little later on, however, the author added: They are not binding upon States, neither are they binding upon the Court. However, no written provision can prevent them from showing authoritatively what international law is, and no written rule can prevent the Court from regarding them as such (p. 22). Consider Tunkin's criticism of Lauterpacht's views in this regard at pages 180–181 of his *Theory of International Law*, translated by W. E. Butler, 1974.

12. *I.C.J. Report 1953*, p. 47.

13. See R. Y. Jennings: *Acquisition of Territory in International Law*, 1963, p. 27 for the view that this case should not be regarded as a happy example of the theory of historical consolidation.

14. This is in line with the arbitral award in the *Island of Palmas Case* 1928, Permanent Court of Arbitration, *Scott's Hague Court Reports*, Vol. 2, p. 83.

15. *I.C.J. Reports 1960*, p. 6.

16. *I.C.J. Reports 1959*, p. 209.

17. See now the Vienna Convention on the Law of Treaties, 1969, Article 48; also, Elias, *Modern Law of Treaties*, pp. 154–6.

18. *I.C.J. Reports 1962*, p. 6.

19. In the *Western Sahara Case, I.C.J. Reports 1975*, p. 12, the issue of sovereignty was considered but the Court would seem to regard the respective claims of Morocco and Mauritania over Spanish Sahara as inconclusive.

20. *I.C.J. Reports 1953*, p. 10.

21. *I.C.J. Reports 1952*, p. 93.

22. *I.C.J. Reports 1961*, p. 9; *I.C.J. Reports 1964*, p. 6; Second phase, *I.C.J. Reports 1970*, p. 3.

23. *I.C.J. Reports 1970*, p. 3, at p. 37 (para. 50).

24. E.g., Vienna Convention on Diplomatic Relations 1961; Vienna Convention on Consular Relations 1963; Convention on Special Missions 1969; Vienna Convention on Relations between States and International Organizations, 1975.

25. *I.C.J. Reports 1950*, p. 59.

26. An account of the evolution of the practice of Capitulations in North Africa will be found in C. H. Alexandrowicz's "The European-African Confrontation", 1973, pp. 83–91. According to this author, the practice originated in Asia in the 16th century where "a Ruler receiving a foreign community of merchants in his territory allowed them to pursue their own way of life and govern themselves by their own law under the jurisdiction of the head of the settlement". This fact was not considered as evidence of inferior civilization. The concessions and privileges were later embodied in bilateral treaties called Capitulations which, however, varied from period to period. The characteristic feature of the capitulations concluded between France and

the North African States was the stipulation of jurisdictional privileges for the French residing in North African States as well as subjects the latter residing in France. See also the same author's article entitled "New and Original States", in *International Affairs*, July, 1969, pp. 465–480.

27. See, e.g. *Aerial Incident of 27 July 1955 (US v. Bulgaria)*, Order of 30 May, 1960, *I.C.J. Reports 1960*, p. 146; also *Compaguie du Port, des Quais et des Entrepots de Beyrouth (France v. Lebanon) I.C.J. Reports 1960*, p. 186.

28. *I.C.J. Reports 1950*, p. 266; also p. 395.

29. *Haya de la Torre Case, I.C.J. Reports 1951*, p. 71.

30. *I.C.J. Reports 1952*, p. 176.

31. *I.C.J. Reports 1953*, p. 111; *I.C.J. Reports 1955*, p. 4.

32. *I.C.J. Reports 1947–48*, p. 15; 53 and 124; *I.C.J. Reports 1949*, p. 4; 237; 244.

33. This decision re-echoed in *Monetary Gold Removed from Rome in 1943, I.C.J. Reports 1954*, p. 19, in which monetary gold removed by the Germans from Rome in 1943 was later recovered in Germany and found to belong to Albania. Under a 1946 agreement, the gold was to be shared among the various countries entitled. The United Kingdom claimed that the gold should be delivered to it in partial satisfaction of the judgment in the *Corfu Channel Case*. Italy raised the preliminary objection that the Court had no jurisdiction to adjudicate upon the validity of the Italian claim against Albania in respect of the same monetary gold. The Court held that it could not deal with the matter since Albania had not consented to, nor taken part in, the dispute before the Court.

34. *I.C.J. Reports 1951*, p. 116.

35. *I.C.J. Reports 1973*, p. 3, 49. *I.C.J. Reports 1974*, p. 3, 175.

36. *I.C.J. Reports 1969*, p. 3.

37. *I.C.J. Reports 1963*, p. 15.

38. *I.C.J. Reports 1950*, p. 128.

39. *I.C.J. Reports 1955*, p. 67.

40. *I.C.J. Reports 1971*, p. 16.

41. The present writer argued the case for the Organization of African Unity.

42. For an interpretation of the 1971 Advisory Opinion in terms of power politics, see G. Schwarzenberger's *International Constitutional Law*, 1976, Vol. III of his *International Law as Applied by International Courts and Tribunals*, pp. 333–335. There are also those who think that the role of the Court is affected by its changing composition — e.g. Judge Petrén, a former member of the Court, in his article, "Some Thoughts on the Future of the I.C.J.", in *Netherlands Yearbook of International Law*, 1976, pp. 59–76.

43. See M. Moskowitz's *International Concern with Human Rights*, 1974, pp. 160–172. We should not overlook the initiative in the Hague Convention Concerning Laws and Customs of War of 1907 with its human provisions for the treatnent of war victims and other affected persons.

44. Egon Schwelb has made a recent study of the problem in his article entitled "I.C.J. and Human Rights of the United Nations", in *A.J.I.L.*, Vol. 66, 1972.

45. *I.C.J. Reports 1949*, p. 174.

46. *I.C.J. Reports 1951*, p. 15.

47. *I.C.J. Reports 1954*, p. 47.

48. A similar decision upholding the competence of the ILO Administrative Tribunal to give decisions in staff matters binding upon UNESCO which had adopted the ILO Tribunal for the purpose of settling such disputes, was reached by the Court in Judgments of the Administrative Tribunal of the ILO upon Complaints made against UNESCO, *I.C.J. Reports 1956*, p. 77.

49. *I.C.J. Reports 1974*, p. 253, 457.

50. *I.C.J. Reports 1973*, p. 347.

51. *I.C.J. Reports 1976*, p. 3.

52. It is unnecessary in the present study to enter into certain unsatisfactory features of the decision in this case.

53. Northedge and Donenalan's *International Disputes: The Political Aspects*, Chapter 10, "The Role of the United Nations", pp. 228–240.

54. For a recent study of the problems see Leo Gross (Ed.) *The Future of the International Court of Justice*, Vol. 1, 1976, Chapter 2 by the editor, entitled "The International Court of Justice: Consideration of Requirements for Enhancing Its Role in the International Legal Order", at pp. 27–87. Also useful is Chapter 4 in the same volume, "The Role of the I.C.J. in the United Nations System: The First Quarter Century", by G. Weissberg, particularly at pp. 168–190.

Chapter 8

HIJACKING IN INTERNATIONAL LAW — A CASE STUDY *

Summary of the Facts

Francisco Xiaviere, a citizen of the Republic of Alterius, hijacks an airliner of Alterius registry and orders it to the Democratic State of Botania. Xaviere, a member of a racial and political minority in Alterius, declares his motive to be publicity for the cause of his "people". A passenger, Robert Yellman of the Coronado Republic, is killed by Xaviere, owing in part to Yellman's having placed himself in a position of danger by trying to disarm Xaviere during both the hijacking and the two-day negotiations with Botanian authorities over asylum for Xaviere, during which time Xaviere allowed no one to board or leave the plane. Yellman had disregarded the airliner crew's standard "in the event of hijacking" instruction to the effect that passengers should remain seated and leave apprehension of the hijacker to the crew, including the sky marshal. Botanian authorities, knowing that Yellman had been wounded and was in critical condition, took no measures to save his life beyond an oral request for Yellman's release during the first day of the negotiations. Botania took Xaviere into custody, but a preliminary hearing on extradition exonerated Xaviere as a "political refugee", and the magistrate refused to bind him over for trial in Botania for either hijacking or murder. Botania, not a party to the 1970 Hague Convention for the Suppression of Unlawful Seizure of Aircraft, refused Alterius' request to have Xaviere returned to Alterius or tried for murder in Botania.

Therefore, Alterius brings action in the International Court of Justice against Botania and against Xaviere. Alterius seeks a mandatory order of the Court to Botania to deliver Xaviere for trial and seeks criminal prosecution of Xaviere for violation of the law of nations. Coronado, on behalf of Yellman's estate, files damage claims against both Xaviere and Botania.

Alterius cites the precedent of the post-World War II International Military Tribunal (Nuremberg) in arguing for

---

* Sponsored by World Association of Judges, World Peace through Law, at its Conference in Abidjan in July, 1973.

International Court of Justice jurisdiction over crimes against the law
of nations. Botania defends, generally citing its territorial inviolability
and challenging the claims that granting asylum to a hijacker violates
the law of nations or that hijacking is a crime against the law of
nations. Xaviere defends, citing his political expression of the plight of
his oppressed people as ground for immunity from any extraterritorial
process against him, and claiming that international law governs only
States and provides no jurisdiction over individuals.

Alterius and Botania further contest the issue of Court jurisdiction
as to the State parties. Both Alterius and Botania are parties to the
International Court's Statute by virtue of UN membership, and each
has deposited acceptance of compulsory jurisdiction of the Court in
all legal disputes concerning:

(a) the interpretation of a treaty;
(b) any question of international law;
(c) the existence of any fact which, if established, would constitute a
    breach of international obligation;
(d) the nature or extent of the reparation to be made for the breach of
    an international obligation.
Provided, that the declaration not apply to: . . . .
(e) disputes with regard to matters which are essentially within the
    domestic jurisdiction of the signatory State; . . . .

Botania argues that asylum is within its domestic jurisdiction. Alterius
contends that the nature of the hijacking crime makes surrender of
Xaviere a question of international law. Coronado claims a right to
maintain its damage claim, and Botania defends on the ground that
an individual cannot use the name of a State to maintain an action in
the Court and that Yellman's estate has not exhausted its local
remedy in Botanian courts. Botania further contends that it was not
negligent in its handling of the asylum negotiations so is not liable for
damages.

Xaviere defends, contending that Yellman's contributory negligence as a matter of law (Yellman having disregarded the anti-
hijacking instructions of the airline crew, which instructions were
promulgated by an administrative agency of Alterius pursuant to
statute) absolves Xaviere from liability. The law of Botania recognizes
such a defence. Coronado maintains that the general principles of law
recognized by nations impose absolute liability on the actor for
injuries resulting from the commission of a crime.

Counsel for Alterius files a brief against Botania and Xaviere on the
mandatory order and criminal charges. Counsel for Botania and
counsel for Xaviere file briefs in response. Counsel for Coronado files

a brief claiming the right to maintain such a damage claim in the International Court, to which both Botania and Xaviere respond through separate counsel.

An International Court of Justice of seven Justices of Nations sat as a "Court" to receive the written briefs and hear arguments of counsel and then decide the issues presented by the above statement of facts.[1]

Opinions of the Court

Oral Judgment of the Court
(Delivered by Dr. T. O. Elias, Presiding Justice, on August 30, 1973)

1. After a very careful consideration of all the submissions of learned counsel for all the parties to this case, we have come to the conclusion that this Court has jurisdiction to entertain the suits brought by Alterius and by Coronado against Botania because, *inter alia*:

(a) the *Asylum* case (1950) ICJ has established that
    (i) the ICJ has jurisdiction in extradition cases and
    (ii) no one State, whether plaintiff or defendant, can *unilaterally* characterize an offence as "political";
(b) the substantive question of defendant's alleged breach of its international obligation is so inextricably bound up with the question of jurisdiction that both must be joined and considered together, as the ICJ did in the case concerning *Right of Passage over Indian Territory (Portugal v. India* [1957]) ICJ 125, at page 150;
(c) important issues of international law, e.g. hijacking, extradition, exhaustion of local remedies, individuals as subjects of international law, are involved, and this Court cannot shirk its responsibility by refusing to entertain the case;
(d) the question of interpretation of certain international instruments relating to jurisdiction has been raised by both sides, which the Court must examine: See Article 38 of the Statute of the Court;
(e) only the ICJ has the power to decide the question whether or not it has jurisdiction in any given case: see Article 36(6) of the Statute of the Court.

2. As regards the main issues, we consider that, in view of the *Tokyo Convention of 1968* and the *Hague Convention of 1970* as well as the General Assembly Resolutions 2551 (XXIV) of 1969 and 2645 (XXV) of 1970, hijacking is an international crime punishable as such by both a municipal court and an international court as may be appropriate. It is an offense *erga omnes*, like piracy at sea, slavery,

crimes against humanity and genocide. These examples are those of what has been described as a rule of *jus cogens* in Article 52 of the Vienna Convention on the Law of Treaties — that is to say, certain peremptory norms of general international law from which States cannot derogate. Moreover the two conventions make it an extraditable offense. Botania is, therefore, under an international obligation to extradite or to punish Xaviere, whatever the latter's motive for hijacking the aircraft from Alterius, and despite Botania's invocation of the exemption clause under its Extradition Treaty with Alterius and its reservation in its Optional Clause regarding matters claimed to be essentially within its domestic jurisdiction. The nature of the international crime of hijacking renders both defenses as well as Botania's claim to right to grant asylum inadmissible in contemporary international law.

3. Botania's contention that it is not bound by the Tokyo and the Hague Conventions or by the General Assembly Resolutions against hijacking is not well-founded because the ICJ has recently ruled in the *Namibia case* (1971) that Member States as well as non-member States of the United Nations are bound by resolutions of the General Assembly on certain fundamental issues such as the right of self-determination. We think that hijacking is in this category. Accordingly, failure on the part of Botania to punish or to extradite Xaviere in the circumstances of this case enagages its international responsibility, and it should make adequate reparation to Alterius, the exact amount of which will be fixed by this Court after the necessary particulars are made available to it by a referee appointed by this Court.

4. In our view, Coronado's espousal of the cause of the estate of its national, Yellman (deceased), entitles it to claim reparation from Botania, the amount of which can be determined only after further details than those so far given are known. We do not consider it appropriate that Yellman's estate should be allowed to bring an independent suit against Botania. Any claim that that estate might have should be settled with its State, Coronado, out of whatever reparation might be made by Botania to Coronado.

5. We have deemed it necessary to announce now these tentative conclusions at which the Court has arrived, pending the preparation of detailed written opinions to be delivered by each of us in due course and published as part of the proceedings of this Court.

Opinion of presiding justice
(Taslim Olawale Elias, Chief Justice of Nigeria, concurred in by Justice Sansern Kraichitti)

The facts of this case sufficiently appear in the preliminary statement of the Honorary Chairman, Mr. T. Berhane of Ethiopia, who at the invitation of the Court, gave a detailed outline. I propose to consider the complicated arguments of plaintiffs and defendants under the following seven broad headings:

I. The Question of Jurisdiction of the Court

I believe that this Court has jurisdiction to entertain the case because:

(a) It has asserted it over an extradition suit in the *Asylum* case (1950) ICJ 266, in which it also held that the State granting asylum cannot unilaterally characterize an offense as a "political", and not a "common", crime.

(b) In the event of a dispute between the parties the Court alone may decide as to whether or not it has jurisdiction. [Article 36(6) of the Statute of the Court].

   This includes its power to interpret instruments governing that jurisdiction: see the *Nottebohm* case (Preliminary Objection) (1953) ICJ 111, 119. The Court may postpone a ruling on jurisdiction and look into the merits of the case: *Panevezys-Saldutiskis Railway* (1939) PCIJ, Series A/B 76; *Electricity Company of Sofia* (1939) PCIJ, Series A/B 77. The substantive question of respondent's breach of an international obligation is so inextricably bound up with the question of jurisdiction that both must be "joined" and considered together, as was done in the case concerning *Right of Passage over Indian Territory (Portugal* v. *India)* (1957) ICJ 125, 159, where a detailed inquiry into the merits was held necessary for the determination of the question of jurisdiction.

(c) Recognizable international rights and obligations are involved in this case; for example, Botania's extradition rights are being asserted against Alterius's jurisdictional rights over Xaviere: see *ILC Draft Declaration on the Rights and Duties of States* (1949), *Article 8 of the Convention to Prevent and Punish Acts of Terrorism*, OAS February 2, 1971.

(d) *The Doctrine of Forum Prorogatum*, i.e. the acceptance of a unilateral summons to appear before the Court, gives the Court unquestioned jurisdiction: the *Corfu Channel case (Preliminary Objection)*, (1948) ICJ 15 (between Great Britain and Albania).

(e) The reservation by Botania in the Optional Clause to the effect that matters within its domestic jurisdiction are not justiciable before the ICJ, is ill-founded.

(f) The exemption of "political crimes" from the provisions of the Treaty of Extradition between Botania and Alterius is invalid in international law.

(g) Exaggerated and out-moded theory of absolute State sovereignty put forward by Botania in respect of its jurisdiction over all persons and things within its territory must be rejected as incompatible with contemporary international law, the exceptions reserved for "immunities recognized by international law" notwithstanding.

II. Aerial Piracy is an International Crime Triable by the International Court of Justice

The judgment of the Nuremberg International Military Tribunal, 1946, and the Tokyo International Tribunal, 1948, are precedents for punishment of crimes against humanity, the perpetrators of which are subjects of international law.

The prohibition of aircraft hijacking pertains to both municipal and international law. It is a multiple crime which endangers the hijacked aircraft and the lives of its crew and passengers without regard to their nationality. It entails a forcible kidnapping of large numbers of innocent people, the threat or use of force against individual crew members and passengers, and the risk of mid-air collision with other aircraft.

Hijacking is directly analogous to sea piracy: aircraft piracy has been thus defined in the United States as "seizure by force or violence or threat of force or violence and with wrongful intent, of an aircraft in flight or air commerce" [49 U.S.C. 1472 (1961)]. Brazil, Portugal and Cuba have similar enactments (see plaintiff's brief). Piracy and skyjacking are virtually synonymous. Pirates are treated as *hostes humanis generis*: the Tokyo Convention on Offenses and Certain Other Acts Committed on Board Aircraft (1968) and the Hague Convention for the Suppression of Unlawful Seizure of Aircraft (1970) both regard hijacking as piracy.

Hijacking is, therefore, an international crime and Botania has committed a breach of an international obligation by refusing to extradite or to punish Xaviere.

III. Aircraft Piracy is not a Political Crime and Extradition is Therefore Obligatory

A. Piracy committed on an aircraft in international commerce threatens all nations.

A right of asylum in a case of piracy is accordingly denied by the two Conventions mentioned under II above. It is not a private matter between Botania and Xaviere, or indeed one exclusively within Botania's domestic jurisdiction. The issues that arise are those of the right of asylum, extradition and punishment of an allegedly international criminal. See U.S. Declaration on Territorial Asylum, Art. 1, para. 2, which expressly denies right of asylum to anyone accused of having committed crimes against humanity [G. A. Res. 2313 (XXII) December 14, 1967]. The OAS Draft Convention on Terrorism and Kidnapping for Purposes of Extortion (1970) expressly provides in its Article 3 that aerial piracy should not be considered as a political offense. The motives that impel aerial pirates to act are irrelevant to the issue of their criminal liability. Political motivation does not necessarily make the resulting offense political. The character of the offense does not depend upon the motive of the offender but rather upon the nature of the rights it infringes.

B. Xaviere's extradition is required by general principles of international law: *aut punire, aut dedere*.

Under the Hague Convention for the Suppression of Unlawful Seizure of Aircraft of December 16, 1970, Article 8, signed by fifty nations, aerial piracy is deemed to be an extraditable offense in any extradition treaty between parties, existing and future. Piracy, genocide, slavery and war crimes are crimes against humanity, not political crimes. Extradition is, therefore, obligatory.

IV. Present Case does not Come within Recognized Requirements for Political Asylum

Botania has failed to allege facts that would bring the present case under the exception for political persecution. The act of hijacking was done merely as a protest, not as a necessary means of flight from political persecution. No hard facts have been adduced to show that Xaviere would receive prejudicial treatment before Alterian courts.

V. Failure to Try and to Punish Air Pirates Violates International Law

There are two main considerations here:

A. The UN General Assembly Resolution on Aerial Hijacking or Interference with Civil Air Travel (Resolution 2645 (XXV), November 30, 1970), Article 2, calls upon States to prosecute and to punish aerial pirates or to extradite them for prosecution and punishment. Since, under customary international law, the absence or inadequacy of municipal law is no excuse for a State not to fulfil its international obligations, Botania must grant extradition or adjust its legal sanctions against hijacking so as to bring them up to the required international standard. A State may be asked by this Court to carry out legislative revision of its penal code in order to allow for the punishment of hijackers. See General Assembly Resolution 2551 (XXIV), December 12, 1969, on Forcible Diversion of Civil Aircraft in Flight; also Article 7 of the 1970 Hague Convention, *cit. supra*. The Montreal Sabotage Convention of 1971 requires punishment or extradition of saboteurs against international civil aviation. See also *Exchange of Greek and Turkish Populations (1925)* PCIJ, *Series B, No. 10*, at p. 20.

The fact that Botania has not signed the 1970 Hague Convention does not relieve it of its liability to be bound by it and by the various UN Resolutions (e.g. 2645 and 2551) against Hijacking: the *Namibia* Advisory Opinion (1971) ICJ 6 shows that both States Members and non-State Members of the United Nations may be bound by majority resolutions of the General Assembly concerning certain fundamental legal issues like the right of self-determination. I consider that hijacking is in the same category. It is analogous to a case of *jus cogens*, that is, certain peremptory norms of general international law from which States cannot derogate: see Article 52 of the Vienna Convention on the Law of Treaties, 1969.

B. Several recent cases cited in the Plaintiff's brief support the established principles: *aut punire, aut dedere*. Jurisdiction is best exercised in the State with the most substantial connection with the crime in question.

VI. The International Court of Justice can Order the Respondent to Try the Offender in its Municipal Courts

The case, though involving criminal law, is justiciable by the Court. States are the only subjects of international law, and the treatment of slaves and pirates is not an exception to that rule. But individuals are subjects of conventional rules of international criminal law — e.g. The Tokyo and The Hague Conventions make individuals subjects of international law. The fact that pirates are triable by national courts does not deprive the offense of piracy of its international character: Kelsen's *Peace Through Law*, p. 76 (1944). Also, the ILC has enumerated the general principles of Nuremberg, pointing out that an international crime remains punishable even though no penalty is imposed by international law: 44 AJIL Supplement 125, p. 127 (1950). Hijacking is an offense against the law of nations, not merely against the particular municipal law under which the hijacker is being tried fortuitously. Failure of a State to try and to punish the offender engages its international responsibility. The International Court of Justice, therefore, has jurisdiction to ensure the asylum State's fulfilment of its international obligations. Botania should, accordingly, make adequate reparation to Alterius, the exact amount of which should be determined by this Court in accordance with the findings of the referee appointed by the Court for the purpose.

There can be no finding of *non liquet* merely because piracy is not an offense under respondent's municipal law or is not adequately dealt with by that law: Article 38 of the Statute of the Court enables it to apply "general principles of law recognized by civilized nations". The obligation that lies upon a State to punish or to extradite is no doubt performed through municipal courts, but it is an obligation owned *erga omnes*.

The respondent's objections on the grounds (a) that the matter was essentially within Botania's domestic jurisdiction and (b) that the plaintiff's action was barred by the rule against non-retroactivity (i.e. nulla poena sine lege) should be overruled by this Court, especially in view of the provision of Article 15(2) of the UN Draft International Covenant on Civil and Political Rights which says that the non-retroactivity rule "shall not prejudice the trial and punishment of any person for any act or omission which, at the time it was committed, was criminal according to the general principles of law recognized by the community of Nations". What Botania had so far done was to have conducted a mere preliminary procedure, not a full criminal trial, as required by international law. Xaviere's appearance before the magistrate had been limited to a determination of the narrow issue of his status as a "political refugee". There has been failure on the part of both the judicial and the executive authorities of Botania to act in accordance with international law.

A magistrate's hearing is procedurally inadequate to satisfy the duty of international law to try and to punish: *South-West Africa case*,

1st Phase, 1962, ICJ and also the 2nd Phase (1966) ICJ 6, at pp. 39, 47 (where the Court made a distinction between plaintiff's claim and his *locus standi* — a "universal and necessary" principle of procedural law): "General principles under Article 38 include procedural and evidentiary principles of substantive law".

VII. By its Refusal to Punish or to Extradite the Offender, Respondent State is Liable in Damages for an International Tort

There is liability for failure to act so as to ensure the safety of international travel, and reparation is payable therefore: the *Corfu Channel (Merits) case* (1948) ICJ 4.

The appellant, Alterius, has asked for U.S. $5 million as special damages for Botania's breach of its international obligation.

In the *Chorzow Factory (Indemnity) case* (1928) PCIJ, *Series A, No. 17,* at pp. 46–48, the Court held that what is necessary to make restitution is the measure of damages. In the United States-Mexico General Claims Commission in *Janes case* (1926), damages were awarded as an "indemnity" to the relatives of the murdered American national because the murderer was not punished.

The Court must consider not only the actual harm done to Alterius's aircraft, but the damage to the airline's reputation regarding the security of future passengers, since non-punishment in the instant case would lead to serious loss of customers by the Alterian airline. Besides, Alterius would be obliged to take expensive measures to prevent future acts of aerial piracy.

Alterius has as much interest to protect by this suit as has the private company which owns the commercial aircraft. A State has the right and the duty to protect its nationals, whether these be natural or artificial persons, against any form of injustice. The interest of both may coincide to the extent that an attack upon the national is an offense against the State in question.

The Court must be dynamic enough to throw its weight on the side of the modern trend towards a consensus against international aerial piracy. The Court should order Botania to extradite or punish under its own law, which must be consistent with international law, or it should be made to pay damages in the sum of U.S. $5 million.

In the view I have taken of the matter, Coronado's espousal of the cause of the estate of its national, Yellman (deceased), entitles it to claim reparation from Botania, the exact amount of which can be determined only after further details than those so far given are known. It is not considered appropriate that Yellman's Estate should be allowed to bring an independent suit against Botania. Any claim that his estate might have should be settled with its State, Coronado, out of whatever reparation Botania would make to Coronado.

Justice Sansern Kraichitti of the Supreme Court of Thailand concurs in this opinion.

NOTES

1. For Arguments of Counsel see Appendix IV.

.

PART III

Human Rights and Humanitarian Law

Chapter 9

HUMAN RIGHTS AND THE DEVELOPING COUNTRIES

I

It is probably unnecessary for us to be reminded that the germ of the idea of human rights and personal liberties is to be found in Article 1 of the United Nations Charter which enjoins the world body to promote "universal respect for, and observance of human rights and fundamental freedoms". It was mainly to fulfil this purpose of the Charter that the UN Organization, very early after its establishment, embarked upon the task of producing and adopting the Universal Declaration of Human Rights of 1948, in which are set out great principles and norms of securing respect for the rights of man everywhere in the world. So universal it is in both its content and message that it soon turned out to be regarded as a "charter of liberties" among the Member States of the UN Organization, especially the newly independent States of Africa and Asia as well as those of Latin America.[1]

These new States soon embodied in their several constitutions fairly elaborate chapters on Human Rights and Fundamental Freedoms guaranteeing the rights to life, freedom from torture or degrading or inhuman treatment, freedom from slavery or forced labor, the right to personal liberty, the right to privacy and family life, freedom of religion and all forms of worship including freedom to hold and propagate opinions, freedom of expression and of speech, freedom of association and assembly including the right to join trade unions, freedom to leave and reenter one's own country, the right of every citizen to own property and to receive adequate compensation on its compulsory acquisition for public purposes, freedom from any form of discrimination on the ground of sex, race, ethnic origin or religion, freedom of the individual to move about within the territory of his own State and live and reside anywhere therein. Other supplementary provisions are made for the further protection of the human rights of the individual in the establishment of an impartial judiciary, the conduct of free and fair elections leading to the establishment of legislatures in which all duly elected persons can participate, public service commissions to ensure fairness and equality in the right to employment in the State's public service, the institution of impartial and well-organized police forces for the maintenance of law and order within the State, and there are other arrangements of a similar character.[2]

Not all the enumerated rights will be found embodied in every one of these new constitutions; some contain more and some less. Nigeria happens to have pioneered this borrowing, not only from the Declaration of 1948 but also from such other sources as the Indian and the Pakistani constitutions; indeed, as pointed out elsewhere,[3] the Nigerian pattern became the example which the other English-speaking African States followed on securing their independence. A good deal of the detailed rules and their elaboration were borrowed from the long-established principles of English Common Law which, though it has yet to adopt a Bill of Human Rights, has always protected personal liberties under the Rule of Law concept. Similarly, many French-speaking African and Asian States borrowed from the Code Napoleon[4] and from the French Revolution ideas derived from Tom Paine's *Rights of Man*. Therefore, it was not the Universal Declaration of Human Rights of 1948 that supplied all the basic principles and precepts by which the Third World countries were guided in enshrining human rights in their constitutions within the past three decades or so. Almost all the new States went beyond the actual provisions of the 1948 Declaration. To be sure, the really detailed and specific provisions were not available in an authoritative form until the Declaration was defined and elaborated in the two epoch-making covenants — the Covenant on Economic, Social and Cultural Rights and the International Covenant on Civil and Political Rights, both entering into force only in 1976.[5]

It may be of interest here to give an outline of the principal provisions of both these covenants before we come to an analysis of the relation between promise and performance in the developing countries. The Covenant on Economic, Social and Cultural Rights provides for many of the rights already enumerated above which were not so fully spelled out by the 1948 Declaration. In addition it binds the parties to the covenant to take steps progressively to achieve the full realization of such new and basic rights as the right to work, the right to social security, the right to an adequate standard of living and of education, the right to the highest attainable standard of physical and mental health, and the right to take part in the cultural life of the nation and of the world. Many of these rights were previously regarded as desirable but legally unenforceable rights and are included in certain constitutions like those of India and Pakistan under the sections headed "Directive Principles of State Policy".

Ghana's independence constitution did not contain a chapter on Human Rights and Fundamental Freedoms, but included instead a section on Directive Principles of State Policy so as to avoid the obligation to enforcement by court action. The UN Covenant on Economic, Social and Cultural Rights, in order to ensure that this would no longer be the case, establishes a review mechanism whereby the Economic and Social Council receives reports from States parties embodying all the measures adopted, progress made and difficulties encountered in the promotion and observance of the rights guaranteed. On the receipt of such reports, the Economic and Social Council calls upon all States parties to take appropriate action to achieve the realization of the rights in question.

The other UN instrument, the International Covenant on Civil and Political Rights, again contains most of the more traditional rights already enumerated above as well as novel ones such as the right to marry. An additional safeguard is provided in an Optional Protocol which establishes a new system for ensuring the implementation of the rights guaranteed in this covenant. The Protocol entered into force on March 23, 1976. The International Covenant on Civil and Political Rights, like its counterpart, also establishes the machinery for the realization of the rights contained therein by instituting a Human Rights Committee which exists for the examination of petitions (called "communications") from individuals who allege violation of the human rights set out in the Covenant. The communications must satisfy fairly rigorous tests, including those of admissibility; each petition must not be frivolous, anonymous or incompatible with the provisions of the covenant; there must have been an exhaustion of local remedies and so on. There can be no doubt that all these procedural safeguards have been borrowed largely from the practice and experience of the European Convention of Human Rights and the European Commission of Human Rights; the third arm, the European Court of Human Rights, has not been copied for the reason that States are far from ready to go so far just yet. An alternative arrangement has, however, been made under Resolution 1503 adopted by the Economic and Social Council on May 27, 1970 instituting a working group of the Commission on Human Rights Sub-Commission on Prevention of Discrimination and Protection of Minorities which should screen all petitions or communications submitted to the United Nations together with any observations from the Member State concerned, so as to determine which of the complaints seem to disclose "a consistent pattern of gross and reliably attested violations of human rights and fundamental freedoms within the terms of reference of the Sub-Commission".

Although this alternative procedure also requires the same detailed requirements of admissibility as that under the Optional Protocol already described above, it is only voluntary and Member States are not bound to follow it. It is unnecessary to emphasize that the Protocol is binding only upon the thirteen or so States that have so far ratified it.

We have now outlined what is usually regarded as the International Bill of Human Rights, consisting of its genesis — the Universal Declaration of Human Rights — and its two complements — the Covenant of Economic, Social and Cultural Rights and the International Covenant on Civil and Political Rights.[6] It seems that the Universal Declaration of Human Rights of 1948 may come to be judged as perhaps the must important document to have emerged from the UN Organization — as the foundation of its existence and indeed its *raison d'être*.[7] If we may give a political document a biological interpretation, it is the nucleus of an organism which is in the process of rapid growth to great dimensions by its own inner dynamism. The UN architects at San Francisco planted in the Charter the seed of the idea of Human Rights as one of the cornerstones upon which the post-1945 world should be built and the Organization lost no time in drafting and adopting the Declaration of 1948, to be later supplemented with the two complementary covenants. By this single act was set in motion the unprecedented process of decolonization and the inevitable principle of the right of self-determination of peoples, thus by the one fell swoop of the adoption of this modern Magna Carta releasing the greater bulk of mankind from political bondage. Without the enlargement of the community of States into the society of States within the framework of the United Nations which only decolonization had made possible so relatively quickly since the founding of the Organization, mankind might have continued to stagnate as it did in preceding centuries, with human rights, such as they were, still limited only to a fraction of the human race.

The Declaration of 1948, in addition to the two covenants to which we have already referred, has been further supplemented by two documents which were adopted earlier. They are the Declaration on the Grant of the Rights of Independence to Colonial Territories and Peoples and the International Convention on the Elimination of all Forms of Racial Discrimination which was *unanimously* adopted by the UN General Assembly on December 21, 1965.[8] It is unnecessary either to elaborate on these epoch-making internationally recognized documents or to add a catalogue of other UN covenants and documents already adopted on the rights of women and children. Nor need we stop here to analyze how most of the activities of the United Nations and its agents and affiliated bodies have been suffused and inspired by this whole preoccupation with the promotion of human rights in the spirit of the Charter as embodied in the Universal Declaration of Human Rights. Since 1948, a new awareness is abroad within the Organization, tending to make Member States regard themselves and their citizens more and more as their "brothers' keepers". Side by side with decolonization, the United Nations has within the last two decades or so been showing increasing concern for the economic, social and cultural betterment of the new States and, through them, their citizens, under the aegis of the Economic and Social Council — the UN organ charged with overall responsibility for the realization of human rights.

II

It is generally agreed that in the field of human rights, we now have a plethora of law-making in the form of declarations, covenants and solemn UN resolutions sufficient to supply the guidelines for safeguarding the rights of man. What is still in need of our serious and continuous attention, however, is the implementation of the rules we already have on the international level. We shall, of course, consider later what we should do at the national level of States vis-à-vis their citizens.

We have mentioned the United Nations' own efforts to establish machinery for the progressive achievement of the global objective of the promotion of human rights through the Economic and Social Council, one of the principal organs of the Organization. We have in this connection briefly outlined the role of the Commission of Human Rights and its sub-commission, including the voluntary procedures and General Assembly Resolution 1503. For many years now, the idea of establishing an International Court of Human Rights has been mooted, without finding much favor with the great majority of the UN members. The reason is obvious. When the International Court of Justice, which is given such limited jurisdiction in respect of contentious cases between States, has received the support of less than one-third of the total membership of the United Nations in accordance with the Optional Clause (Article 36 of the Statute of the Court), is there any hope that States would accept a new international court of human rights with jurisdiction empowering it to entertain complaints from the individual citizens of their respective countries? It is not realistic to expect this to happen in present-day circumstances.[9] Even a more modest approach to institute a UN High Commissioner for Human Rights to supervise petitions or communications from aggrieved individuals from Member States has had little success precisely because States are understandably reluctant to entrust so sensitive an area of their sovereignty to what is to them a supra-national authority.

If the institution of judicial and investigative bodies for the promotion and enforcement of human rights has made little headway, what about regional efforts in the same direction? Unfortunately, regional attempts, with the exception of those of Europe, have not achieved any worthwhile measure of success. Europe has to its credit a European Convention of Human Rights, a Commission as well as a Court of Human Rights, albeit binding only among the nineteen Member States of the Council of Europe. This laudable complex of machinery for the implementation of human rights no doubt has its problems, but it is the only joint human effort in this field that has worked. Another regional arrangement is beset with teething troubles. We refer, of course, to the Inter-American Commission of Human Rights under the auspices of the Organization of American States and with headquarters in Washington.[10] The Commission receives complaints from individuals, from non-governmental organizations and from other governments. It began by dispatching its Executive Secretary or a Mission (and sometimes both) to the country against which complaints of violations of human rights had been made, in order to carry out an on-the-spot investigation. The Commission has had to content itself in recent years with evidence obtained from outside the State concerned, together with such comments as may be submitted thereon by that State; this is because Member States have been showing great reluctance in permitting local investigation of complaints. Indeed, the Commission would appear to have come under great pressure from Member States to limit its activities.[11]

Africa and Asia have yet to establish institutions for the promotion of human rights in both regions. The Organization of African Unity has no Declaration of Human Rights and not even a Convention. An attempt was made in 1961 when, at the First International Conference on the Rule of Law for African States, held in Lagos, Nigeria, in January of that year, 194 judges, practicing lawyers and teachers of law from twenty-three African nations as well as nine countries of other continents declared in the Law of Lagos, *inter alia*;

(a) that the fundamental human rights, especially the right to personal liberty, should be written and entrenched in the constitutions of all countries and that such personal liberty should not in peacetime be restricted without trial in a Court of Law;

(b) that in order to give full effect to the Universal Declaration of Human Rights of 1948, this Conference invites the African Governments to study the possibility of adopting an African Convention of Human Rights in such a manner that the *Conclusions* of this Conference will be safeguarded by the creation of a Court of appropriate jurisdiction and that recourse thereto be made available for all persons under the jurisdiction of the signatory States; and

(c) that in order to promote the principles and the practical application of the Rule of Law, the judges, practicing lawyers and teachers of law in African countries should take steps to establish branches of the International Commission of Jurists.[12]

Unfortunately, apart from the subsequent establishment of the African Commission of Jurists with headquarters at the Secretariat of the Organization of African Unity in 1963 after the Commission was first formally founded in Lagos by both English-speaking and French-speaking African lawyers, this enthusiastic blueprint was never implemented. The African States have not shown any readiness for this enterprise.

It remains to observe that, while certain regions of the world have still to take concrete steps to establish human rights implementation machinery, some international as well as national efforts have already been made. The first is the International Institute of Human Rights founded in Strasbourg by René Cassin, the eponymous hero of the universal protection of human rights. His great work with the United Nations in this field needs no encomium, but it is necessary to underline the significance of his initiative and foresight in establishing a forum for the education as well as edification of nations and individuals about human rights. For the failure of effort noted above in certain areas of the world, and even in areas where partial success has been achieved so far, has been the inevitable result of a lack of or insufficient education in respect of human rights and fundamental freedoms. The reluctance of States to institute machinery for the promotion and implementation of human rights, whether at the international or at the national level, can be traced in no small measure to the insufficient appreciation of the human values that are at stake.

This noble example of the René Cassin Institute has quite recently been followed by a few States, notably the United Kingdom, which now has the British Institute of Human Rights. It is somewhat ironical that a country, with a justifiably proud record in the field of the Rule of Law and human rights, should not only be one of the cornerstones of the European Commission and the European Court of

Human Rights but also one of the first to establish an Institute of
Human Rights. It is probably because of the René Cassin Institute
that France, another redoubtable defender of the rights of man, has
not weighed in with its own national institute of human rights. There
is no doubt that other countries, including the developing ones, will
sooner or later take a cue from their more developed counterparts in
establishing at least some modest institutions for the promotion of
human rights in their part of the world.

The UN Organization has itself, however, struck boldly in the
direction of promoting the dissemination of knowledge about human
rights, particularly in developing countries, by the holding of joint
seminars with their governments; for example, Seminars on Human
Rights on Developing Countries were held in Kabul (Afghanistan) in
May 1964,[13] in Dakar (Senegal) in February 1966[14] and in Dar-es-
Salaam (Tanzania) in October-November 1973,[15] each having been
devoted to the problems and needs of the various regions concerned.
The seminar in Tanzania was held specifically on the Study of New
Ways and Means of Promoting Human Rights in Africa. Other
significant seminars have been held; for example, the one in Teheran
discussed human rights on a worldwide basis and the conference was
well-attended. The International Institute of Human Rights in
Strasbourg, in collaboration with the International Commission of
Jurists and the International Association of Democratic Lawyers, held
an International Conference on Namibia and Human Rights at
Dakar early in January 1976 at the invitation of the Senegalese
Government and under the sponsorship of the UN Commissioner for
Namibia. The delegates included many African representatives, a
number of national liberation movements, particularly the South
West Africa Peoples' Organization (SWAPO), and several inter-
governmental and non-governmental organizations; there were also
several individual experts and well-known jurists in the field of
human rights from all parts of the world. The two significant
documents resulting from the Conference were the Declaration of
Dakar on Namibia and Human Rights embodying specific principles
of human rights, and a Program of Action calling upon States, non-
governmental organizations and intergovernmental organizations to
do all in their power to secure early independence for Namibia.[16]

We have probably now given a sufficient outline of the various
efforts, both universal and regional, that have been and continue to
be made to establish institutions and machinery for the promotion of
human rights, especially for the dissemination of knowledge and
understanding of the rules and the procedures that have been laid
down. The educational values of the institutes and the seminars are

incalculable if the end we all so much desire is to be rightly sought after.

III

Let us next examine the gap between promise and performance. As we have noted above, the UN Declaration of 1948 as well as its complementing covenants have been the models upon which most independence constitutions and organic laws have been patterned. As the various UN seminars have revealed, however, the reactions of the several regions have not always coincided, in that there have been some varying degrees of emphasis. But the keynote appears to the present writer to have been rightly struck in the following passage from the Kabul seminar report:

> It was considered as self-evident by all the speakers that the existence of adequate material means and a high standard of economic development were essential prerequisites of the full and effective enjoyment of economic, social and cultural rights, and contributed to the promotion of civil and political rights. As was pointed out by several speakers, man needed to be adequately fed and clothed before he could be realistically expected to concern himself fully with human rights. To mention only one instance which was stressed by several speakers, the right to work was meaningless in countries where employment opportunities were grossly inadequate owing to overpopulation combined with economic under-development.[17]

This view is basic to any proper appraisal of the problems of human rights in developing countries. While the statement is largely true in the case of many of the economic and cultural rights, it is not necessarily true of most social and political rights which require other criteria than the possession or lack of wealth; indeed, to make the enjoyment of such rights dependent upon wealth is positively harmful and may be a clear negation of individual human rights. We may illustrate from the same publication this excerpt with regard to the Right to a Fair Trial:

> It was pointed out that the right to a fair trial presupposed the definition of all criminal offences by law and the giving of publicity for such laws. Criminal law should not be retroactive. Some speakers thought that delegations of power by the legislative organs to the executive, especially in the field of criminal law, were potentially very dangerous for human rights, if such delegations of power were too broadly worded and did not provide for a strict control of the legality of regulations by the courts.[18]

Similarly, the Seminar recorded this view:

There was a general agreement that there should be no distinction between the developed and the developing countries in the recognition of the right of everyone to freedom of opinion and expression and freedom of information.[19]

At the second seminar held in Dakar in 1966, again under the United Nations' auspices, much the same grounds were canvassed as at Kabul. The emphasis was on the establishment of the institutions and procedures for ensuring the promotion of and respect for human rights in developing countries, although certain rights such as the right to own property, the right to education, freedom from slavery or torture, freedom from unlawful arrest, the right to a fair hearing, to participate in political activities and to choose one's employment were first discussed. One noticeable feature of the Dakar seminar was that, while most delegates acknowledged the principle of the right to own property subject to certain restrictions on its exercise, the question whether the Western concept of the right was applicable to Africa gave rise to a very lively debate:

The Universal Declaration of Human Rights of 1948 was itself challenged. Some speakers wondered whether the Declaration corresponded with the present state of society in the Third World. After raising doubts about this, the speaker expressed the view that the economic and political requirements of Africa could not be met within the framework of the Declaration. He pointed out that changes were taking place in the concept of property and recalled that, at the international level, the Protocol to the Rome Convention of 1950 had already gone beyond the principles of the Universal Declaration and contained a provision according to which the right to own property should be subject to its use in the general interest. Another participant pointed out that, as the Universal Declaration dated from 1948, it did not therefore take into account the problems raised by the independence of African countries. Furthermore, it had been drawn up on the basis of the ideas and needs of States whose economic and social structures were radically different from those of the African countries. Yet another participant proposed that in view of the obstacles to development which might arise from the principles of the Universal Declaration relating to property, the Seminar should call for a revision of the 1948 Declaration in order to adapt it to African realities.[20]

Surely, the short answer to this type of argument is that the Declaration lays down only broad principles of action which are adaptable to differing circumstances irrespective of date or clime and that, in any case, many African States have already made all the adjustments which their particular situations demanded so long as the fundamental issue of fairness to individual property-owners and public interests are safeguarded. There are many Asian and African legal systems that allow free scope to succession and inheritance, side by side with modern mores and laws in these areas.

The Tanzanian seminar of 1973 presented yet another twist to the human rights debate. Representatives from Africa, Europe, the specialized agencies, the Economic Commission for Africa, UNITAR, the UN High Commissioner for Refugees and a number of African liberation movements invited by the host Government were present. The seminar was, at the invitation of the Tanzanian Government, organized by the UN Secretary-General under the program of advisory services in the field of human rights established by General Assembly Resolutions 926 (X) for the study of suitable activities which could be undertaken in celebration of the 25th Anniversary of the Universal Declaration of Human Rights. In addition to a few rights like the right to work, the right to an adequate standard of living, the right to health and to education, and cultural rights, the delegates discussed at some length the right of self-determination, stressing in particular the right to political independence, and the question of sovereignty over natural resources. Speakers maintained that "until all African peoples could freely determine their political status, freely pursue their economic, social and cultural development, and freely dispose of the natural wealth and resources of their countries, talk of other political rights was merely academic . . . the right to self-determination was an inherent and legal right, and no judicial machinery existed whereby it might be protected[21] . . . Denial of the right . . . was the most serious problem of the continent.[22] Rather ominously, the seminar added: "It was the consensus of opinion that unless the right of self-determination was attained by African peoples still under colonial domination, there would be continuing violations of human rights".[23] The seminar also made another pronouncement of great interest:

> With regard to the question of sovereignty over natural resources, some participants expressed the view that the problem raised by foreign investment and the granting of special privileges to non-citizens and foreign corporations were inherited problems which could not be solved by reference to United Nations human rights instruments. The primary task of the African countries was to remove all privileges and to permit all to share equally . . . .[24]

The seminar did not recommend expropriation, but it would seem to favour joint exploitation under OAU auspices. How exactly this would be carried out was not stated. The problems of refugees were next discussed and it was pointed out that "there was an urgent need for ratification by African States of the UN Convention and Protocol Relating to the Status of Refugees of 1967, and to the OAU Convention Governing the Specific Aspects of Refugee Problems in Africa of 1969. There was also a need . . . to establish special

procedures in order to establish the bona fides of refugees and others
requesting asylum in view of the problems of security faced by the
host countries".[25] Because of its importance to the question of human
rights, we may quote the following passage which shows that some at
least of the participants indicated some unease about denial of human
rights within certain African countries:

> Some participants referred to problems arising out of conflicts in personal law,
> inheritance law and nationality law, as well as to the conflicts arising out of
> differences between modern legislation and customary law. Others mentioned the
> problems arising from the persistence of ancient customs and traditions, such as
> the payment of brideprice, the inheritance of widows and the exploitation of child
> labor. Reference was also made to conflicts which arose out of confusion between
> the State itself and the Government of the State. It was pointed out that
> frequently legitimate efforts of individuals to influence or change the regime in
> power had been construed as being directed against the authority of the State,
> and the individual had been censured or punished for exercising a perfectly
> legitimate political right.[26]

There are two major issues here: one is the extent to which certain
internal customs and practices should be harmonized with the
requirements of human rights, and the other is the exploitation of
human beings, for example, through permission of child labor and the
inhuman treatment meted out to those who voice dissent or wish to
change a government by peaceful means. While the first problem can
be solved by the adoption of remedial laws such as many African
States have introduced in more recent times, the second question
would seem to be one of the thorny problems of contemporary
government in the Third World as a whole, namely, the need for
present rulers to appreciate that attempts to secure a change of
government, provided the means adopted is legitimate, are not
necessarily bad in themselves and should not result in the ruthless
suppression of human rights to participate in the achievement of
political changes from time to time. The crucial question is to be sure
at the same time that those who wish to change a government in fact
adopt a legitimate method of achieving that goal.

IV

It must not be supposed, however, that the countries of the Third
World, although they have not established effective regional human
rights machinery, have been insensitive to the clarion call of the
Universal Declaration of Human Rights of 1948. We have already

noted the widespread incorporation, in Third World constitutions, of most of the principles embodied in the International Bills of Human Rights and, in many well-known cases, municipal legislation has been enacted to make the local laws conform to the requirements of international standards. In particular, the criminal law and procedure has been the area in which great attention deserves to be, and has in some cases been, paid to human rights issues.[27]

A number of the developing countries have established two major reforms of their criminal law and procedure in recent years. These reforms are the institutions of Legal Aid and of the Ombudsman or Parliamentary Commissioner. Hitherto, there has hardly been a legal aid scheme to assist impecunious litigants in civil matters and only in murder cases was there any provision for the defendant or the accused. As a corollary to the constitutional provisions for the protection of human rights to be found in many developing countries, legal aid must be seen as one of the best means of guaranteeing and implementing these rights, if they are to have any meaning at all. Unfortunately, perhaps largely on the ground of the expense likely to be involved but also because of natural reluctance on the part of governments because they might be subsidizing litigation or even subversion against themselves if accused persons were given any financial assistance, legal aid is still not a popular means of protecting human rights in developing countries. And, yet, here is an important area where, both nationally and internationally, better and more thoughtful education and widespread practice in the field of human rights could be of positive value.[28]

The Ombudsman institution is similarly not popular with many developing countries and this is not surprising because, apart from his Scandinavian habitat, the Parliamentary Commissioner is not yet a popular phenomenon in Europe. There are only a very few countries in Africa and Asia that have adopted the institution and even then, with the usual limitations either that the Ombudsman must carry out his functions through his Member of Parliament or Assembly, or that he must confine his task to local government officials. In either case, his annual report is subject to Parliamentary surveillance. But, in spite of these limitations, the institution of Ombudsman, if properly run and efficiently directed, could be very useful in checking ministerial or other official abuses of power in relation to human rights.

While on this subject, we may note that a few developing countries have also established and regularly operate a system of Public Officers Complaints Bureaus, thus enabling individual citizens to report, *inter alia*, cases of violation of human rights or other abuses to an inspectorate network of highly qualified officials of proven integrity and dedication.

An institution which is a logical complement of this, and which has been established in Britain and probably elsewhere, is the Police Complaints Board to which police officers may be reported by aggrieved citizens either for abuse of power or for corruption in the discharge of their functions.[29] This system is in addition to, not a substitute for, the other means, and arrangements of protecting individual rights so far enumerated. The justification for singling out the police officers for this special form of surveillance is that on them primarily depends the promotion and implementation of human rights and fundamental freedoms at the grassroots level. An honest and efficient police force is indispensable to every civilized system of administration of justice under law.

V

There are some countries in the Third World which, partly because of a fairly long experience of parliamentary practice and Rule of Law, have managed to show respect for human rights to an acceptable degree. These have tried to preserve, in many instances, more than the outward forms of democratic practices and standards. Many now have military regimes that have established tribunals trying even purely civil offenders, while some of these States have avoided such tribunals, preferring to maintain the ordinary judicial processes according to the Rule of Law. For instance, Nigeria may be mentioned as one such country and it is to its credit that, when the military regime took over in 1966 and set aside most of the constitution, the constitutional provisions relating to fundamental human rights were expressly preserved and are still applied and protected by the country's judiciary. Much the same position exists in Ghana. In both countries, it must be admitted, however, that military trials of soldiers have been held before military tribunals from time to time.

Of the non-military regimes, the Ivory Coast, Senegal, the Cameroons, India (despite the recent unhappy interlude), Malaysia, Singapore and a few other Asian and South-East Asian States and some Latin American countries like Venezuela and Mexico, are regarded, by and large, as democratic and respectful of human rights. There are occasional dark spots here and there, but the general picture in each of these States is tolerably passable and should improve if there is no reversal of the situation.

On the other hand, military or military-backed regimes like Chile,[30] Argentina, Brazil, Colombia and Uruguay have not come out well in recent reports on human rights violations or alleged violations, whether at the United Nations or at non-governmental international bodies like the International Commission of Jurists or Amnesty International. Chile is reported to have refused even an investigating mission from the United Nations to enter the country to carry out an on-the-spot assessment of the situation.[31]

There is a question whether Angola's public trial of a group of captured mercenaries is or is not an instance of the observance of the Rule of Law. Uganda has in recent times had a consistently bad press concerning allegations of murders and fratricides. We need not lay it on too thickly regarding that much-troubled country's current problems.[32] Nor must we linger over the well-worn but nevertheless ignoble tales of man's inhumanity to man constituted by the practice of apartheid in Zimbabwe, Namibia and South Africa. All we can hope is that practical meaning and reality will be given quite soon to the International Convention on The Suppression and Punishment of the Crime of Apartheid which came into force on July 18, 1976 and which proclaims apartheid, like genocide, to be a "crime against humanity".[33] The subject of apartheid has been discussed *ad nauseam*, in the United Nations, in all seminars and conferences on human rights and self-determination, in almost all Third World thinking and activities, so much so that one might say that implementation of human rights is synonymous with abolition of apartheid.

We may now turn to one problem that deserves a brief comment in the context of practices in the field of human rights in developing countries. The problem of one-party States in relation to human rights was discussed recently at an international seminar in Tanzania. The moot point is to determine to what extent, if at all, human rights are compatible with one-party States, of which there are many in the developing countries. The International Commission of Jurists organized the seminar with the approval of the Tanzanian Government whose national representative presided over the meeting held in private and attended only by the invitees of the Commission. The meeting was held in Dar-es-Salaam from September 23–28, 1976; the six States that participated were Sudan, Tanzania, Zambia, Botswana, Lesotho and Swaziland. The report on the seminar is still awaited from the Commission with which an understanding had been reached beforehand that it should only be released with the consent and as approved by the Governments of the six participating States. Meanwhile, it may be asked if it is a fact that military regimes do not raise the same type of problems of human rights as do one-party

States. The question is a loaded one.

Another question of contemporary relevance to the human rights issue in developing countries is the existence of or the extent to which one can say that there is a right to struggle for freedom as well as the right to be helped to achieve it. The Organization of African Unity as well as similar bodies in the Third World maintain that the right of self-determination is meaningless without both of these necessarily concomitant rights. Professor Ronzilli recently advanced the view that the UN General Assembly Declaration on Friendly Relations has created "a new rule of international law forbidding States to use force to suppress national liberation movements . . ."; a similar conclusion was reached by Dr. Toman in his own "La conception sovietique des guerres de liberation nationale".[34] There is no direct provision in the International Bills of Human Rights on the subject of liberation movements, but even the UN Organization is known to have welcomed movement representatives to a number of General Assembly meetings.

VI

Summary and Conclusions

We have now arrived at the stage at which we can say that all human rights questions must be discussed and analyzed from the standpoint of the UN's Universal Declaration of Human Rights of 1948 and its supplementary international covenants and declarations on the subject. In the light of this collective International Bill of Human Rights we have noted the various efforts already and still being made at the international level to implement the quite substantial laws and institutions that have been respectively laid down and established. The procedures have not yet received universal or even widespread acceptance among the States which are still reluctant to welcome any supranational authority in this field as in others under contemporary international law. The worthwhile examples of the European Court of Human Rights and of the Court of the European Communities have yet to be followed in other regional bodies and in the United Nations. In this regard, the developing countries have a good leeway to make up, since institutional structures under a regional convention like a Court of Human Rights or even a Commission of Human Rights have not been established or effectively established for the protection of individual freedoms. We have outlined, at the State level, what several developing countries have achieved, or failed to achieve, especially in the matter of criminal law and procedure insofar as the various individual rights are concerned.

It must be admitted that, despite what has been done at both international and national levels, not enough public debate at seminars and conferences on human rights and their observances has taken place among the countries of the Third World. This over-cautious approach might be out of sympathy for the under-standable preoccupation of many developing countries with the acute problems of development and decolonization; it might also be for fear of wounding their susceptibilities, since they are often intolerant of criticism of many of their actions or inactions within their State borders. One sometimes wonders whether, when condemning — and quite rightly so — the atrocious things being done in Zimbabwe, Namibia and South Africa, we may not spare a thought for the improvement of the human conditions in our own individual countries. It seems that, with the liberation of Southern Africa in sight, there should from now on be increasing public discussion of issues of human rights in developing countries, even if, to begin with, it is only in respect of purely non-economic rights.[35]

Such a shift in emphasis, if imaginatively handled by the UN bodies and other international organizations, could lead to the making of a greater cooperative endeavor in the sober examination of the rules and procedures already laid down in order to see whether, as we have noted above, there is any real justification to consider the suggestion that the Declaration be revised, or whether it is we who should readjust our thinking and perspectives about some of the problems in the way of implementation in our respective countries.

The educational role of the Declaration and its supporting covenants, declarations and resolutions should certainly be intensified by their wide dissemination and through comparative studies, participation in which at both high and low levels of every community in every State ought to secure. In view of the record of the regional differences noted in the foregoing survey of the human rights field today, it seems that we must remind ourselves of the pioneering words of the General Assembly when, on December 10, 1948, it proclaimed the Universal Declaration of Human Rights "as a common standard of achievement for all peoples and all nations, to the end that every individual and every organ of society, keeping this Declaration constantly in mind, shall strive by teaching and education to promote respect for these rights and freedoms and by progessive measures, national and international, to secure their universal and effective recognition and observance, both among the peoples of Member States themselves and among the peoples of territories under their jurisdiction".[36] When greater maturity has been gained as a result of the education and edification of both developed and developing countries, especially the latter, there will be less and less of man's inhumanity to man in the world of today. This inhumanity may arise from oppression or discrimination or domination, and may be practiced in any country after decolonization is over. As Lord Wright once had occasion to warn us:

> The civilized nations have abolished slavery in the economic sense but the world now presents the appalling spectacle of a new slavery, the slavery of the spirit. Freedom to think and to believe and to say what we deem right, subject only to the recognition of the same freedom on the part of others — that is the charter of liberty which our ancestors won for us, not without toil and tears. That same liberty we now see threatened by a new tyranny which seeks to reduce the citizen to a soulless machine, to moral and intellectual servitude. But whether it takes the form of the dictatorship of the despot or of the ruthless domination of one section of the community over the others, it is the sworn foe of justice.[37]

To the same end, it is clear, is directed the message of the Secretary-General of the United Nations on December 10, 1975 at the Human Rights Day observance, when he said, *inter alia*:

> There are many ways to help promote human rights . . . We must bring an end to ccolonialism . . . We must wipe out racial discrimination. We must insist upon equal rights for women and a broader recognition of the rights of the child. We must promote equal treatment of minorities and of disadvantaged groups. We also have a duty to give more meaning to basic human rights by doing more to meet basic human needs and to assure greater equity in the use of available resources.[38]

These are no doubt large tasks set for us all to undertake. The problems are complex and, indeed, daunting. But, to improve the human condition, we must persevere.

NOTES

1. See, generally, M. Moskowitz's *Human Rights and World Order*, 1953, New York.

2. For a typical example of these constitutional provisions see my "The New Constitution of Nigeria and the Protection of Human Rights and Fundamental Freedoms" in *The Judicial Review*, 1960, Vol. II, No. 2, pp. 30–46; see also M. Moskowitz's *Human Rights and World Order*, 1953, New York, pp. 25–26.

3. Elias: *Nigeria — Development of its Laws and Constitution*, 1967, Stevens and Sons Ltd., London, pp. 165–167.

4. See e.g. G. Mangin's "Problems of the Judiciary in the 'Communaute' in Africa" in the *Journal of the International Commission of Jurists*, Vol. II, No. 2, pp. 75–94, *passim*, and in particular at p. 81: "the principle of the separation of powers would be applied in penal matters and the indigenous peoples would enjoy the same guarantees of personal liberty as the French".

5. For a fairly detailed summary account of the two covenants see Elias', *Africa and the Development of International Law*, 1972, pp. 188–201.

6. See Frank Newman's article entitled "The International Bill of Human Rights: Does it exist?" in which the author argues that it does and points out that its content is to be found in the UN Declaration and the two covenants which, according to him, interpret the human rights provisions of the Charter and thus, through the Charter, are binding on Member States. (See Antonio Cassese's *Current Problems of International Law: Essays on the UN and the Law of Armed Conflict*, Milan, 1975, Chapter III.)

7. As far back as 1929, the *Institut de droit international* published a Declaration of the International Rights of Man proclaiming, *inter alia*, "that the juridical conscience of the civilized world demands the recognition for the individual of rights preserved from all infringements on the part of the State; that it is important to extend to the entire world international recognition of the rights of man", *A.J.I.L.*, 1941, p. 662.

8. For an account of US policy regarding this Covenant see Nathanson and Schwelb's *The U.S. and the U.N. Treaty on Racial Discrimination: A Report for the Panel on International Human Rights Law and its Implementation*, St. Paul, West Publishing Company, 1975, pp. 94ff. A.S.I.L. Studies in Transnational Legal Policy No. 9.

9. US resistance to the ratification of UN Human Rights Conventions was under discussion. An example of the attitude of powerful States is shown in the remarks of Senator Bricker from Ohio: "There are two reasons, Mr. Chairman, why the Senate Joint Resolution has attracted such widespread support. The American people want to make certain that no treaty or executive agreement will be effective to deny or abridge their fundamental rights. Also they do not want their basic rights to be supervised or controlled by international agencies over which they have no control"; (Hearings on S.J.I. and 43 before the Sub-Committee of the Senate Committee on the Judiciary, 83rd Cong., 1st Session 1 *et seq.*, 1953.

10. There is an Inter-American Declaration of Human Rights based on the UN model of 1948.

11. See *The Journal of the International Commission of Jurists*, No. 16, June 1976, pp. 23–24 where an account is given of three disturbing examples of the findings of the Commission in respect of torture in Brazil, illegal execution and detention in Cuba and illegal killings and torture of persons in Chile following the military coup there in 1973.

12. *The Journal of the International Commission of Jurists*, Vol. III, No. 1, p. 10. The "Conclusions" referred to in the text of the Resolution are stated in pp. 11–15, and the Conclusions of the International Congress of Jurists on the Rule of Law are given in an appendix at pp. 16–18. Draft outline for the National Reports for the African Conference on the Rule of Law entitled "Human Rights and Government Security — the Legislative, the Executive and the Judiciary" is at pp. 19–21. Gabriel D'Arboussier of Senegal wrote on "Significance of the Lagos Conference" at pp. 22–24 on behalf of French-speaking delegates.

13. See ST/TAO/HR21. Kabul, 1964.

14. ST/TAO/HR25. Senegal, 1966.

15. ST/TAO/HR. 48, Tanzania, 1973.

16. The Declaration deplored, in particular, the use of the veto by the United States, the United Kingdom and France to prevent the adoption by the Security Council of three resolutions attempting to impose sanctions against South Africa for

its continued illegal occupation of Namibia. The General Assembly adopted a resolution in 1976 inviting the Economic and Social Council to examine the "Consequences of the Use of the Veto" by France, the United Kingdom and the United States on the enjoyment of human rights by oppressed Africans, *UN Press Release WS/791*, 3 December 1976.

17. ST/TAO/HR21., para 133.

18. Ibid., para. 71.

19. Ibid., para. 97.

20. ST/TAO/HR25., para. 92.

21. It is only fair to point out that the judicial situation has changed for the better since the advisory opinion in the *Namibia case* (*I.C.J. Reports 1971*, p. 16) and the *Genocide Convention case* (*I.C.J. Reports 1951*, p. 15).

22. ST/TAO/HR.48, paras. 43 and 44.

23. Ibid., para. 47.

24. Ibid., para. 46.

25. Ibid., paras. 48–50.

26. Ibid., para. 60.

27. See International Bar Association: Ombudsman & Other Complaint Handling Systems Survey, 1975–1976 U.S.A. Pennsylvania.

28. See Cappelletti, M. et al.: *Toward Equal Justice: A Comparative Study of Legal Aid in Modern Societies*, Oceana, 1975, for an imaginative treatment of the subject.

29. See Police Act, 1976.

30. Compare what happened recently at Strasbourg when the United Kingdom was put on trial on a charge of torture in Northern Ireland. Could this have taken place in Africa, Asia or Latin America? Of course, it must be admitted that Europe has come a long way to this very modern position only recently attained by the nineteen member countries of the Council of Europe.

31. The UN *Ad Hoc* Working Group on Human Rights in Chile recommended the setting up of a UN Fund to aid people in Chile who were persecuted under the "stage of siege" legislation. Hundreds of witnesses and extensive documentation supported the Group's conclusion in its report that there had been no sign of progress in the restoration of human rights in Chile. The Chilean Government described the report as based on "fictions" and "flights of fancy" about torture and abuse of power in the country, *UN Press Release WS/787* of 5 November 1976, p. 6.

32. E.g. the country's then Chief Justice disappeared without trace and the Archbishop died in a motor car incident, both in rather mysterious circumstances.

33. See *UN Chronicle, February 1977, Vol. XIV*, p. 15, 21, 29. In this connection, it may be recalled that the ECOSOC agreed to arrangements for the preparatory sub-committee established in May 1976 for the World Conference to Combat Racism and Racial Discrimination scheduled to take place in Accra, Ghana in 1978 (ibid., p. 20).

34. See Antonio Cassese's *Current Problems of International Law: Essays on the UN and the Law of Armed Conflict*, Milan 1975; also Prof. Ronzilli in the 11th Essay and Dr. J. Toman in the 12th Essay.

35. The International Labor Organization is doing a magnificent job of education and persuasion in this area, especially in developing countries. See "The ILO

Examination of Human Rights Situations", *International Commission of Jurists Journal*, No. 12, pp. 40–49.

36. See *The Impact of the Universal Declaration of Human Rights*, United Nations Sales No. 1953, XIV, 1; and René Cassin's Preface to M. Moskowitz's *Human Rights and World Order*, New York, 1958. Professor Cassin was a former Chairman of the UN Commission on Human Rights and one of the architects of the Declaration.

37. Lord Wright: *Legal Essays and Addresses*, London, 1945.

38. HRD/108, 110; G.A./5544; SG/SM/2393; Note No. 4032.

Chapter 10

DEVELOPMENT OF INTERNATIONAL HUMANITARIAN LAW

Introduction

If customary international law may be dated back to the break-up of Western Christendom following the Treaty of Westphalia in 1648, the development of the relatively much more recent branch of it now termed International Humanitarian Law may be regarded as having begun with the Geneva Convention of 1864. No doubt some rudimentary forms and norms applying to inter-State relations antedated 1648 in the case of customary international law, just as some of the notions underlying modern international law may be discerned in the concepts and practices of "just" and "unjust" wars as adumbrated in the writings of the Schoolmen in the Middle Ages.[1]

Since at least the time of Hugo Grotius[2] when distinctions were first made between war and peace, the notion of the difference between just and unjust or lawful and unlawful wars would seem to have led to the speculation as to whether just or lawful wars sanctioned the inhumane manner of their execution while unjust and unlawful wars did not. It is not quite clear from the literature on the subject that the historical dichotomy between war and peace has yielded any sufficient evidence that the conduct of war, whether regarded as just or unjust, lawful or unlawful, has produced any detailed rules or norms of humanitarian principles applicable in particular instances.[3]

According to recorded history, the Crusades and other religious wars between the 12th and 16th centuries must often have been fought with such ferocity and ruthlessness that humanitarian considerations for combatants and non-combatants alike would have counted for little in these old-world struggles for men's souls and goods.

Under the traditional laws of war, the requirements of reciprocity based upon a balance of power meant that war was a continuation of politics by other means and that any necessary use of force or wanton acts of cruelty might obstruct any eventual peace settlement. Also failure by belligerents to respect non-belligerents could result in a war between two States developing into a total war. The traditional laws of war, if they made any real distinction at all between just and unjust wars, would have been concerned more with the *origin* of the conflict rather than with the scope and *manner* of their execution.[4] It soon became necessary that the freedom of States to resort to war, a *jus ad bellum*, was qualified by the principle of some restraint in the conduct of armed forces; a *jus in bello*.[5] Clearly, this trend shows the inadequacy of such a law of war and the need for more definite and more meaningful rules based upon developed humanitarian principles. The rules of warfare, so long as they permitted the use of force or any other violent means to achieve the absolute defeat of the enemy as quickly as possible were later modified only by considerations of *humanity*, which was against violence and cruelty, and by *chivalry*, which dictated some degree of fairness in both offensive and defensive warfare.[6] This is, of course, no longer the case,[7] but the historical evolution is worth noting.

Since about at least the 17th century, however, numerous treaties have been concluded between States concerning the treatment of each other's wounded and the exemption of army surgeons from detention or imprisonment. But there was no customary law on the subject until 1863 except one which prohibited the killing, mutilation or ill-treatment of the wounded. It fell to the lot of Jean Henry Dunant to initiate a change for the better. As a Swiss citizen from Geneva, he had been an eyewitness to the Battle of Solferino in 1859 and seen thousands of wounded die who would not have died had they been better looked after. He published a pamphlet entitled "Un souvenir de Solferino" in 1861 and a second edition in 1863. In consequence of this publication, an International Congress under the joint auspices of the Geneva *Société d'Utilité Publique* and the Presidency of Gustave Moynier, was held in Geneva in 1863 to consider the greatly felt need for better arrangements for tending the wounded on the battlefield. Following this Congress, the Swiss Government invited all European and several American States to a congress in Geneva in 1864, which resulted in the adoption of the Convention for the Amelioration of the Condition of Soldiers wounded in Armies in the Field, signed on August 22, 1864. The better known First Hague Conference in 1899 built partly upon this foundation.[8] Soon after the ratification of this 1864 Geneva Convention, its principles were adapted to the requirements of naval warfare in non-ratified additional Articles of 1868, nine of which attempted to fill the gap. The object was not achieved, however, until the special and more definitive Hague Convention of 1899.[9]

The Hague Conventions and Regulations, 1899 and 1907: Beginnings of International Humanitarian Law

It was at the Hague Peace Conference of 1899 that the Powers met to discuss the codification of the laws of war. The Conference adopted a Convention which was ratified by most of the participants. The Convention was later revised by the Second Peace Conference of 1907, its place being taken by Convention IV which made it clear that it was not intended as a complete code of the laws regarding land warfare. Customary law still governs cases not covered by it. Convention IV is usually referred to as the Hague Regulations, which are intended to be binding upon the belligerants, although they are not exhaustive. They form the basis upon which the signatory Powers are expected to frame their instructions to their respective armed forces. Article I provides as follows: "The High Contracting Parties shall issue instructions to their armed land forces, which shall be in conformity with the Regulations respecting the Laws and Customs of War on Land annexed to the present Convention." It should, however, be noted that Article 2 which contains the so-called "general participation clause" provides that the Regulations shall be binding upon the contracting Powers only in respect of wars between the Parties *inter se*, and shall not apply in wars to which non-contracting Powers take part.

There were three Hague Declarations concerning expanding bullets, projectiles and explosives launched from balloons, and projectiles diffusing asphyxiating or deleterious gases. There was also the Hague Convention for the adaptation to sea warfare of the principles of the Geneva Convention of 1864, which was revised by the Second Peace Conference and the Hague Conventions of 1907 concerning the commencement of hostilities, the status of enemy merchantmen at the outbreak of hostilities and their conversion into men of war, the laying of automatic submarine contact mines, the bombardment of naval forces in time of war, certain restrictions on the exercise of the right of capture in maritime war, and the rights and duties of neutral Powers and persons in land and sea warfare.

The codification of the laws of war in these Hague Conventions and the Regulations represents the first almost universal attempt at laying down general principles regulating the conduct of armed conflicts, especially as regards the treatment of the victims of wars by the belligerents. These are placed under certain rules of behavior, in that they must respect undefended civilian populations in towns and villages; belligerents are also to respect those that have belligerent status, and are required to take certain measures in occupied territories for the protection of their non-combatant inhabitants. Also carefully laid down are the rights and duties of neutral States and their personnel in time of war.

The Hague Conventions and Regulations, for all their good intentions and purposes, contain inadequate provisions for giving effect to the rules prescribed therein. This is despite the fact that the Protecting Power system was established towards the end of the 19th century to enable a non-belligerent State to undertake to supervise the operation of the laws of war as they are applied to the nationals of weaker States in armed conflicts between belligerent States. We shall return later to this important development in international humanitarian law.

Development of International Humanitarian Law between the Two World Wars

The laws of war that were first regulated by international action in 1864, thanks to the pioneering initiative of Jean Henry Dunant, were codified in a fairly comprehensive manner at the First and Second Hague Conferences in 1899 and 1907. A number of important additions and improvements to the Hague Conventions and Regulations continued to be made after the end of the First World War in 1918, largely as a result of the experiences gained during the conflict itself. The Treaty of Versailles may in a sense be the beginning of the changed attitude of the conquerors and the vanquished alike to the often irremediable catastrophe of wars produced by the madness of men.

Under the League Covenant an attempt was made to limit the resort to war by introducing a system of collective security which, however, lacked the necessary universality to make it work. This serious defect was shown, for instance, by the failure of application of sanctions in 1936 during the Italo-Ethiopian War.

In 1923, an International Commission for the Revision of the Rules of Warfare drew up a few Rules on Air Warfare in which an attempt to limit aerial bombardment to military objects was made, but these rules never became law. In 1925, a Conference adopted a Protocol on the Prohibition of the Use in War of Asphyxiation, Poisonous or Other Gases and of Bacteriological Methods of Warfare. It was, however, doubted by some whether the Protocol bound non-parties.

In 1928 the Kellogg Pact outlawed war as a means of national policy, except for self-defense. This Treaty, though nearly universal in scope and intendment, has remained in doubt as to whether it is binding on non-parties. But whereas the law before World War I made no distinction between offensive and defensive wars, the Pact nevertheless provided a test of the lawfulness of resort to war.

In 1929, at the instance of the International Committee of the Red Cross, two Conventions were adopted, namely the Convention on the Amelioration of the Condition of Wounded and Sick in Armed Forces in the Field and on Prisoners of War. These instruments marked useful improvements in the development of humanitarian ideas in armed conflicts. In 1936, the London Protocol was adopted concerning the use of submarines against merchant vessels; the London Naval Treaty of 1930 provided in Part IV that, in the Parties' action with regard to merchant ships, submarines were required to conform to the established rules of customary international law governing surface vessels, and that, *inter alia*, "except in case of persistent refusal to stop on being summoned, or of active resistance to visit or search a warship, whether surface or submarine, may not sink or render incapable of navigation a merchant vessel without having first placed passengers, crew and ship's papers in a place of safety". It was provided that the Treaty shall remain in force without any time limit.[10]

The intervention of the war of 1939–45 gave international humanitarian law such a jolt that mankind was obliged to take another serious look at the whole field of the laws and usages of warfare. The most important steps were the Geneva Conventions of 1949, but certain tentative conclusions had already been reached before that date.

Growth of Humanitarian Law under the UN Charter and Practice and Under the Geneva Conventions of 1949

As soon as the Second World War came to an end, the first important steps were taken under the Charter of the United Nations which in Article 2 (4) extended the Kellogg Pact (1928) prohibition of the resort to force to the threat and use of force for the settlement of international disputes. Articles 51, 53, 103 and 107 contained express limitations in the interest of collective defence under UN auspices for the maintenance of world peace. Another step taken by the United Nations was the unanimous adoption by the General Assembly in 1947 of the Nuremberg Principles which embodied the rulings of the International Military Tribunal (Nuremberg) set up under the London Charter of 1945. Branches of the laws of war were thus extended to crimes against humanity. Traditional laws of warfare were, however, more definitively circumscribed and made more humane by the *Four Geneva Conventions of 1949 on the Protection of War Victims*, adopted under the auspices of the International Committee of the Red Cross. These Conventions relate to:

(i) the Treatment of Prisoners of War;
(ii) the Amelioration of the Condition of the Wounded and Sick in Armed Forces in the Field;
(iii) the Amelioration of the Condition of Wounded, Sick and Shipwrecked Members of Armed Forces at Sea, and;
(iv) the Protection of Civilian Persons in Time of War.

They are regarded as "binding upon belligerents under all circumstances and conditions, except in the case of reprisals as retaliation against a belligerent for illegitimate acts of warfare by the members of his armed forces or his other subjects".[11] The purpose of these Conventions is to ensure that persons who are not combatants be treated in a humane manner by the prohibition of such practices as the taking of hostages, illegal executions of certain categories of those involved in armed conflicts and the use of reprisals against persons who are protected by the Conventions. There are also provisions for ensuring adequate standards of care of prisoners of war, while deportation and indiscriminate destruction of property in the territories occupied by the victors are expressly prohibited.

These Geneva Conventions have been supplemented, as far as the postwar development of international humanitarian law is concerned, by the Convention on the Protection of Cultural Property in the Event of Armed Conflict, in 1954, under the sponsorship of UNESCO.

In its advisory opinion in *Reservations to the Convention on the Prevention and Punishment of the Crime of Genocide*,[12] which Convention was prompted mainly by the extermination of some six million Jews in Nazi Germany during the Second World War, the Court observed as follows:

"The origins and character of the Convention, the objects pursued by the General Assembly and the contracting parties, the relations which exist between the provisions of the Convention, *inter se*, and between those provisions and these objects, furnish elements of interpretation of the will of the General Assembly and the parties. The origins of the Convention show that it was the intention of the United Nations to condemn and punish genocide as "a crime under international law" involving a denial of the right of existence of entire human groups, a denial which shocks the conscience of mankind and results in great losses to humanity, and which is contrary to moral law and to the spirit and aims of the United Nations (Resolution 96I of the General Assembly. December 11, 1946). The first consequence arising from this conception is that the principles underlying the Convention are principles which are recognized by civilised nations as binding on States, even without any conventional obligation. A second consequence is the universal character both of the condemnation of genocide and of the cooperation required "in order to liberate mankind from such an odious scourge" (Preamble to the Convention). The Genocide Convention was therefore intended by the General Assembly and by the contracting parties to be definitely universal in scope. It was in fact approved on December 9, 1948, by a resolution which was unanimously adopted by fifty-six States. The objects of such a convention must also be considered. The Convention was manifestly adopted for a purely humanitarian and civilizing purpose.

The Protecting Power System of the ICRC

The foregoing survey of the Hague and the Geneva Conventions shows that, like the Universal Declaration of Human Rights of 1948 and the two Covenants on Political and Civil Rights and Economic and Cultural Rights, they now have a plenitude of rules and provisions, but still lack adequate implementation machinery. The Human Rights group of conventional instruments are, however, far ahead of the Hague and Geneva ones, not only in regard to reasonable fullness in detailed rules and their coverage but also in the various machinery procedures for implementation, weak though these still are. The current Geneva Conference on International Humanitarian Law is clear evidence of the many gaps in the existing rules of warfare, whereas most people are now agreed that the existing Human Rights conventional rules are fairly adequate, at least for the present. It can also be said of the various provisions which the Human Rights instruments contain that they are at least worthwhile efforts towards a measure of implementation of the rules.

There are as yet no similar rules in all the Hague and Geneva Conventions laying down any machinery for the strict observance of the not inconsiderable rules they embody for the humanitarian protection of combatants and non-combatants alike. No doubt, part of the problem arises from the nature as well as the manner of war itself; it is neither easy to nor susceptible of control. A High Commissioner for Human Rights might be feasible, as has been suggested at the United Nations for some time, now, but a supervising agency acceptable to the majority of States has yet to be established for the supervision of the Hague and the Geneva Conventions. All that has so far happened has been the gradual introduction of the system of Protecting Power.[13]

Historically, the function of a Protecting Power was mainly to ensure diplomatic representation of the interests of one State towards another between which there were no diplomatic relations, or where the State whose interests were being protected had no diplomatic mission in the other State concerned. This arrangement was usually made by the State requiring protection appointing a third State to act for it in the State in whose jurisdiction the exercise of the protection was to be carried out, always with the latter's consent. It was only during the First World War that a Protecting Power was allowed to exercise the power to visit prisoners of war camps.

The institution of the Protecting Power in the laws and customs of war antedates both the Hague and the Geneva Conventions. The system grew up whereby big Powers voluntarily undertake to supervise the waging of wars between two or more States so that the weaker ones might be protected against blatant violations of the customary rules of warfare. Until 1870 (the Franco-Prussian War), Protecting Powers enjoyed no special rights, and even until 1930 such rights as they exercised were not clear.

In addition to the services rendered by the Protecting Powers during World War I, the ICRC and National Red Cross Societies rendered unofficial supervision of the laws of war by providing medical assistance for those detained in the State of residence of the victims.[14]

It may be mentioned in parenthesis that the ICRC, which consists of itself and over one hundred Red Cross or Red Crescent societies working under a League, holds international conferences of all these elements, although the national societies operate mostly on their own. The ICRC is the most active in the application of the Geneva Conventions, especially in natural and man-made disasters short of war. It often has to work under superhuman conditions, such as in the Nigerian civil war (1967–70), in Bangladesh (1971), in the Indo-Chinese conflict (1962) and during the 1967 and 1973 Middle East Wars. The ICRC, it will be noticed, although sometimes acting as a Protecting Power in armed conflicts, also often works in these other disaster situations.

The real weakness of the Protecting Power system lies in the requirement of consent of both the Protecting Power and the State holding the victims. The mandatory system proposed by the ICRC to the 1929 Conference was not adopted, but Article 86 was accepted and this ensured a measure of international obligation for States.

During the Second World War, Switzerland and Sweden acted as the Protective Powers for almost all belligerents. The ICRC also provided significant humanitarian services which supplemented the work of the Protecting Powers. Three changes were made in the work of scrutiny at the 1949 Geneva Conference. A common clause in all the four Conventions was introduced which provided that they were to be applied "with the cooperation and under the scrutiny of the Protecting Powers whose duty it is to safeguard the interests of the Parties to the conflict". Secondly, provision was made for a Substitute, whereby another State should act for the Protecting Power.

Thirdly, where there was no agreement as to the appointment of a Protecting Power, a detaining Power could request or accept the services of a humanitarian organization like the ICRC to perform the functions normally rendered by a Protecting Power.

Since the Geneva Conventions of 1949, the institution of Protecting Power has been made use of in three notable situations of armed conflict. The first two occurred when the ICRC, in pursuance of Common Article 10, attempted to secure an official substitute for a Protecting Power: during the *Suez Affair* in 1956 when the ICRC vainly sought to have itself accepted as an official substitute, and also during the *Goa Affair* in 1961 when there was a similar result. In the *Bangladesh Affair* in 1971, however, the ICRC and Switzerland agreed to share functions as the Protecting Powers.[15] But States are still reluctant today to accept the role of Protective Powers in their wars. The system under the 1949 Geneva Conventions has not worked and the need for improvement remains with the current Conference of 1974.

Apart from the institution of Protecting Power, the only other means of strengthening the application of the Geneva Conventions in the direction of humanitarianism would be the limited deterrent effects that war crimes trials like those of Nuremberg and Tokyo might have on would-be war-makers of our time. We have referred to this subject earlier and we shall have cause to refer later to the Angola Trials of 1976 in connection with international humanitarian law and Africa. But the really needful step to take would be for the on-going Geneva Conference to adopt a new rule establishing an International Tribunal for the trial of law-breakers like mercenaries and other offenders.

Development at the Current Conferences on International Humanitarian Law (1974 till the present)

For the purpose of updating the laws of war since the adoption of the four Geneva Conventions in 1949, the Swiss Government invited delegates from 126 States and ten national liberation Organizations to the Diplomatic Conference on the Reaffirmation and Development of International Humanitarian Law which held its first session from February 20th to March 29th, 1974.

Recent liberation movements and guerrilla wars led to three significant resolutions — the first by the 1969 UN Conference of Human Rights in Teheran, the second by the UN General Assembly calling upon the ICRC to undertake the task of bringing the law up to date, and the third by the XXI International Conference of the Red Cross Societies in Istanbul in September 1969. At the first session of the 1974 Conference, the ICRC tabled two draft Additional Protocols to the 1949 Geneva Conventions, the first Protocol giving additional protection in armed conflicts between States, while the second provided detailed rules for wars not of the traditional kind between States. The issue then became one in which Committee I posed the question whether wars of national liberation could be regarded as of international character. Many Western European countries, the United States, Japan, Argentina and Pakistan wanted the First Protocol to apply only to wars between States, while Arab States, many African States like the Cameroons, Ivory Coast, Zaïre and Nigeria, as well as Norway, Australia and Yugoslavia, would prefer it to include wars of colonial liberation. There was thus a direct confrontation between the traditionalists (mostly Western European States) who argued that only conflicts between States which were the subjects of international law could be regarded as international conflicts, and the modernists (mostly the Third World and the Eastern Bloc) who contended that wars between Colonial Powers and those in colonial territories struggling for the right of self-determination or liberation should be considered also as international conflicts entitled to the benefits of the Geneva Convention.[16] Various amendments were proposed to the second paragraph of Article I of Protocol I, but, although none was eventually carried at that Conference, any final version must contain a reference to liberation wars as international conflicts.

It will be recalled that Article 2 which is common to all the four Geneva Conventions of 1949 provides that they shall apply to "all cases of declared war or of any other conflict which may arise between two or more of the High Contracting Parties". The ICRC's First Draft

Additional Protocol provided in Article 1 that the Protocol "shall apply in the situations referred to in Article 2". This was considered to be insufficient to cover cases of liberation movements or guerrilla groups which clearly are not States but for which any modern rules for the protection of war victims must now provide. All the amendments proposed would expand the coverage of the Protocol to wars of national liberation, but only in such a way that "wars of secession" would not be included. This was because of the recent experiences of some of the Third World countries as well as a few of the older Western States. Brazil's suggestion that any liberation movement that has some defined territory under its control should be entitled to pursue the conflict between it and the State in question was not accepted; nor was the suggestion of New Zealand, Norway and Spain that Protocol I should apply to all armed conflicts which have reached a certain "level of intensity" being regarded as international and therefore, entitled to come within the coverage of the Geneva Conventions.[17]

Although the majority of the Conference delegates favored the inclusion of the national liberation wars in the concept of international conflicts, the final text that would make this part of the codes was not adopted at the session, largely because of the fear on the part of some Western States that the wording proposed had too much of the flavor of political motivation.

The *Second Session* held from February 3rd to April 18th, 1975 adopted sixty-nine Articles in whole or in part, compared with only three so adopted at the first session. There were notable absences from this second session, China, Albania and South Africa and about five other States; it is believed that this was one of the factors that promoted the consensus.

There was, however, the debate on whether or not to seat the Provisional Revolutionary Government of Vietnam alongside the Government of South Vietnam. The United States opposed and, after a series of votes on procedure, the PRG was denied a seat.

The second session also dealt with the problem of Protecting Powers and attempted to clarify their legal status and rights beyond the provisions of the 1929 Convention on Prisoners of War and the common clause inserted in Article 8 of Conventions I, II and III and Article 9 of Convention IV. The First Committee attempted to strengthen the Geneva Conventions in a number of ways:

(a) The Protecting Power System: Article 5 of the Draft Protocol places a duty on the parties to an armed conflict to secure the invocation of the Protecting Power System, or to appoint one without delay or, if there is no such appointment, the ICRC or other humanitarian body should offer its good offices or act as a Protecting Power. The parties are under a duty to accept the offer.

(b) A conference of all the Parties to the Protocol to "consider general problems concerning the application of the Conventions and of the present protocol". The requirement of a request of one or more Parties on approval of two-thirds of the Parties to the Protocol. As the motion for this was adopted by *consensus*, the future of the proposal was uncertain at that stage of the Conference.

(c) Another safeguard concerns the requirement that Parties to the Protocol should report on measures they have taken to disseminate the contents of the Conventions and the Protocol to the Swiss Confederation as the depositary every four years.

(d) Yet another provision was adopted which would assimilate to civilian journalists on dangerous missions in war zones.

(e) Penalties are provided for enforcing criminal liabilities for breaches of the Conventions and the Protocol.

The Committee at this Second Session made greater progress than in the First Session mainly because it dealt with less controversial matters like the care of the sick, the wounded, the shipwrecked, detained persons and medical staff, thereby updating the existing rules in these subjects.

The task of the Third Committee was to adapt humanitarian law to the technological needs of modern methods of warfare and to ensure the protection of the civilian population from attacks against such installations as dams, dikes, and nuclear electrical-generating stations. There are provisions for demilitarized zones in areas of conflict, and attacks on "non-defended localities" are prohibited.

The First Committee adopted a compromise text on the inclusion of civil wars as international conflicts, but no final agreement was reached on the inclusion of guerrilla wars.

The Second Session ended with a suggestion on the one hand that the two Additional Protocols be merged into one, and another suggestion that the guarantees and obligations which each Protocol would eventually carry should be such as to command common support from the majority of all the States parties to the Conference.

The Ad Hoc Committee on Prohibition or Restriction of Certain Conventional Weapons did not make much progress because of the attitude of the Major Powers towards controversial issues of disarmament.[18]

The Second Protocol on non-international armed conflicts did not achieve the desired progress because of the problems posed for Third States by civil wars and the threats of secessions in those States. The debate was confined to situations in which the rebel group must be seen to control a part of the territory of the State concerned. An Ad Hoc Committee was still to finalize its recommendations on possible Prohibition or Restriction of some Conventional Weapons.

The *Third Session* was held in Geneva from April 21st to June 11th, 1976. It did not complete the work set for it, and at least another session was needed. The most important hotly-debated topic was the question of the right of guerrilla fighters to prisoner-of-war status, but the conference failed to adopt a text. A good many of the more difficult problems had been put off from the first two sessions for final consideration by this Third Session. Six new States admitted to the United Nations since the second session were invited to this session. Only 106 out of the 153 invited attended the Conference. There were too many sub-committees under the three main committees; the complicated procedures adopted tended to slow down the work of the Conference. Committee II had made great progress with its work on the protection of the wounded, sick and shipwrecked persons, identification and transportation of medical and civil defense personnel, exchange of information on missing persons as well as the recovery of dead bodies. Committee I was faced with the question of repression of breaches of Protocol I and an independent investigating body. Breaches of the Protocol and of the 1949 Geneva Conventions were made war crimes by Article 74. Still remaining to be considered is the proposal that a permanent International Enquiry Commission be set up to investigate alleged violations of the Conventions and the Protocols.

Committee III had the task of finding the terms for the definition of *Guerrilla fighters* which would enable them to benefit from the protection of the Conventions and the Protocols. The 1949 Geneva Convention on Prisoners of War provides for militias, volunteer corps and organized resistance movements, but they must fulfil *four conditions*. These are:

(1) that the guerrillas, freedom fighters and similar groups must be under the command of a person who is responsible for its subordinates;
(2) that they must have a fixed distinctive sign or emblem which is recognizable at a distance;
(3) that they must carry their arms openly, and
(4) that they must conduct their activities according to the laws and customs of war.

According to the Geneva Conventions, failure to fulfil these conditions render them liable to be treated as common criminals. The majority view at this Conference is seriously to question the relevance of existing international law in the context of these Geneva rules. Hence the demand for change. In view of their circumstances in having to fight often superior forces, guerrillas could not satisfy all these conditions, but the majority view was that they should nevertheless enjoy prisoner of war status.[19]

Nigeria's proposal that *Mercenaries* be denied combatant and prisoner of war status was not adopted after a long and strenuous debate, but the debate continued at the next session where Article 42 was to be dealt with.[20] The Conventions together with the two Protocols (when adopted) would constitute the Bill of Rights of Humanitarian Law.

The Fourth and final Session of the Geneva Conference, which lasted from March 17th to June 10th, 1977, adopted on June 8th two protocols additional to the Geneva Convention of 1949 which are yet to be ratified. It is provided in Article 47(1) of Protocol 1, however, that a mercenary cannot be a combatant or a prisoner of war (as pointed out earlier in the proposal of Nigeria) while paragraph 2 of the same Article contains a slightly modified form of the same Nigerian proposal. But there is no provision in the Protocol outlawing mercenarism as an international crime.

Under Article 75, certain "fundamental guarantees" are entrenched: for example, persons who fall into the power of a Party to a conflict and who do not benefit from more favorable treatment are to be treated humanely in all circumstances. All those detained are to be released without delay. No punishment is to be meted out to anyone found guilty of a penal offence related to any armed conflict except pursuant to a sentence pronounced by an impartial and regularly constituted court. There is, therefore, no provision for a trial by an international tribunal. However, under Article 90, an International Fact-Finding Commission of fifteen members is to be established to: (a) enquire into any facts alleged to be grave breaches under the Geneva Conventions and Protocol I; and (b) facilitate, through its good offices, the restoration of an attitude of respect for the Conventions and Protocol I. The Commission is required to institute an enquiry at the request of a Party to the conflict only with the consent of the other Party or Parties concerned. There is the following interesting provision in Article 90(2)(a) which is curiously reminiscent of Article 36 of the Statute of the International Court of Justice:

The High Contracting Parties may, at the time of signing, ratifying or acceding to the Protocol, or at any other subsequent time, declare that they recognize *ipso facto* and without special agreement, in relation to any other High Contracting Party accepting the same obligation, the competence of the Commission to enquire into allegations by such other Party, as authorized by this Article.

If and when this provision comes into force after ratification of the Protocol, it will be interesting to watch its application in practice, especially the procedure for the setting up of the chamber to conduct the enquiry.

There is penalty provided in Article 91 against a Party to the conflict which violates the provisions of the Geneva Conventions and Protocol I, in that, if the case demands, it may be liable to pay compensation. It shall be made responsible for all acts committed by persons forming part of its armed forces.

Protocol II contains modest provisions concerning the protection of victims of non-international armed conflicts, and deals mainly with questions of the humane treatment of those who do not take a direct part or who have ceased to take part in hostilities; it also provides in Article 4 that, whether or not their liberty has been restricted, they are entitled to respect for their person, honor and convictions and religious practices. They are to be treated humanely in all circumstances. It is prohibited to order that there shall be no survivors. In other words, victims of non-international armed conflicts are granted almost the same amount of protection of humane treatment as those of international conflicts under Protocol II. Protocol II, however, contains no express definition of what constitutes "non-international armed conflicts", and there is no direct reference to national liberation guerrilla movements.

Conclusion

In the light of the foregoing survey, international humanitarian law can be seen to have taken its modern roots in the Geneva Convention of 1864 thanks to the vision and the initiative of Jean Henry Dunant, which set the pace for the whole development of the Hague Rules and Regulations of 1899 and 1907. Various further steps in the form of international conferences and conventions were taken in the years between the two World Wars to advance and enlarge mankind's awareness of the need for improvement of the conditions under which armed conflicts, national as well as international, should be carried on and, in particular, the treatment of the victims of war and of the civilian populations generally. Since the establishment of the UN

Organization in 1945, much has been happening under its auspices, including a number of resolutions and declarations which have, beginning with Article 2, paragraph 4 of its Charter, had the effect of making the laws and customs of war more and more humane. We may recall, in particular, the General Assembly resolution on the Convention on the Prevention of the Crime of Genocide and on the Nuremberg Trials as well as the Universal Declaration on Human Rights, 1948 and the effect these and similar measures have had on international relations and international law generally during the past thirty years.

The four Geneva Conventions of 1949 are the first universal attempt to codify the laws and customs of international armed conflict on a scale and in a manner never attempted before, and they remain the basic texts upon which rests the new international humanitarian law. Yet, international law has been affected in modern times by two major phenomena: the first is the frightening advance of technology which has outpaced the Geneva rules and the traditional modes of warfare, and the second is the problem of self-determination, largely under UN auspices, which has led to an unprecedented increase in civil wars, guerrilla wars and resistance movements, and wars of national liberation. There is also the concomitant issue of mercenaries which has raised problems not previously dealt with in customary international law.

All these relatively recent developments have called for the review and the up-dating of the Geneva Conventions of 1949 with a view to evolving a more universally acceptable system under contemporary conditions of armed conflicts. The Swiss Government and the International Committee of the Red Cross deserve our thanks for setting in motion the necessary machinery for achieving the desired goals, and we can only hope that success will attend the efforts of the on-going Diplomatic Conference on the Reaffirmation and Development of International Humanitarian Law upon which, in the absence of an effective international ban on any kind of war, mankind's hopes for a better and saner world largely depend.

NOTES

1. Certain germs of these ideas may be noted in, e.g. Ayala, *De Jure et Officus Bellicis et Disciplina Militari Libri Tres* (1582) Book I; Grotius, *De Jure Belli ac Pacis Libri Tres* (1625), Book III.

2. See his *De Jure Belli ac Pacis Libri Tres* (1625).

3. This would seem to be so even if we accept Schwarzenberger's view that "the

juxtaposition of peace and war is an oversimplification . . . Corresponding to the continuum between peace and war, there is a continuum between war and peace, and a relativity of war and peace. It is as much legally relevant as the state of intermediacy between peace and war" (see *International Courts*, Vol. 2, Armed Conflict, p. 723).

4. It is significant that, at the first session of the 1974 Conference in Geneva, China took the view that there was even today a distinction between "just" and unjust" wars in the application of humanitarian law. China, apparently, decided to withdraw from the subsequent sessions of this important conference on this account, although other reasons had been suggested, e.g. lack of expertise among the Chinese delegation.

5. Schwarzenberger: *Dynamics of International Law*, 1976, p. 77, 85.

6. See e.g. Lauterpacht's *Oppenheim's International Law*, Vol. 2, 8th edition, pp. 335–347, on the legality or illegality of the use of atomic weapons on Hiroshima and Nagasaki.

7. Ibid., pp. 217–218; since the Covenant of the League of Nations, the Kellogg-Briand Pact and the United Nations Charter.

8. See Lauterpacht, ibid., pp. 353–354.

9. Ibid., at p. 500.

10. See Lauterpacht, ibid., pp. 489–491.

11. Lauterpacht, ibid., p. 231.

12. *I.C.J. Reports 1951*, p, 15.

13. See D. P. Forsythe's "Who Guards the Custodians?: Third Parties and the Law of Armed Conflict", *A.J.I.L.*, Vol. 70, No. 1, pp. 41–61.

14. See S. Suckow, Conference on Humanitarian Law — Phase II, *International Commission of Jurists*, No. 14, June 1975, pp. 46–47.

15. See Forsythe, ibid., at pp. 46–47.

16. See G. Abi-Saab's "Wars of National Liberation and the Laws of War", *Annales d'Etudes Internationales*, Vol. 3, 1972.

17. See, generally, S. Suckow's "Development of International Humanitarian Law", in *I.C.J. Review*, June 1974, No. 12, pp. 50–57.

18. See S. Suckow's "Conference on Humanitarian Law — Phase II", in *I.C.J. Review*, June 1975, No. 14, pp. 42–54.

19. See S. Suckow's "Conference on Humanitarian Law — Phase III", in *I.C.J. Review*, June 1976, No. 16, pp. 51–61.

20. For an interesting account of the question of Mercenaries see H. W. V. Deventer's article in *A.J.I.L.*, October 1976, Vol. 70, No. 4, pp. 811–816.

Chapter 11

INTERNATIONAL HUMANITARIAN LAW AND AFRICA

So far as International Humanitarian Law is concerned, there are three phenomena that have posed major problems in contemporary Africa: wars of national liberation from colonialist and racist regimes, civil wars within States, and the employment of mercenaries. The national liberation movements have raised the legal problem as to whether they can be regarded as coming under the umbrella of "international armed conflicts" which alone are covered by the Four Geneva Conventions of 1949. The ICRC put forward to the recent Conference two Protocols, one dealing with traditional conflicts of an international character, while the other deals with non-international armed conflicts. The newly independent African States and their Third World allies claim that wars of national liberation are international wars coming within the first Article of the First Protocol, but the majority of the major Powers who are parties to the 1949 Conventions would not agree. Committee I of the Conference failed to agree on a text that would give liberation movements the protection of the Geneva Conventions.[1] These movements, it has been argued, should not be recognized since they are not sovereign States, which are the only subjects of international law. The majority at the Conference, however, were in favor of wars of national liberation being regarded as international wars and the rebel fighters as entitled to prisoner-of-war status. Some of the delegates suggested two tests (a) control of a definite part of the territory of the State in which the struggle is taking place, and (b) the attainment of a certain "level of intensity" in the armed conflict, whether international or national. There was no agreement on these tests of determining recognition. Multinational, multi-racial or multi-cultural States all opposed the extension of the coverage of the Geneva Conventions to "wars of secession", even after satisfying the traditional tests: (a) that they are commanded by a person responsible for his subordinates, (b) that they have a distinctive sign recognizable at a distance, (c) that they carry arms openly, and (d) that they conduct military operations in accordance with the laws and customs of war.[2] Wars of self-determination, as distinct from the rights of peoples to self-determination, are not often easy to define or acknowledge.

Committee I, after prolonged negotiations, adopted a consensus text which, by eliminating conflicts subject to the First Protocol and conflicts arising from situations of internal disturbances and tensions, came to the middle range constituting civil wars. This is Article I of Protocol II. It is clear that guerrilla wars are excluded from the protection of the proposed Protocol, until the "level of intensity" has reached the stage that the fighters have controlled a part of the territory.[3] The proposed definition would seem to have covered only the type of civil wars recently waged in Nigeria and Zaïre (in Africa) and Iraq, the Philippines and South Vietnam (in Asia).

Mercenaries in Africa

Mercenaries constitute an important element both in wars of liberation in colonialist and racist regimes and in civil wars in Africa. How to define a mercenary? One definition put forward by the Nigerian delegation at the Third Session of the current Conference on International Humanitarian Law in Geneva (in 1976) is:

> A mercenary includes any person not a member of the armed forces of a party to the conflict who is specially recruited abroad and who is motivated to fight or to take part in armed conflict essentially for monetary payment, reward or other private gain.[4]

The idea was that a party to the conflict need not treat a mercenary as a prisoner of war or as someone possessing combatant status. As there was no consensus on the subject, the matter was placed on the agenda of the next session of the Conference.

In its report[5] published in London in August 1976, the Diplock Committee, set up by the UK Government as a result of the growing involvement of British citizens in mercenary activities in Angola, came to the conclusion that mercenarism should not in itself be made a crime in the United Kingdom, since in its view it was difficult to achieve a satisfactory definition of a mercenary. The dominant idea up to the time of the report was not to regard mercenarism as an offense by reference only to motivation. Based on this approach, the Diplock Committee recommended that the UK Government should make, not mercenarism itself, but the recruitment in the United Kingdom of persons as mercenaries in order to take part in foreign armed conflicts, a criminal offense. This conclusion would not meet the strong view held on the subject in Africa in particular and in the

Third World and some other parts of the world in general. As Colin Legun observed: "Since modern mercenaries are deployed in the territories of the Third World, it is plain folly to ignore the attitudes of their Governments towards intervention by foreign soldiers; or to ignore the fact that it is *their* courts which will conduct the trials of any British citizens caught by them . . . It might not be a crime in the United Kingdom to be a mercenary, but most African countries take a different view."[6]

In this connection it may be recalled that the test of motivation was shown to be too narrow at the Diplomatic Conference on the Reaffirmation and Development of International Humanitarian Law Applicable in Armed Conflicts, where the consensus reached by the Third Committee was that a mercenary is a person motivated to fight primarily by the desire for monetary gain, whether it be higher pay than is given to the regular armed forces or by way of bonuses for persons killed or captured, and that this does not include a person enlisted as a regular member of the armed forces because he is attracted by good pay. The consensus was also that the mercenary must have been recruited to take part in the fighting itself, thus excluding technical experts like instructors (although some delegations would include these). It was also agreed that a mercenary should have been "recruited on behalf of one of the parties to the conflict of which he is not a national in order to participate in a particular conflict". This definition and its various refinements have resulted from the Nigerian proposal which initiated the debate, as it was the Nigerian Civil War (1967–70) that first witnessed the emergence of mercenaries on a significant scale in recent years.

The Conference further agreed, as part of its debate on Article 42 of Draft Protocol I, that the mercenary should not have the status of a combatant or a prisoner of war under the Geneva Conventions. Opinion was divided as to whether it should be left to a capturing power to grant such status in particular cases. At any rate, the majority of the delegations were of the view that mercenaries should be treated humanely in accordance with the domestic law of the capturing power. It is significant that the Conference did not adopt any proposal that mercenarism be treated as a crime.[7]

Evolution of the African Attitude to Mercenaries

The strong resentment felt throughout Africa towards mercenaries may be understood when viewed against the background of the recent history of this phenomenon. The mercenary is seen as the representative of colonialism and racist repression on the continent, assassins hired to kill freedom fighters in the wars of national liberation and against oppression. Thus, at Kinshasa in 1967, the Organization of African Unity roundly condemned mercenary activities in the Congo and made a strong appeal to all nations, especially Western European Powers, to make the recruitment and training of mercenaries a crime. At Addis Ababa in 1969, the African Heads of State and Government again adopted a resolution calling upon all nations to cease recruitment and training of mercenaries. At the meeting of the OAU Council of Ministers held in Lagos in 1970, another passionate condemnation of mercenaries was registered and a draft resolution was submitted to the next Assembly of Heads of State and Government. In 1971, the "scourge" of mercenarism was again condemned. The OAU, in adopting its well-known declaration on the subject, expressed dismay and disgust at what seemed to them a consistent effort on the part of those recruiting and training mercenaries to defeat the United Nations endeavors to foster self-determination and freedom from colonial domination. In the Declaration the OAU resolved to "prepare a legal instrument for coordinating, harmonizing and promoting the struggle of the African peoples and States against mercenarism".[8] In pursuance of this aim, a draft convention was adopted at Rabat in 1972 in which the elimination of mercenaries from Africa was advocated and a clarion call was made for the making of mercenary activities a crime. It is not certain whether the convention has since been ratified by the OAU Member States.

The African struggle against the presence of mercenaries has been carried to the UN General Assembly, where at least four important resolutions to the same effect as the OAU resolutions and declaration have been adopted.[9]

The Angola Trial

All fair-minded persons who have studied the Angola Trial are, it is believed, agreed that the procedure adopted was reasonably good but that the law applied by the tribunal was controversial.[10] As to procedure, let us quote the following summary from Riley Martin:[11]

> In his report[12] Mr. Lockwood concluded that procedurally the trial was, in the main, a fair one: the defendants' right to know the charges against them was observed, as was the defendants' right to examine the case file, right to question witnesses for the prosecution, right to be heard, right to present favorable

witnesses, right to counsel and right to a public trial. The Report also observes that the presiding judge took pains to be fair towards the defendants, was incisive in his questioning and ruled astutely on the motions. As in other civil law countries, neither prosecution nor defense were restrained from asking leading questions and hearsay evidence was admitted. Mr. Lockwood's main criticism was that a documentary film which depicted war scenes and recruitment of mercenaries in Britain was introduced although there was no evidence which connected this film to the specific defendants on trial. There was relatively little direct evidence against the defendants and much of it was poor in quality. However, all the defendants admitted to being mercenaries and two of them admitted having executed fellow mercenaries.[13].

But as to the law applied in the trial, even Mr. Lockwood described it as raising "difficult and contentious" problems. It is to be noted that the thirteen persons on trial were specifically charged with (a) being mercenaries and (b) crimes against the peace, including murder and maltreatment of civilians, prisoners of war and other mercenaries. Nine of them, six British, one American, one Irish and one Argentinian, were sentenced to terms of imprisonment ranging between sixteen and thirty years; twelve days later, the remaining four (three British and one American) were ordered to be executed by firing squad on July 10, 1976. Of these four, two had been specifically charged with, and had personally admitted having committed, murder. The main difficulty about the law which the Peoples' Revolutionary Tribunal applied was that the defendants had committed the crime of mercenarism, an offense not at that time part of the municipal law of Angola.[14] It was not even a crime in relation to the OAU, as the Rabat Draft Convention had yet to be ratified by the Member States; neither the various OAU resolutions nor those of the United Nations declaring mercenarism a crime had established such an offense definitively; and the last session of the current Geneva Conference had not even dealt with the question of mercenarism as a crime. All but two of the thirteen found guilty of this offense had been punished by reference to an *ex post facto* legislation, not laid down in advance of the trial by an Angolan decree but by a decision of the revolutionary tribunal that mercenarism "consists of specific crimes known to all penal systems". It was the view of those outside observers at the trial that a draft international convention on the prevention and suppression of mercenary activities be drawn up to meet the need felt for such a situation. The sub-committee, thus set up, did draw up a convention, Article 1 of which provides:

The crime of mercenarism is committed by the individual, group or association, representatives of State and the State itself which, with the aim of opposing by armed violence a process of self-determination, practises any of the following acts:

(a) organizes, finances, supplies, equips, trains, promotes, supports or employs in any way military forces consisting of or including persons who are not nationals of the country where they are going to act, for personal gain, through the payment of a salary or any other kind of material recompense;

(b) enlists, enrolls or tries to enroll in the said forces;

(c) allows the activities mentioned in paragraph (a) to be carried out in any territory under its jurisdiction or in any place under its control or affords facilities for transit, transport or other operations of the above-mentioned forces.[15]

This rough-and-ready attempt at a definition shows the response of outside observers to the tribunal's findings in the face of an inadequate Angolan law which should be strengthened to meet a situation such as the activity of mercenaries presented under contemporary international law. Is the above definition really sufficient by requiring that the mercenary should necessarily have the "aim of opposing by armed violence a process of self-determination"? Fortunately this restrictive concept was not, as we have seen, adopted at the Third Session of the Geneva Conference. A broader consensus formulation was adopted.

The legality of the Angolan Trial should be viewed, however, in the light of the precedents existing in international law. The Nuremberg Trial, no doubt, has certain parallels in that the basic law was also *ex post facto*, having been laid down by the victorious powers after the end of the Second World War in the London Act of 1945. The Tokyo Trials were even nearer to the Angolan Trial in that they were based on a law laid down by the Allied Commander in Japan. It must be said, however, that in both cases, the law, such as it was, predated the trials themselves and were not formulated by the tribunals themselves, as was the case in Angola. Nevertheless, all three species of trial shared the common character of defendants being accused of acts which were not crimes at the time of their commission, and the crimes charged — crimes against humanity and against peace in the Nuremberg and the Tokyo Trials as well as the crime of "mercenarism" in the Angolan Trial — were all newfangled and not part of customary international law at the material times

Conclusion

There is, therefore, much to be said for the establishment of an International Criminal Tribunal or something like it, if the *ad hoc* tribunals which have been set up by victors over the vanquished after most of the cases of armed conflicts in recent years all over the world are not to be condemned as purely motivated by revenge. This is why the current Diplomatic Conference of the Reaffirmation and Development of International Humanitarian Law Applicable in Armed Conflicts seems to the majority of international lawyers to be taking the right step in the right direction when, in Article 65 of Protocol I, it included a Bill of Rights of Humanitarian Law. It will be recalled that Article 10 provides, *inter alia*, that criminal offenses be tried before independent and impartial tribunals, that the defendants be charged with individual responsibility, that there be a presumption of innocence and that defendants should not be prosecuted under retroactive laws. The Article also provides that the death penalty must not be pronounced against persons under the age of eighteen years at the date of the commission of the offense. There should be no execution of any pregnant women or mothers of young children. The Article ends up with the important provision that, at the end of an armed conflict, the victorious side should always grant amnesty to as many as possible of those who participated therein. Nigeria did exactly that at the end of its Civil War in January 1970 when neither military trials nor civil prosecutions were held, and a general amnesty was proclaimed and granted.

NOTES

1. See S. Suckow's "Development of International Humanitarian Law" in *I.C.J. Review*, No. 12, June 1974, pp. 50–57. The same author's two articles in the same *Review*, Nos. 14 and 16, contain useful summaries of the Conference Proceedings.

2. See H. W. V. Deventer's "Mercenaries at Geneva" in *A.J.I.L.*, Vol. 70, No. 4, October 1976, pp. 811–816, at p. 812.

3. And yet, as E. Kossoy argues, in *Living with Guerrilla: Guerrilla as a Legal Problem and Political Fact*, 1976, non-compliance with the four conditions would not necessarily exclude guerrillas.

4. For a discussion of Article 4 of the 1949 Geneva Convention see Lauterpacht's *Oppenheim's International Law*, 7th edition, Vol. II, pp. 214–216.

5. The Report of the Committee of Privy Council to Enquire into the Recruitment of Mercenaries, August 1976.

6. "Why Britain Must Keep Mercenaries Out of Africa", in *The Observer*, August 8, 1976.

7. See H. W. V. Deventer's "Mercenaries at Geneva", in *A.J.I.L.*, Vol. 70, No. 4, October 1976, pp. 811–816.

8. See OAU Declaration on the Activities of Mercenaries in Africa, Eighth Summit Heads of State Conference, Addis Ababa, June 1971.

9. See UN General Assembly Res. 2395 (1968), Res. 2465, Res. 2548 (1969) and Res. 3103 (1973).

10. Cf. the trial of Rolf Steiner in the Sudan in August 1971: see "In the Trial of F. E. Steiner — A Court Martial", *Sudan Law Journal and Reports* 147 *et seq.* (1971). Steiner was sentenced to death but the Sudanese President commuted the death penalty to twenty years' imprisonment. He was soon after released in an act of clemency.

11. "Mercenaries and the Rule of Law" in *I.C.J. Review*, No. 17, December 1976, pp. 51–57 at p. 55.

12. Report on Trial of Mercenaries, Luanda, Angola, June 1976 (unpublished).

13. A detailed account of the Angola Trial will be found in "The Laws of War and the Angolan Trial of Mercenaries: Death to the Dogs of War", in *Case Western Reserve University Journal of International Law*, Vol. 9, Spring 1977, pp. 323–406, particularly p. 333ff. 352, by J. D. Hoover.

14. Article 3 of the Angolan Rules of Procedure provides only that "war crimes and crimes against humanity" are triable — not mercenarism as such.

15. The Draft Convention containing the definition was sent to the United Nations, the OAU and the Angolan Government for necessary action. Nothing has so far been done thereon.

PART IV

Appendices

Appendix I

Resolution 171 (III) of the United Nations General Assembly
14 November 1947

Need for Greater Use by the United Nations and Its Organs of the International Court of Justice

A
The General Assembly,

Considering that it is a responsibilty of the United Nations to encourage the progressive development of international law;

Considering that it is of paramount importance that the interpretation of the Charter of the United Nations and the constitutions of the specialized agencies should be based on recognized principles of international law;

Considering that the International Court of Justice is the principal judicial organ of the United Nations;

Considering that it is also of paramount importance that the Court should be utilized to the greatest practicable extent in the progressive development of international law, both in regard to legal issues between States and in regard to constitutional interpretation.

Recommends that organs of the United Nations and the specialized agencies should, from time to time, review the difficult and important points of law within the jurisdiction of the International Court of Justice which have arisen in the course of their activities and involve questions of principle which it is desirable to have settled, including points of law relating to the interpretation of the Charter of the United Nations or the constitutions of the specialized agencies, and, if duly authorized according to Article 96, paragraph 2, of the Charter, should refer them to the International Court of Justice for an advisory opinion.

C
The General Assembly,

Considering that, in virtue of Article 1 of the Charter, international disputes should be settled in conformity with the principles of justice and international law;

Considering that the International Court of Justice could settle or assist in settling many disputes in conformity with these principles if, by the full application of the provisions of the Charter and of the Statute of the Court, more frequent use were made of its services,

1. Draws the attention of the States which have not yet accepted the compulsory jurisdiction of the Court in accordance with Article 36, paragraphs 2 and 5, of the Statute, to the desirability of the greatest possible number of States accepting this jurisdiction with as few reservations as possible;

2. Draws the attention of States Members to the advantage of inserting in conventions and treaties arbitration clauses providing, without prejudice to Article 95 of the Charter, for the submission of disputes which may arise from the interpretation or application of such conventions or treaties, preferably and as far as possible to the International Court of Justice;

3. Recommends as a general rule that States should submit their legal disputes to the International Court of Justice.

Appendix II

Resolution 3232 (XXIX) of the United Nations General Assembly
12 November 1974

Review of the role of the International Court of Justice

The General Assembly,

Recalling that the International Court of Justice is the principal judicial organ of the United Nations,

Bearing in mind that, in conformity with Article 10 of the Charter of the United Nations, the role of the International Court of Justice remains an appropriate matter for the attention of the General Assembly,

Recalling further that in accordance with Article 2, paragraph 3, of the Charter, all Members shall settle their international disputes by peaceful means in such a manner that international peace and security, and justice, are not endangered,

Taking note of the views expressed by Member States during the debates in the Sixth Committee on the question of the review of the role of the International Court of Justice at the twenty-fifth, twenty-sixth, twenty-seventh and twenty-ninth sessions of the General Assembly,

Taking note also of the comments transmitted by Member States and by Switzerland in answer to a questionnaire of the Secretary-General in accordance with General Assembly resolutions 2723 (XXV) of 15 December 1970 and 2818 (XXVI) of 15 December 1971, and of the text of the letter dated 18 June 1971 addressed to the Secretary-General by the President of the International Court of Justice,

Considering that the International Court of Justice has recently amended the Rules of Court, with a view to facilitating recourse to it for the judicial settlement of disputes, *inter alia* by simplifying the procedure, reducing the likelihood of undue delays and costs and allowing for greater influence of parties on the composition of *ad hoc* chambers,

Recalling the increasing development and codification of international law in conventions open for universal participation and the consequent need for their uniform interpretation and application,

Recognizing that the development of international law may be reflected, *inter alia*, by declarations and resolutions of the General Assembly which may to that extent be taken into consideration by the

International Court of Justice,

Recalling further the opportunities afforded by the power of the International Court of Justice, under Article 38, paragraph 2, of its Statute, to decide a case *ex aequo et bono* if the parties agree thereto,

1. Recognizes the desirability that States study the possibility of accepting, with as few reservations as possible, the compulsory jurisdiction of the International Court of Justice in accordance with Article 36 of its Statute;

2. Draws the attention of States to the advantage of inserting in treaties, in cases considered possible and appropriate, clauses providing for the submission to the International Court of Justice of disputes which may arise from the interpretation or application of such treaties;

3. Calls upon States to keep under review the possibility of identifying cases in which use can be made of the International Court of Justice;

4. Draws the attention of States to the possibility of making use of chambers as provided in Articles 26 and 29 of the Statute of the International Court of Justice and in the Rules of Court, including those which would deal with particular categories of cases;

5. Recommends that United Nations organs and the specialized agencies should, from time to time, review legal questions within the competence of the International Court of Justice that have arisen or will arise during their activities and should study the advisability of referring them to the Court for an advisory opinion, provided that they are duly authorized to do so;

6. Reaffirms that recourse to judicial settlement of legal disputes, particularly referral to the International Court of Justice, should not be considered as an unfriendly act between States.

Appendix III

Resolution concerning the Internal Judicial Practice of the Court
(RULES OF COURT, ARTICLE 33)
ADOPTED ON 12 APRIL 1976

The Court decides to revise its Resolution concerning the Internal Judicial Practice of the Court of 5 July 1968[1] and to adopt the articles concerning its internal judicial practice which are set out in the present Resolution. The Court remains entirely free to depart from the present Resolution, or any part of it, in a given case, if it considers that the circumstances justify that course.

Article 1

(i) After the termination of the written proceedings and before the beginning of the oral proceedings, a deliberation is held at which the judges exchange views concerning the case, and bring to the notice of the Court any point in regard to which they consider it may be necessary to call for explanations during the course of the oral proceedings.

(ii) In cases where two exchanges of oral arguments take place, after the first such exchange has been concluded, a further deliberation is held having the same objects.

(iii) The Court also meets in private from time to time during the oral proceedings to enable judges to exchange views concerning the case and to inform each other of possible questions which they may intend to put in the exercise of their right under Article 57, paragraph 3, of the Rules.

Article 2

After the termination of the oral proceedings, an appropriate period is allowed to the judges in order that they may study the arguments presented to the Court.

Article 3

(i) At the expiration of this period a deliberation is held at which the President outlines the issues which in his opinion will require

---

1. Prior to 1968, the internal judicial practice of the Court was governed by the Resolution of the Permanent Court of International Justice of 20 February 1931 (as amended on 17 March 1936), by virtue of a decision of the International Court of Justice of 1946 to adopt provisionally the practice of the Permanent Court.

discussion and decision by the Court. Any judge may then comment on the statement or call attention to any other issue or question which he considers relevant, and may at any time during or at the close of the deliberation cause to be distributed a text formulating a new question or reformulating a question already brought to notice.

(ii) During this deliberation any judge may comment on the pertinence of any issues or questions arising in the case. The President also invites judges to indicate their preliminary impressions regarding any issue or question.

(iii) Judges will be called on by the President in the order in which they signify their desire to speak.

Article 4

(i) At a suitable interval of time after this deliberation, each judge prepares a written note which is distributed to the other judges.

(ii) The written note expresses the judge's views on the case, indicating, *inter alia*:

(a) whether any questions which have been called to notice should be eliminated from further consideration or should not, or need not, be decided by the Court;

(b) the precise questions which should be answered by the Court;

(c) his tentative opinion as to the answers to be given to the questions in *(b)* and his reasons therefor;

(d) his tentative conclusion as to the correct disposal of the case.

Article 5

(i) After the judges have had an opportunity to examine the written notes, a further deliberation is held, in the course of which all the judges, called upon by the President as a rule in inverse order of seniority, must declare their views. Any judge may address comments to or ask for further explanations from a judge concerning the latter's statement declaring his views.

(ii) During this deliberation any judge may circulate an additional question or a reformulation of a question already brought to notice.

(iii) On the request of any judge the President shall ask the Court to decide whether a vote shall be taken on any question.

Article 6

(i) On the basis of the views expressed in the deliberations and in the written notes, the Court proceeds to choose a drafting committee by secret ballot and by an absolute majority of votes of the judges present. Two members are elected who should be chosen from among those judges whose oral statements and written notes have most closely and effectively reflected the opinion of the majority of the Court as it appears then to exist.

(ii) The President shall ex officio be a member of the drafting committee unless he does not share the majority opinion of the Court as it appears then to exist, in which case his place shall be taken by the Vice-President. If the Vice-President is ineligible for the same reason, the Court shall proceed, by the process already employed, to the election of a third member, in which case the senior of the elected judges shall preside in the drafting committee.

(iii) If the President is not a member of the drafting committee, the committee shall discuss its draft with him before submitting it to the Court. If the President proposes amendments which the Committee does not find it possible to adopt, it shall submit the President's proposals to the Court together with its own draft.

Article 7

(i) A preliminary draft of the decision is circulated to the judges, who may submit amendments in writing. The drafting committee, having considered these amendments, submits a revised draft for discussion by the Court in first reading.

(ii) Judges who wish to deliver separate or dissenting opinions make the text thereof available to the Court after the first reading is concluded and within a time-limit fixed by the Court.

(iii) The drafting committee circulates an amended draft of the decision for the second reading, at which the President enquires whether any judge wishes to propose further amendments.

(iv) Judges who are delivering separate or dissenting opinions may make changes in or additions to their opinions only to the extent that changes have been made in the draft decision. During the second reading they inform the Court of any changes in or additions to their opinions which they propose to make for that reason. A time-limit is fixed by the Court for the filing of the revised texts of separate or dissenting opinions, copies of which are distributed to the Court.

Article 8

(i) At or after a suitable interval following upon the termination of the second reading, the President calls upon the judges to give their final vote on the decision or conclusion concerned in inverse order of seniority, and in the manner provided for by paragraph (v) of this Article.

(ii) Where the decision deals with issues that are separable, the Court shall in principle, and unless the exigencies of the particular case require a different course, proceed on the following basis, namely that:

(a) any judge may request a separate vote on any such issue;

(b) wherever the question before the Court is whether the Court is competent or the claim admissible, any separate vote on particular issues of competence or admissibility shall (unless such vote has shown some preliminary objection to be well-founded under the Statute and the Rules of Court) be followed by a vote on the question of whether the Court may proceed to entertain the merits of the case or, if that stage has already been reached, on the global question of whether, finally, the Court is competent or the claim admissible.

(iii) In any case coming under paragraph (ii) of this Article, or in any other case in which a judge so requests, the final vote shall take place only after a discussion on the need for separate voting, and whenever possible after a suitable interval following upon such discussion.

(iv) Any question whether separate votes as envisaged in paragraph (ii) of this Article should be recorded in the decision shall be decided by the Court.

(v) Every judge, when called upon by the President to record his final vote in any phase of the proceedings, or to vote upon any question relative to the putting to the vote of the decision or conclusion concerned, shall do so only by means of an affirmative or negative.

Article 9

(i) Although because of illness or other reason deemed adequate by the President, a judge may have failed to attend part of the public hearing or of the Court's internal proceedings under Articles 1 to 7 inclusive of this Resolution, he may nevertheless participate in the final vote provided that:

(a) during most of the proceedings, he shall have been, or remained, at the seat of the Court or other locality in which the Court is sitting and exercising its functions for the purposes of the case under paragraph 1 of Article 22 of the Statute;

(b) as regards the public hearing, he shall have been able to read the official transcript of the proceedings;

(c) as regards the internal proceedings under Articles 1 to 7 inclusive, he shall have been able at least to submit his own written note,

read those of the other judges, and study the drafts of the drafting committee; and

(d) as regards the proceedings as a whole, he shall have taken a sufficient part in the public hearing and in the internal proceedings under Articles 1 to 7 inclusive to enable him to arrive at a judicial determination of all issues of fact and law material to the decision of the case.

(ii) A judge who is qualified to participate in the final vote must record his vote in person. In the event of a judge who is otherwise in a fit condition to record his vote being unable because of physical incapacity or other compelling reason to attend the meeting at which the vote is to be taken, the vote shall, if the circumstances permit, be postponed until he can attend. If, in the opinion of the Court, the circumstances do not permit of such a postponement, or render it inadvisable, the Court may, for the purpose of enabling the judge to record his vote, decide to convene elsewhere than at its normal meeting place. If neither of these alternatives is practicable, the judge may be permitted to record his vote in any other manner which the Court decides to be compatible with the Statute.

(iii) In the event of any doubt arising as to whether a judge may vote in the circumstances contemplated by paragraphs (i) and (ii) hereof — and if this doubt cannot be resolved in the course of the discussion — the matter shall, upon the proposal of the President, or at the request of any other Member of the Court, be decided by the Court.

(iv) When a judge casts his final vote in the circumstances contemplated by paragraphs (i) and (ii) of the present Article, paragraph (v) of Article 8 shall apply.

Article 10

The foregoing provisions shall apply whether the proceedings before the Court are contentious or advisory.

Appendix IV: Oral Arguments of Lawyers for the Parties

Argument

By Chesterfield Smith,
United States of America

On behalf of the Republic of Alterius

May it please the Court:

In accordance with the Statute governing this Court and those States party to it, the Republic of Alterius asks this Court to address itself to a question of international law — a question of grave concern not only to Alterius but to the entire family of nations. Within this context the Republic of Alterius further asks this Court to exercise its jurisdiction to determine the nature and extent of the reparation to be made for the breach of this international obligation about to be described.

Most broadly stated, the issue is suppression of crime. More narrowly, the focus is upon aerial hijacking. Few problems have so plagued the community of nations this past decade as this crime of the aerospace age. In a very real sense, these are "crimes against humanity" since they inevitably cause unnecessary suffering and may cause useless destruction of human lives. The multitude of nationalities among the passengers using a modern commercial airliner, whether in international or in domestic aviation, makes every safety hazard a matter of international concern. Acts of individual aerial hijackers assume the status of international law.

Alternatively, aerial hijacking might be viewed as one manifestation of international terrorism, a matter which has concerned nations with increasing frequency and which led the UN General Assembly to adopt in December of 1972 a Resolution on Measures to Prevent International Terrorism.

In an ideal world an aerial hijacker will be referred to an international criminal court for prosecution. Indeed this was the solution envisioned by twin conventions signed in 1937, the Convention for the Prevention and Punishment of Terrorism on the one hand, on the other the Convention for the Creation of an International Criminal Court. Unfortunately both Conventions were casualties of World War II. They were not ratified and interest in the problem faced a long period of dormancy.

Since ours is not yet an ideal world it is necessary to seek a solution to this pressing problem through institutions now available. Among existing institutions none is so well qualified as this Court to articulate the norms of international law relevant to aerial hijacking, norms we believe already exist and which are adequate to the Court's and society's needs.

The United Nations, of which this Court is a principal organ, is deeply rooted in the protection of human rights and values. These are delineated from time to time by Resolutions of both the General Assembly and the Security Council. Both bodies have addressed themselves to aerial hijacking. The Security Council, on September 9, 1970, "Gravely concerned at the threat to innocent civilian lives from the hijacking of aircraft . . . Calls on States to take all possible legal steps to prevent further hijackings . . ." The General Assembly, on November 30, 1970, adopted, without a single negative vote, a Resolution:

> Recognizing that such acts . . . constitute a violation of . . . human rights, . . . Condemns, without exception whatsoever, all acts of aerial hijacking . . . [and] Requests concerted action on the part of States . . . towards suppressing all acts which jeopardize the safe and orderly development of international civil air transport.

Member States responded enthusiastically to the Assembly's call to adopt a convention on the unlawful seizure of aircraft. At a conference at The Hague in December 1970 the Convention for the Suppression of Unlawful Seizure of Aircraft was signed by States representing broadly the world's different regions and political philosophies.

Alterius submits that the civilized nations of the world have thus declared in favour of human rights and against terrorism and the international crime of aerial hijacking. Society's goal has been articulated and, assuming there are international legal norms to support it, this Court has the jurisdiction and the duty to implement this goal.

The Statute of this Court directs it to apply international conventions, international custom and the general principles of law recognized by civilized nations. In addition, reference may be made to judicial decisions and the teachings of the most highly qualified publicists of the various nations, as subsidiary means for the determination of rules of law.

While it is true that Botania is not a party to the 1970 Hague Convention and while we recognize that United Nations' resolutions may not have binding effect, Alterius contends that this Court may declare and apply the applicable law without recourse to international conventions and United Nations' resolutions.

Alterius submits that ample authority exists both in international custom and in the general principles of law recognized by civilized nations for the Court to hold that aerial hijacking is an international crime of the aerospace age and that its punishment is a proper subject for the law of nations and this Court.

It has been wisely said that a satisfactory account of customary international law involves the acceptance of law as process and an understanding of the basis of obligation as consensus, that is, the attribution of law to a particular standard of behavior that has wide but not necessarily universal or long-standing support by governments. The resolutions and conventions we have described are a part of this process and certainly they represent a consensus that aerial hijacking is an international crime.

Preeminently, however, the 1970 Hague Convention shows how customary rules of international law may be generated by treaty. This process was the subject of brilliant exposition in the *North Sea Continental Shelf cases* in 1969. There this Court for the first time gave explicit substantiation to the thesis that provisions in treaties can generate customary law, that they can be of a "norm-creating character". There is no doubt, as this Court put it, that the norm-creating process "is a perfectly possible one and does from time to time occur: it constitutes indeed one of the recognized methods by which new rules of customary international law may be formed".

In the *Continental Shelf* decision this Court recognized that not all provisions in treaties generate customary law binding upon non-parties. The Court said the test is whether the relevant provision "should, at all events potentially, be of a fundamentally norm-creating character such as could be regarded as forming the basis of a general rule of law".

Professor D'Amato, relating this abstract proposition concerning customary norm generation by treaty to the concrete case represented by the *Shelf* decision, suggests that the question then becomes: has the 1958 Continental Shelf Convention itself expressed the equidistance principle in such a form as to manifest the convention's intent to have that principle generate a rule of customary law to the same effect? To answer this question, this Court told us to look at the form in which the rule is cast as well as the structural relation within the treaty of the rule to other provisions in the convention. After considering the form in which the provision concerned was cast, this Court looked to the structure of the convention as a whole, discovered as well that reservations were permitted to the provision concerned, and finally held that, while the first three articles (to which no reservation was permitted) possessed "norm-creating character", the provision concerned did not.

If this methodology is applied to the 1970 Hague Convention, the Court will examine the impact of Articles 1, 2, 4, 6, 7 and 8 upon the general fabric of customary law. The Court will surely find that the Hague Convention has expressed the principle *aut punire aut dedere* in such a form as to show the convention's intent to have that principle generate a rule of customary law to the same effect. The Court will also note that reservations are permitted only with respect to Article 12 dealing with the mechanics of arbitration.

Pouring "Practical Content" Into the Theory

The question remains as to how this new customary law is to be enforced in this Court. Since States alone can be parties before the Court, a recognition of the still viable concept that individuals are only objects of international law, this Court can and should hold that a nation into which one responsible for such a seizure comes incurs international responsibility either to try and punish or to extradite the offender.

The doctrinal basis for the mandatory nature of prosecution and the Court's jurisdiction to ensure that prosecution meets minimum standards of international custom is that, in the act of aerial hijacking, an offense against the law of nations has been committed, and not merely an offense against the municipal laws under which the offender is being tried, more or less fortuitously.

Before an International Court a respondent State cannot plead that its municipal law contains rules which conflict with international law, nor can it plead absence of any legislative provision or rule of internal law as a defense to a charge that it has broken international law. The obligation to punish the offender is one that devolved upon the respondent State when it chose not to extradite. This obligation it owes to all nations.

The "Damages" Issue

The breach of any international obligation constitutes an illegal act or international tort, and the commission of an international tort involves the duty to make reparation. The Republic of Alterius has asked for U.S. $10 million special damages if the Respondent State refuses to perform its international obligations.

Not only was the airline in this incident harmed, but the security interest of the Republic of Alterius in the safety of its airways is seriously jeopardized by the encouragement given to terrorists on the part of the Democratic State of Botania. Expensive new measures to prevent hijacking will have to be taken and this responsibility will devolve upon Alterius as well as upon its airlines.

Any amount of compensation paid to Alterius less than $10 million would not be adequate to deter other States from encouraging aerial hijacking by holding out the possibility of asylum.

Final Submissions

The Court is asked:

A. To adjudge and declare:
   (1) that unlawful seizure of aircraft in flight is a violation of customary international law and the general principles of law recognized by civilized nations:
   (2) that a nation into which one responsible for such a seizure comes incurs international responsibility either to try and punish or to extradite the offender;
   (3) that a nation failing to meet this international responsibility must respond in damages to the injured nation.
B. To adjudge and declare that the Democratic State of Botania must respect this obligation.
C. To adjudge and declare that the Democratic State of Botania has acted and continues to act contrary to the obligation recalled above.
D. To call upon the Democratic State of Botania:
   (1) to try and punish this offender, or
   (2) to pay damages to the Republic of Alterius in the amount of U.S. $10 million.

Argument

By Professor Fernando Della Rocca, Italy

On Behalf of the Coronado Republic for the Estate of Robert Yellman, Plaintiff (Civil Suit)

Mr. Presiding Justice, Honorable Justices:

It is a great privilege for me to present shortly the oral arguments in favor of the State of Coronado with reference to the written brief which is already in your hands.

The facts assumed in our case are very clear and I think we can all admit that substantially there is no disagreement about them among the parties concerned.

I shall deal with the matter in two sections: the first concerns procedural problems especially in respect of the jurisdiction of the International Court, while the second concerns the merit of the case, i.e. the "liability".

1. First of all we have to consider the principle laid down in Article 93 of the Charter of the United Nations, by which the jurisdiction of this High Court arises, subjectively, when the parties, as in our case, are members of the United Nations. Because of this membership, they are, *ipso facto*, members of the Court, which was designated by that Charter as the "principal judicial organ" of the United Nations (see Article 7, paras. 1 and 92). We must also bear in mind another principle. It is to be found in Article 34, para. 1 of the Statute of the Court and provides that "only States may be parties in cases before the Court".

I, now, come to the objective aspect of the jurisdiction of the ICJ. It is unquestionable if a case is of international significance. In the case before us I formally assume that the facts of it involve truly international rights and obligations. And in this connection I must refer to Article 36 of the Statute of the Court, which does not apply to "disputes with regard to matters which are essentially within the domestic jurisdiction of the signatory State".

In my brief I have recalled an important decision taken by the ICJ in the *Mavrommatis Palestine Concessions case*. On that occasion, among other statements, the ICJ pointed out that "it is an elementary principle of international law that a State is utilized to protect its subjects when injured by acts contrary to international law committed by another State, from whom they have been unable to obtain satisfaction through the ordinary channels". Therefore when a government espouses the claim of one of its nationals who has been injured, or denied justice by a foreign government, the espousing government makes the claim its own. It is thus acting in its sovereign capacity and not as an agent for the claimant, or as a trustee for the claimant.

And by doing so in our case, the Coronado Republic seeks not only to cure the injury which has been suffered by one of its subjects but also to discourage subsequent injuries to any other of its subjects.

2. In the matter of hijacking we are definitely confronted with an international crime. It therefore properly comes under the jurisdiction of the ICJ. We must say more. The brief on behalf of the Republic of Alterius has brilliantly emphasized that the consciousness of all peoples regards such crimes as crimes against humanity. The declaration of human rights reflects this principle. Furthermore, the UN Assembly of November 25, 1970 unanimously condemned "all acts of aerial hijacking". And it is of no avail to object that the Democratic State of Botania did not subscribe to the Hague Convention for the Suppression of Unlawful Seizure of Aircraft (1970). Granted! But the fact remains that, even if international conventions cannot be invoked in this case, the Court has to apply international custom (as evidence of general practice accepted as law) and the general principles of law recognized by civilized nations (see Article 38 of its Statute). Hijacking, as a form of piracy, is a crime *jure gentium* in customary law. And we must not forget that the "customary international rules are a direct, immediate, spontaneous expression of the conscience of the members of the international community" and that, according to the teaching of Prof. Giuliano, "it is not difficult to determine, not only the degree of the common conscience of peoples, but also a uniform standard of internal legislative provisions or of decisions by international judicial authorities, such as reflect the existence of a general international rule" in order to "identify whether a general practice accepted as law exists to adopt the forceful expression which we find in Article 38 of the Statute of the ICJ". In applying the forms of evidence in order to establish the existence of an international custom, what is sought for is a general recognition among States of "a certain practice as obligatory", as Prof. Brierly says.

Consequently hijacking, as an international crime which operates against humanity, is a proper subject for the jurisdiction of the ICJ and this jurisdiction covers "all the elements of the case", as the Permanent Court of International Justice stated in the *Serbian Loans case*, which I recalled in my brief.

3. In this case I respectfully submit that there is no need to go through the really futile formality of exhausting local remedies in Botanian Courts. We must, primarily, admit the principle that it is right to prefer the use of local remedies for two reasons: (a) on the national level, the rule is intended to allow local Courts to do justice in their own way and to be aware of the international responsibility of their own state judiciary; (b) on the international level, it provides a uniform procedural framework so that the ICJ will truly be a Court of

last instance. But we must also consider, together with Sir Hersch Lauterpacht, whose separate opinion was expressed in the *Norwegian Loans case*, which was decided by the ICJ on July 6, 1957, that "the requirement of exhaustion of local remedies is not a purely technical or rigid rule" and that "it is a rule which international tribunals have applied with a considerable degree of elasticity" and moreover "in particular, they have refused to act upon it in cases in which there are, in fact, no effective remedies available owing to the law of the State concerned or the conditions prevailing in it". Now, it is obvious that an adequate remedy in Botanian Court is quite unavailable. There has been no trial and the local magistrate has not even found grounds for the minimal kind of probable cause required to initiate criminal proceedings. Hence it is clear that the State of Botania wants to preserve Xaviere from any criminal or civil prosecution. Furthermore, through the "asylum" which has been granted to him, Xaviere has been fully exonerated as a political criminal or political refugee, regardless of the "common crimes" involved in this case. This situation leads us to the inescapably severe conclusion that to all intents and purposes no legislative remedies exist at all under Botanian laws.

Therefore I come back to the references I made to the *Norwegian Loans case* and I maintain that we have here a first reason to make an exception to the principle of the "preference" for local Courts.

But there is another reason for making an exception. Where the original wrong alleged to have been suffered by an alien is up against a gross deficiency in the systematic administration of judicial or remedial process, then it is completely pointless to expect the claimant to pursue further remedies within that system. We need only recall that the State of Botania, as is clearly shown by the evidence, took no prompt or vigorous action either to save the deceased or to punish his murderer.

Finally, as yet another reason for making an exception to the principle which gives preference to local remedies, there is the so called "link" theory which is also in our favor — a link, be it citizenship, residence or contract, between the injured individual and the respondent State. But no such link exists in the precedent case!

4. We have thus clarified the status of our judicial case as to the procedural problems regarding the jurisdiction of the ICJ, and must now turn to the question of liability.

As a starting point we must recall Article 38 of the Statute of the ICJ, which enumerates the sources of the law to be applied.

Besides what we have already said on the role of international customary law, let us remember that the Court must carefully consider the teachings of the most authoritative commentators on international law and the general principles of international law as recognized by civilized nations.

5. In asserting whether the State of Botania has committed an international tort it should be remembered that whether a State has a municipal law that incorporates international law as "a part of the law of the land" or not, the norms of international law are always intrinsically superior to municipal law.

Now, the liability of the State of Botania rests on its failure in two areas: (a) its failure to vigorously negotiate for the release of the deceased, while there still existed a chance of saving his life (and the testimony of those present during the period of negotiating is among the judicial acts at the disposal of the Honorable Court); (b) its failure to provide even reasonably adequate legal redress to the survivors to the estate of the deceased.

As regards the first failure, we have to consider that hijacking is an international crime and that the State of Botania is under an international obligation not only to prevent its occurrence, but to suppress and minimize its harmful impact. And since Botania breached this duty in its almost casual approach to negotiating for the release of the deceased — the total absolution of Xaviere's foul acts is most significant — its negligence constitutes the act of a joint tortfeasor who must be held jointly and severally liable for the wrongful death of the deceased.

As to the second failure, i.e. the State of Botania's denial of justice, I would like to make a special reference to the brief presented by my eminent colleague Chesterfield H. Smith on behalf of the co-plaintiff the Republic of Alterius. The State of Botania is under a clear obligation to prosecute and punish hijackers, both civilly and criminally, and failure to do so constitutes an international tort for which reparation must be made.

6. As for the liability of Xaviere I maintain that it is beyond dispute.

Hijacking has been denied, over the years, the status of "political crime". However even if this were a "political crime", that would only affect the issue of Xaviere's extraditability, not his ultimate liability.

And Yellman's failure to comply with airline emergency procedures can have no juridical bearing on the issue. Indeed, the regulation instructing passengers to remain seated and to leave the capture of hijackers to the proper authorities is intended for the protection of passengers; it does not create a legal standard of care for passengers that are terrorized at gun point.

As I have pointed out in my brief, under the conditions present inside that aircraft, Yellman's actions were both foreseeable and not unreasonable; in no sense do they constitute a superseding, intervening cause of his death so as to relieve Xaviere of liability. The entire three-day hijacking was an assault upon the crew and passengers.

7. The murder of Yellman by Xaviere, Botania's negligent non-attempt at securing the release of the deceased and Botania's failure to prosecute and punish the offender: these are three compelling reasons for imposing full liability.

Therefore I ask this Honorable Court to hold the defendants, Francisco Xaviere and the Democratic State of Botania, jointly and severally liable for the wrongful death of the deceased, Robert Yellman.

Argument

By J. B. Piggott, Australia

On behalf of Botania ATS Alterius and Coronado (Yellman Estate)

May it please the Court:
   The following deductions can be made from the stated facts:

1. Xaviere is a member of an oppressed racial minority in Alterius which denies basic human rights to this class of its citizens.
2. Freedom of speech being denied to these citizens of Alterius Xaviere sought to publicize the plight of his people by the act complained of.
3. To escape what would have been a political trial in Alterius, Xaviere sought asylum in the Democratic State of Botania.
4. Botania exercised its territorial sovereignty in the matter and tried Xaviere in its Magisterial Courts on the application of Alterius for extradition which was refused on the ground that Xaviere was a political refugee.
5. The Botanian magistrate also refused to commit Xaviere for trial for the diversion of the aircraft or for the murder of Yellman.

Presumably hijacking was neither an extraditable offense under the treaty between Alterius and Botania nor a specific crime in Botania. As to the charge of murder there was evidence that could have supported a finding of accidental death in respect of Yellman.

6. The Alterian authorities provided an Air Marshal for the flight but made no search or no sufficient search of travelling passengers including Xaviere who was carrying firearms. (For all one knows, Alterians, like Americans, carry firearms around with their tooth-brushes.)

7. Botania is not a signatory to the Hague or Montreal Conventions on suppression of hijacking.

8. Botania has excluded matters of essentially domestic character from its acceptance of the compulsory jurisdiction of the International Court of Justice.

It is contended on the facts that the effective causes of the tragedy in this case were:

(a) the failure of Alterius to take reasonable precautions within its own territory to prevent the hijacking;
(b) Alterius' denial of fundamental human rights to its racial minority.

Law

The Plaintiff's case rests upon the following assertions:

1. The ICJ has jurisdiction by its Statute in all legal disputes concerning (*inter alia*) questions of international law and facts constituting a breach of an international obligation, and the Court has power to order reparation for the breach of an international obligation.
   This is admitted.
2. It is an international obligation of States to punish or surrender hijackers.
   This is denied.
3. Botania has breached this international obligation and should make reparation.
   This is denied.

Two major issues therefore arise:

(a) has the ICJ jurisdiction to try this case?

(b) If so, has Botania breached an international obligation?

The answers to both these questions can be stated in four legal propositions:

1. Many domestic questions at first appear to have an international flavor but this does not make them amenable to international jurisdiction as questions of international law. For example, in the field of immigration law all questions relating to the admission of foreigners to a State look like international questions but immigration is a subject peculiarly within the domestic jurisdiction of a State. Thus, in Botania's reservation to acceptance of the compulsory jurisdiction of the ICJ, the declaration speaks of "matters essentially within the domestic jurisdiction" of Botania. The important word is "essentially".

2. Questions concerning extradition and asylum are questions which have always been regarded in international law as questions essentially within the domestic jurisdiction of States.

Extradition

(a) Throughout the history of international law there has never been either a duty to surrender a fugitive or a duty not to surrender a fugitive even in respect of common offenses. It has always been said to be a matter of imperfect obligation and, in the absence of a treaty, the grant of extradition is purely a matter either of reciprocity or courtesy.

(b) Hence, the object of the Hague, Tokyo and Montreal Conventions for the suppression of hijacking is to make hijacking a defined international crime carrying automatic extradition or punishment *per se*.

(c) International law concedes that the grant of and procedure for extradition are matters of municipal law and thus part of the territorial sovereignty of a State.

(d) The extradition treaty between Alterius and Botania exempts political offenders from extradition and the magistrate in Botania found, in the circumstances, that Xaviere was a political refugee.

Asylum

(a) Every State has a national sovereign right to extend asylum not only to social, religious or political refugees but to criminal offenders also.

(b) Asylum is a humanitarian institution recognized and enjoined on States by the Universal Declaration of Human Rights and the Declaration on Territorial Asylum of the General Assembly of the United Nations (1967).

(c) Botania's right can only be cut down by its extradition treaty with Alterius but this treaty preserves Botania's right to grant asylum to political refugees from Alterius.
(d) Thus, the grant of asylum to Xaviere is a matter for Botania alone and in the absence of any applicable regional or international convention the decision as to who is a "political refugee" is for Botanian Courts alone to judge.

Chairman of the Court: In the case of Colombia v. Peru this Court rejected the submission of Colombia that it alone could determine that Haya de la Torre was a political refugee and the Court assumed jurisdiction in the case.

Counsel for the Defense: In that case my recollection is that there was a regional treaty between the parties concerning asylum. In any event, it was a case of diplomatic, not territorial, asylum and the parties were not objecting to the jurisdiction of the Court nor had they made reservations in this respect.

3. The trial and punishment of Xaviere was also a matter for the Courts of Botania because the alleged offenses partly took place in the air space or territory of Botania and it alone had custody of the alleged offender.
4. Xaviere was in fact tried in Botania in accordance with the judicial processes of that State.

Conclusion

1. The Plaintiff's case rests on wishful thinking as to what international law ought to be, rather than on what it is. Otherwise there would be no need for the great international activity now going on to secure acceptance and ratification by States of the Conventions on the suppression of hijacking. Although it is conceded that the ICJ can interpret and extend doctrines of International Law which have existed for centuries, there are only three ways in which new rules can become part of the corpus of International Law and thus binding on States —

(a) by embodiment in a treaty entered into in accordance with the constitutional processes of the State parties (treaty);
(b) by general action upon them in the practice of States out of a conviction that those States are bound by them (custom). The

onus to establish such a custom would be upon Alterius and there has been no proof of any such custom;

(c) adoption by a judicial or like tribunal authorized to declare and apply the law of nations (judicial process). Since what is contended for by the Plaintiffs is contrary to the law of nations (as it is) this Court cannot make entirely new law on the subject. With respect, for the ICJ to do otherwise would not enhance its reputation, for law needs to be respected, to be obeyed and, furthermore, such a legislative act would not encourage ratification of the anti-hijacking conventions and it is their ratification which constitutes the new method of tackling the problem.

2. Hijacking is a serious problem of the modern technological world arising from many different causes — extortion, terrorism and hijacking of planes by those seeking asylum from oppression or by the mentally disturbed for the expression of their psychoses. It can only be tackled by:

(a) Worldwide ratification of the anti-hijacking treaties making hijacking an international crime against humanity analogous to piracy or war crimes. (In spite of this, only thirty-two States have so far ratified the Montreal Convention of 1971 and this number does not include the United States).

(b) Multilateral agreement for retaliation and coercion against States refusing to extradite or punish offenders.

(c) International machinery to enforce an international criminal code.

(d) Enforceable International Safety Regulations to strengthen preventative measures.

3. The Defense has contended that Alterius's denial of human rights to Xaviere was the effective cause of the tragedy. Moreover, in international law the denial of human rights by a State to its citizens has been held by this Court to be a breach of an international obligation. In the Advisory Opinion of *South-West Africa* of the ICJ (1970) the Court said (concerning apartheid)

> No factual evidence is needed to determine whether apartheid is in conformity with the international obligations assumed by South Africa under the Charter of the United Nations . . . . It has pledged itself to observe and respect human rights and fundamental freedoms . . . . and to establish distinction based on race, color, descent or national or ethnic origin is a flagrant violation of the purposes and principles of the Charter.

Thus, Alterius has breached the international obligations it assumed in membership of the United Nations to provide human rights and fundamental freedoms to Xaviere and Alterius should be ordered to make the reparations sued for on behalf of the relatives of Yellman.

Argument

By Juan Manuel Fanjul Sedeno, Spain

In Defense of Francisco Xaviere against the suit for damages presented by the Republic of Coronado

May it please the Court:

With the permission of the Court and in defense of Francisco Xaviere to oppose the claim presented against him by the Republic of Coronado, which has assumed the rights of the heirs of the subject of said State, Mr. Yellman, claiming compensation for damages for his death during the seizure.

I consider it unnecessary to repeat here the causative facts of this claim, as they are already in the official resume which each of the parties has received; they have been set forth in previous court appearances and have been published in the suit of the Republic of Coronado. The Court, therefore, is well acquainted with them.

I do, however, consider it appropriate to set forth here some circumstances of critical importance for the interpretation of our defense:

(a) Yellman was wounded while the plane was still on the ground, at the Botania airport. Yellman was wounded when he tried to disarm Francisco Xaviere in violation of the instructions of the crew, which had ordered all passengers to make no act of opposition to the seizure or to take any positive posture toward the hijacker. The proof of this is that the rest of the passengers who remained quiet, obeying the crew's orders, were unharmed.

(b) The claim of the Republic of Coronado does not raise a criminal issue; this is beyond the scope of our suit; we are referring solely to that which is called civil liability; specifically, to compensation for damages for Yellman's death.

(c) Yellman's heirs are not filing their claim as individual persons, rather the State to which he belonged, the Republic of Coronado as said sovereign State, is suing Francisco Xaviere and the

Democratic State of Botania; my role is merely the defense of
Francisco Xaviere as an individual person.
(d) The claim of the Republic of Coronado is raised before the
International Court of Justice.

I. From the relation of the facts and of these special circumstances,
there arises with indisputable vigor a clear exception of a procedural
nature: the Court is incompetent. And the Court is incompetent by
reason of the persons and by reason of the subject.

(a) The court is incompetent by reason of the persons because the
International Court of Justice only has jurisdiction when the issue
is a claim between States, but is not competent if one or both of
the litigants are private individuals. Thus, Article 34 of the Statute
of the International Court of Justice says, literally, in its first
paragraph:

1. Only States may be parties in cases before the Court.

In this case the claimant meets the criterion, since it concerns a
State, the Republic of Coronado, but the criterion is not met with
regard to the defendant, who is an individual. That is, the
claimant is a legal entity but the defendant is not.
(a) We recognize with regard to the first aspect the principle called
"diplomatic protection", by virtue of which any State may take
upon itself the private interest of one of its citizens and take a
claim for his rights before the International Court of Justice. But
this principle demands a strict interpretation to the extent that the
States must "take upon themselves" the right for which they are
suing, and not merely act in representation of it. In that regard,
the doctrine has foreseen the risk of procedural fraud, requiring
that the State act when it assumes the right, but never when it is
only representing it.

Therefore we recognize the legal capacity of the Republic of
Coronado to take upon itself the rights of Yellman's heirs; Now
then, why does it assume that private interest? To file suit. But to
file suit against whom? Necessarily, in accordance with Article 34
of the Court Statutes, it can only be used to file suit against
another State.

There are the cases of Nottebohm, in which Liechtenstein filed
suit against Guatemala; and of Boll, in which Holland sued
Sweden; but in no cases does a private individual appear as
claimant or defendant.

Consequently, if the claim made is not against another State, but against an individual, the Court is incompetent by reason of the persons, and by directing its suit against Francisco Xaviere, the Republic of Coronado has disqualified itself from a hearing before the Court. It can continue the process to the extent of suing Botania, but not as a suit (which is what concerns me) against Francisco Xaviere.

(b) The Court is also incompetent by reason of the subject matter. The claim asserts that the justification on which the compensation suit against Francisco Xaviere is based arises from the fact of a crime of aerial piracy, which is an international crime. Gentlemen of the Court, this assertion brings us to the logical form known as "petition of principle", because the affirmation that it is an international crime is presented as an argument in a debate in which that is precisely what we are discussing, whether the piracy committed by Francisco Xaviere is an international crime. Here, at this very moment, the various parties involved are discussing this theme. For until a decision is issued affirming that it is a matter of an international crime, this fact cannot be admitted as an argument as to the competence of the International Court. This theme has been submitted to the Court independently; it is not within my purview. But I do affirm that *hic et nunc*, here and now, while a decision has not yet been handed down, one cannot use as an argument a declaration which, as yet does not exist. But I want to go even further in my dialectical concessions, Gentlemen of the Court, and, admitting as a hypothesis that the Court might be competent with regard to subject matter, it would also turn out to be incompetent pursuant to Article 36 of the Statute of the International Court of Justice.

This article requires recognition by the litigant State of the jurisdiction of the Court and indicates the subject matters of a legal nature to which the generic jurisdictional recognition refers.

The interpretation of this precept conforms to the doctrine; it is also restrictive, because the broad nature of that submission would affect the sovereignty of the States.

Professor Medina of the Complutensian University of Madrid, who is with us in this Conference, comments in this respect in his work on the United Nations:

"In conformity with Article 2/7 of the Charter, no provision authorizes the United Nations to intervene in matters which are "essentially within the jurisdiction of the States" or to "subject said matters to ruling procedures".

And he adds:

"Whenever the Court recognizes the existence of a question of national competence it should declare its incompetence without this reservation having to be expressly stated."

We find, therefore, in the area of "national competence" that it is neither vulnerable nor avoidable without the express acceptance of the State involved: proof of this is its reinforcement through what is called the reserve clause of national competence, which the most important States have established to declare for themselves which matters cannot leave the jurisdiction of their courts.

I ask myself, Gentlemen of the Court, where it would lead us, particularly in civil matters (civil liability, although derived from a crime, is of a private nature), where it would lead us to set aside the national competence clause; we would come to an extension of international competence over all subjects and over all individual persons. And this would convert the International Court of Justice into a Tribunal which, being above the national courts, would make itself freely available to powerful litigants against the poor litigants who could not afford to pursue a case before it. It would overrule the right of sovereignty of the States and of their courts and would open a door to the world of the powerful over the weak not only between States but between persons.

Therefore, Gentlemen of the Court, I consider as an unacceptable defense any attempt to violate the principle of national competence, which requires the use and exhaustion of the internal procedural resources of each State before a matter is brought before the International Court of Justice.

The theme is so clear that the plaintiff State, the Republic of Coronado, understands what shaky ground it is on in raising the claim against Francisco Xaviere before the International Court of Justice and anticipates this by observing: "I cannot bring my claim before the courts of Botania because they are prejudiced; because they have already refused to judge Francisco Xaviere for the criminal act which he committed and, because faced with the political tension which has been produced as a consequence of the demand for extradition from Alterius, there is a predisposition by the courts of Botania to find in favor of Francisco Xaviere".

In response to this, we must make an important clarification of the adverse claim: what the courts of Botania have refused to do is to try Francisco Xaviere for a crime, what they have refused to do is to grant the extradition of Francisco Saviere for a crime, but what they have not refused to do, because nobody has suggested it, for nowhere in any of the courts of Botania is there a trace of any suit, is to intervene in a civil damage suit in the death of Mr.

Yellman. Thus the refusal to judge Francisco Xaviere for a crime cannot serve as an argument, because no one raised the right of Yellman's heirs to compensation for damages for the damage caused to their constitutent. For all these reasons I maintain the incompetence of the International Court of Justice to entertain the demand of the Republic of Coronado against Francisco Xaviere in a civil damage suit.

II. Neither can the demand of Coronado against Francisco Xaviere succeed for basic reasons.

(a) Observe, Gentlemen of the Court, that we find ourselves (insofar as this defense is concerned) not faced with punishment for a crime, nor with penalization for some transgression, but — only and exclusively — with the requirement of a civil obligation. The universal doctrine (with slight variations in one legislature or another) holds that obligations arise from the Law, from contract, from crimes and from acts or omissions in which guilt or negligence play a role.

In this case we know that there is no law or contract which impels, or from which is derived, the requirement of the obligation which is postulated; we do not know if there is an international crime, because this problem is being resolved contemporaneously in the issue in which we find ourselves. If there is a definitive declaration of the existence of fraud, that will exclude guilt or negligence. Only, therefore, when the criminal sentence is handed down will we know if there is any possibility of discussing the existence of those things as the source from which arises the obligation of compensation which is demanded in this suit.

The fact on which the Republic of Coronado bases its demand for compensation is the death of one of its subjects, Yellman, but until the criminal court makes its decision the civil process will have to be continued, because that is the only way in which light can be shed on the existence and circumstances of this civil liability.

In Spanish law and in Continental law in general, the civil process is suspended when a criminal process is instituted on the same set of facts, therefore the judgment of the criminal court in fact has civil consequences.

Observe that in the criminal decision being pursued concurrently with this one, compensation for damages is being demanded — in a criminal process — which, if granted and depending on how stipulated, could be incompatible with that being demanded here in a civil process.

(b) The claim of the Republic of Coronado — alleging that the general principles are the applicable law — in accordance with Article 38, Section (c) of the Statute of the International Court of Justice, alleges the general principles in the abstract, but doesn't say specifically which of them should be applied. The general principles in themselves are a definition of a generic nature, and within them must be specified which ones may be relevant to the debated supposition and to the demand obligation. Do not forget that in international law the burden of proof of the right which is alleged to be applicable falls upon the plaintiff, but this plaintiff has not specified anything in his demand.

(c) Now that we are into the basic thesis, demand for an obligation to compensate, derived from guilt or negligence (that derived from a criminal act is being dealt with by other esteemed colleagues), we must reject the claim that it is sufficient to obtain a verdict of guilty, to allege the existence of damage and, consequently, the obligation for compensation; we cannot accept that automatic application. We do not deny the influence of Anglo-Saxon law with regard to objective civil liability, but we must also keep in mind the classic laws in which there is an evident need to accredit the act or the omission which brought about the damage, the damage itself, and the causative connection between the one and the other from which the obligation to indemnity is derived.

The civil juridical problem raised by the Republic of Coronado is much more complex than it was explained to be It is not enough (as burden of proof of the applicable law) to cite Article 38 of the Court Statute and, in general, the general principles of law. These would be, let us not forget, as the precept says, those recognized by civilized nations. And I then tell you that we must ascertain which of these principles of law is the one applicable, under what conditions, by arrangement with what interpretive doctrine, in accordance with what body of laws. Coronado has told us none of this in either its written claim or the statement of its lawyer.

Thus it happens that, although the Court may be competent to judge, it would not know which standard to apply because no standard of them has been cited and developed by the claimant.

But let us go still further in the destruction of the case of the Republic of Coronado. We admit, hypothetically, the existence of guilt on the part of the defendant, Francisco Xaviere. That brings us inevitably to a consideration of the theory of concurrence or compensation of guilt.

The theory varies in different countries and according to different doctrines. In general it is not accepted within the field of Criminal Law, but it is in the field of Civil Law.

Well then, in the working documents which we have been given for this process it says peremptorily that the Law of the Republic of Botania (the place where the act was committed from which arose the case of civil liability which is being claimed) denies the right to compensation for damage when there is guilt on both sides. What applies here is what is called the doctrine of "avoidable consequences" under which compensation is denied to any person who, while violating rules of conduct formulated for his protection, deliberately exposes himself to a known danger. In accordance with the circumstances to which we have alluded at the outset, you must recognize, Gentlemen of the Court, that the crew of the aircraft gave orders that no passenger should carry out any act or initiate any defense, but should remain passive. Mr. Yellman disobeyed this order, violating these rules of conduct formulated for his protection, as Botanian Law says; he provoked the hijacker, trying to disarm him. This imprudence resulted in the shot being fired and his subsequent death two days later. Mr. Yellman died while the other passengers, who obeyed the orders of the crew, were unhurt.

Therefore the doctrine of compensation of guilt, the doctrine of avoidable consequences, is clearly applicable, and therefore even if it should result, contrary to our belief, that the Court is legally competent, it cannot take action against Francisco Xaviere in a demand of civil liability.

Gentlemen of the Court, I do not wish to end without expressing my human adherence to Mr. Yellman's gesture, without lamenting the injurious consequences which resulted from his behavior; Mr. Yellman was a brave man, he was a determined man, he was a heroic man. We recognize that. But we also recognize that heroes' compensations are written into the book of history, but not in the resolutions of the Courts of Justice. That is all.

Argument

By Fernando Fournier, Costa Rica

On behalf of the Democratic State of Botania, Defendant

May it please the Court:

Botania acquired jurisdiction over Defendant Xaviere, a citizen of Alterius, when the airliner he had hijacked landed in Botania. Both the Magistrate who conducted a hearing under Botanian law, and the Botanian executive who refused to extradite Xaviere on the demand of Alterius were correct in concluding that the Extradition Treaty between Alterius and Botania exempts "political" crime and that the crime of hijacking, under the facts in this case, is a political crime.

This Court is bound by the Statute of the International Court of Justice to refuse jurisdiction.

Botania has accepted the compulsory jurisdiction of the International Court of Justice, but such jurisdiction does not include extradition for political crimes, which is a question for decision within Botania's domestic jurisdiction exclusively.

When one consults the decisions of the International Court of Justice and the writings of the great experts in the field of international law, it will be found that internal affairs of a nation are not the proper subject of international inquiry. Indeed, it is its sole jurisdiction over its territory that Botania here seeks to vindicate.

International law recognizes no right to extradition apart from a treaty. It is true that Grotius and other writers in the past have taken the view that under the usage of civilized nations — customary law — every sovereign State is obliged to grant extradition freely and without qualification or restriction. That view no longer prevails. The law today is that right to demand extradition exists apart from the provision of an international agreement or treaty.

The treaty between Botania and Alterius having to do with extradition exempts political crimes from its provisions, as I have said. Thus Botania concurs in the position of Xaviere that he is not extraditable.

Political offenses are not crimes as they are not the result of malignant intention. They are rather the effects of a society suffering from maladjustments which drive people to despair and violence. This is why extradition is granted as to common crime, but refused as to political crimes.

The Inter-American Convention on Territorial and Diplomatic Asylum of 1954 clearly states that the right of decision as to extradition belongs with the recipient State Thus Botania in deciding to grant Xaviere asylum exercised its lawful right to take such a decision.

The 1970 Hague Convention for the Suppression of Unlawful Seizure of Aircraft is not binding on Botania because Botania has not signed the Convention. In fact, that Convention has not yet been signed by a majority of the nations of the world, so that Convention is irrelevant to the claims brought before this Court. The several UN Resolutions condemning hijacking are also irrelevant to the issue before this Court as those resolutions create no law binding on this Court.

Neither the 1970 Hague Convention for the Suppression of Unlawful Seizure of Aircraft, nor the UN Resolutions supporting the goals of that Convention are binding on Botania as expressions of "international customary law" within the meaning of the Statute of the International Court of Justice. There has been no proof of such custom or of a uniform usage as practiced by States. The treatment of hijacking by States does not meet the test of a constant and uniform usage which is thereby elevated to customary status under international law.

The conflicting precedents referred to by our distinguished adversaries in their respective briefs confirm that the question of international custom in this area is far from settled.

Botania has brought Xaviere to justice by giving him a Preliminary Hearing before a magistrate. The decision of that magistrate that Xaviere's act was a political crime is binding upon this Court. This adjudication by the magistrate fulfills Botania's duty under international law.

The political action of Xaviere does not violate international law on crimes against the law of nations. Citations of principles developed in Nuremberg and other similar courts does not apply here.

The exoneration of Xaviere by the magistrate is the upholding of his basic human rights as adopted by the international community. I refer to the provisions of the European Convention on Human Rights, Article VI, which provides that "everyone is entitled to a fair and public hearing within a reasonable time by an independent and impartial tribunal established by law".

Here, the magistrate provided such a hearing and such a decision. Our adversaries are wrong in contending that such a decision is a violation of international law.

The ruling of the magistrate in Xaviere's favor was totally in accordance with Botania's internal law, and was the result of an independent and free judicial inquiry which this Court should respect and uphold.

A second trial would violate Xaviere's right against double jeopardy. I call upon the Court to recognize that the prohibition of double jeopardy is recognized universally. It is written into the International Convention on Civil and Political Rights of 1966, Article XIV.

It is clear that under international law Botania has jurisdiction over Xaviere, and it has the lawful duty to prevent his being placed twice in jeopardy. An alien in Botania has a right to be protected by local law in Botania. I call attention to the right of political refugees to the full protection of the law of the nation of which they are a refugee.

Therefore, I urge that Xaviere's legal responsibility in this matter is exclusive and that it was properly carried out under Botania's domestic jurisdiction. Botania here has exercised that jurisdiction in a lawful manner. Any further action by Botania or any other nation, would violate the rule of double jeopardy.

This Court should deny the claim of Plaintiff's to obligatory extradition and deny as well Plaintiffs' alternative claim that Botania be compelled to conduct further legal proceedings in this case in Botania's municipal courts.

Argument

By Toye C. Barnard, Liberia

On behalf of Francisco Xaviere, Defendant

May it please the Court:

We here consider a unique political act undertaken by Xaviere to publicize the oppression of his political and religious minority group in Alterius. The Defendant's actions were not motivated by personal gain or other impulses. The magistrate, in exonerating Xaviere, has upheld Xaviere's contention that he was and is a political refugee. It was on this basis that the magistrate ordered that no further criminal proceedings for either hijacking or murder could be brought against Xaviere in the Botanian Courts.

That Xaviere's motive was to publicize the plight of his racial and political minority group cannot be denied. It is unfortunate that passenger Robert Yellman was wounded attempting to disarm Xaviere. His death is deeply regretted.

What we have here is a legal question involving the jurisdiction of this Court — as an international court of justice — over an individual, and acts committed by that individual to carry out his political beliefs. We have a legal question of an international court assuming to review domestic action of a State over domestic matters.

There is no question that the Statute of the International Court of Justice, as is stated by the many writers on the subject, in our brief, contains no provision whereby individuals may be given access to that Court or become parties to cases before that court. The subject matter, the Court's sole jurisdiction, is the rights and duties of nations arising under international law when they act as States, solely and exclusively.

The crime of hijacking is not an international crime, or a crime under international law. Hijacking is a national crime, and even if it were a crime under international law, this Court would lack jurisdiction to try the alleged hijacker, Defendant Xaviere.

The Nuremberg principles which are cited in my brief, and the Eichmann Decision in Israel, are not precedents for the trial of individuals for crimes under international law. No international Court has jurisdiction over individuals for crimes such as are stipulated by Article VI of the Chapter of the International Military Tribunal. Such a Court would have to be created by international treaty and could, of course, obligate only the States or nations who are parties to the treaty. The law incorporated into the treaty would not be binding on other States who did not sign the treaty or become parties to the treaty.

The charges made at Nuremberg and the law under which they were tried are clearly distinguishable from the charges before this Court if it were to assume jurisdiction over this case. The Nuremberg Court was a military tribunal created by victorious nations engaged in governing conquered territory. It exercised national jurisdiction in the name of the then defunct German State.

The subsequent endorsement of the general principles of Nuremberg by the General Assembly of the United Nations does not provide jurisdiction in the International Court of Justice over a case like the instant case. Certain individuals were held responsible at Nuremberg for war crimes and crimes against humanity as set forth in the Code of Offenses Against the Peace and Security of Mankind. These principles did not alter what has been the traditional nature of jurisdiction with regard to international or national crime, i.e. the permissive grant of jurisdiction by every State.

Eichmann was tried before a national court of Israel. That case cannot serve as a precedent of bringing Defendant Xaviere before this International Court of Justice.

In this case, it should not be forgotten that Botania has forthrightly exercised its legitimate domestic sovereignty and territorial jurisdiction by bringing Defendant Xaviere before its magistrate for a Preliminary Hearing, and that magistrate exonerated him.

This is all that international law requires of Botania. That magistrate's decision serves as a bar to this Court's jurisdiction.

Hijacking is not a crime against international law; this is clear from the fact that sea piracy is not a crime or offense under the law of nations. Under international law, piracy is special ground for the exercise of State jurisdiction, of jurisdiction by every State. The law of nations applying to sea piracy justifies State action within limits and fixes limits. That piracy is not a crime under the law of nations is made clear by the references in my brief to the statements of the International Law Commission and to Harvard's research into international law.

Xaviere's action in hijacking the plane was a political crime and is not extraditable under the Extradition Treaty between Botania and Alterius which exempts political crimes specifically and therefore Xaviere cannot be extradited.

Xaviere has declared throughout that his motive in committing the hijacking was to publicize the oppressed status of his minority and political group in Alterius. The facts support him.

In what I have said in my brief, I have set forth the comments by many experts on what constitutes political motives, political action or the political character of an action. I believe that from these various authorities one can conclude that an action such as that of Xaviere here is clearly within the meaning of "political" offense or political "crime" as it has been viewed by the Courts and learned writers on the subject.

Under the applicable law, we urge that an act which has been defended as a political offense must be analyzed in terms of the motives and objectives of the offender together with the circumstances surrounding the act in question. Here, those elements are predominantly political, and there is a direct connection between the crime charged and Xaviere's background in politics. So asylum is appropriate and extradition is inappropriate.

Under the facts here, it is clear that Botania's determination as to the political nature of Xaviere's offense is reasonable and that the decision both of the Botanian Executive and magistrate should not be overruled by this Court without evidence of bad faith or incompetence, and neither of those is present.

If Xaviere is extradited to Alterius he will be prosecuted for his political motivations and actions. Such prosecution of Defendant Xaviere is political prosecution which violates the principles of the Human Rights Conventions based upon the Universal Declaration of Human Rights.

Because this Court, under its Statute and international customary law, lacks jurisdiction over Xaviere and any alleged offenses which he may have committed, and because his acts in any event were political, this Court is asked to reject the claim of jurisdiction and uphold both the decision of the magistrate and denial of extradition conducted pursuant to both Botanian and State law.

SELECTED BIBLIOGRAPHY

Alexandrowicz, C. H., The European-African Confrontation, 1973.

Asamoa, O. Y., The Legal Significance of the Declarations of the General Assembly, 1966.

Brownlie, I., Principles of Public International Law, 1966.

Cappelletti, M. (et al), Toward Equal Justice: A Comparative Study of Legal Aid in Modern Societies, 1975.

Cassese, A., Current Problems of International Law: Essays on the UN and the Law of Armed Conflict, 1975.

Casteneda, J., The Legal Effects of United Nations Resolutions, 1969.

Churchill, R. (ed), New directions in the Law of the Sea, Vol. III, 1973.

Elias, T. O., Nigeria — Development of its Laws and Constitutions, 1967.

Elias, T. O., Africa and the Development of International Law, 1972.

Elias, T. O., Modern Law of Treaties, 1974.

Gross, Leo, (ed), The Future of the International Court of Justice, Vol. I, 1976.

Hollick, A. I., and Osgood, R. E., New Era of Ocean Politics, 1974.

Jenks, C. W., The Prospects of International Adjudication, 1962.

Jennings, R. Y., Acquisition of Territory in International Law, 1963.

Kossoy, E., Living with Guerrilla: Guerrilla as a Legal Problem and Political Fact, 1976.

Lachs, M., The Law of Outer Space, 1972.

Lauterpacht, H., The Development of International Law by the International Court, 1958.

Lauterpacht, H., Oppenheim's International Law, Vol. 2, 8th edn.

Lord Wright, Legal Essays and Addresses, 1945.

Moskowitz, M., Human Rights and World Order, 1953.

Moskowitz, M., International Concern with Human Rights, 1974.

Mosler, H., and Bernherdt, Judicial Settlement of International Disputes — An International Symposium, 1974.

Nathason and Schwelb, The US and the UN Treaty on Racial Discrimination: A Report for the Panel on International Human

Rights Law and its Implementation, 1975.

Niucic, Djuva., The Problem of Sovereignty in the Charter and in the Practice of the United Nations, 1970.

Northedge and Donelan, International Disputes: The Political Aspects, 1971.

Sahovic, M. (ed), Principles of International Law concerning Friendly Relations and Cooperation, 1972.

Schwarzenberger, G., International Constitutional Law, 1976, Dynamics of International Law, 1976.

Scott, Hague Court Reports, Vol. 2.

Sinclair, I., The Vienna Convention on the Law of Treaties, 1973.

Smith de, S. A., Judicial Review of Administrative Action, 1975, 3rd edn.

Tabibi, A. H., The Right of Transit of Land-locked Countries, 1968.

Tunkin, G. I., Theory of International Law, 1974.

GENERAL INDEX

The letter-by-letter system has been adopted.
Familiar acronyms such as GATT, UNCTAD etc. are regularly used, including ICJ
(International Court of Justice).
Pronouncements will be found under Conventions; Covenants; Declarations and
Principles.
As to the names of countries, the modern ones have been used in the index, i.e., Republic
of South Africa, Namibia, etc.